FIGHTER COMMAND

FIGHTER COMMAND

1936 - 1968

Chaz Bowyer

J M Dent & Sons Ltd

London   Toronto   Melbourne

First Published 1980
© Chaz Bowyer 1980
All rights reserved. No part of this publication may
be reproduced, stored in a retrieval system, or
transmitted, in any form or by any means,
electronic, mechanical, photocopying, recording or
otherwise, without the prior permission of
J M Dent & Sons Ltd.

Printed in Great Britain by
Billing & Sons Ltd, Guildford, London, Oxford & Worcester
for J M Dent & Sons Ltd
Aldine House, Welbeck Street, London

This book is set in 11 on 13½pt VIP Baskerville by
D. P. Media Ltd., Hitchin, Herts.

British Library Cataloguing in Publication Data

   Bowyer, Chaz
   Fighter Command.
   1. Great Britain. Royal Air Force. Fighter
   Command – History
   I. Title
   358.4'3'0941   UG635–G7

   ISBN 0-460-04388-9

Contents

	List of Illustrations	9
	Introduction	11
1	Ancestry	13
2	Spreading Wings	21
3	Debacle	37
4	So Few	58
5	Dark of Moon	77
6	Seek and Destroy	86
7	Aces and Kings	98
8	Side-shows	107
9	By Day, by Night	116
10	Shield and Buckler	130
11	From the Cockpit	146
12	Phoenix Rising	161
13	Beyond Sound	175
Appendix 1	AOCs-in-C, Fighter Command	186
Appendix 2	Squadron dispositions	187
	Bibliography	196
	Picture Credits	199
	Index	201

The English will suffer for a time, but in the end they take such bloody payment as may well serve for an example; nor can they be played with . . . England is the best guarded country in the world. Otherwise it neither would nor could maintain itself.

Froissart: 1356

List of Illustrations

Between pp. 64–5

1 Bristol Bulldogs of B Flight, 3 Squadron.
2 Gloster Gauntlet of 46 Squadron.
3 Hawker Fury IIs of 25(F) Squadron.
4 Gloster Gladiator of 73 Squadron in pre-1938 finish.
5 Bentley Priory – Fighter Command's headquarters.
6 Hugh Dowding, Group Capt. Nichols and ACM Sir Guy Garrod.
7 Keith Park, who commanded 11 Group during the Battle of Britain.
8 Hawker Hurricane fighters under mass production.
9 Spitfire I, P9450, on air test in April 1940.
10 Heinkel III brought down on British soil.
11 Chain Home (CH) radar, 1940.
12 Operations Room at Bentley Priory.
13 Pilot Officer A. G. Lewis, DFC of 85 Squadron.

Between pp. 80–1

14 Eric James Brindley Nicolson, the only fighter pilot to be awarded a Victoria Cross during 1939–45.
15 Spitfire of 602 Squadron, AAF being re-armed.
16 The victory tally of Roland Tuck, DFC in late 1940.
17 Adolph 'Sailor' Malan.
18 'Sailor's Rules' Rules.
19 'Night Fighter' – Squadron Leader R. P. Stevens, DSO, DFC.
20 Crews of 604 Squadron, AAF, outside their Officers' Mess.
21 Night fighter pilots of 85 Squadron relaxing at dispersal.
22 Douglas DB7 'Havoc', an American design used as an 'interim' night fighter.
23 Bristol Beaufighter VIF of 307 (Polish) Squadron.

24 Chocks away!
25 They also served . . .
26 Night shift.
27 HM King George VI greeting pilots from a Spitfire squadron on 29 April 1942.
28 Spitfires of 122 Squadron take-off from Fairlop.
29 Australian Spitfire pilots of 452 Squadron, RAAF.

Between pp. 128–9
30 Spitfire Vb, R6923, serving in 92 Squadron.
31 Hurricane pilots of 402 Squadron, RCAF 'scrambling' at Digby, 1941.
32 Hurricane IIb, BE417, AE-K at Warmwell in early 1942.
33 Twin 20mm cannon wing installation of a Hurricane II.
34 Hawker Typhoon with four 20mm cannon battery in the wings.
35 Wing Leader Alan Deere, DSO, DFC.
36 AVM T. Leigh-Mallory, commander of 12 Group in 1940.
37 Spitfire Mk XIIs of 41 Squadron.
38 'Through the camera.'
39 AM Sir Roderic Hill.
40 The Hawker Typhoon.
41 'Mosquito bite.'

Between pp. 160–1
42 Night crews of 29 Squadron's Mosquitos at Hunsdon, 1944.
43 Squadron Leader Joseph Berry, DFC.
44 Point-blank range fire.
45 J. E. Johnson, DSO, DFC, top-scoring RAF fighter pilot in the European operational zone.
46 Gloster Meteor EE528.
47 Standard Meteor F4s of 66 Squadron, 1949.
48 De Havilland Venom NF2s of 23 Squadron.
49 North American Sabre jet fighters of 112 Squadron.
50 Gloster Javelin FAW7s of 23 Squadron.
51 Bristol Bloodhound ground-to-air defence missile.
52 Hawker Hunter F6s in tight echelon.
53 English Electric Lightning interceptor.
54 'Feeding time.'
55 Fighter Command's principal fighters, 1939–68.

Introduction

Fighter Command, RAF came into existence on 14 July 1936, and ultimately lost its individual entity on 30 April 1968. This book is an attempt to place on record an appreciation of its essential history, and something of the character of those years. It is, perforce, a story of men and machines, but primarily a saga of some three main generations of young men, their achievements, failures and problems. Despite the modern worship of the machine, man remains the creative genius and motivation behind every computer or any other form of inanimate technology.

The time parameters placed upon my text are deliberate; only in the years 1936–68 was RAF Fighter Command a distinct formation. Also intentional on my part is the wide emphasis upon the period 1939–45, for only in those years did the command have occasion to fulfil its prime and *original* purpose. Thus my text is neither a history of Britain's aerial defences *per se*, nor simply a chronology of RAF fighter aircraft; though aspects of both subjects are necessarily threaded throughout the narrative. Instead it is meant as a simple record and appreciation of the birth, life and actions of a specific body of men – the fighter pilots of the Royal Air Force during the period 1936–68.

Fighter pilots – of any nation and era – have always evoked an image of fulsome 'glamour' in a layman's mind. The aura of succinct individualism commonly associated with this popular image is inevitably coloured by a myriad of highly publicised exploits of certain pilots in the history of combat in the arena of the heavens. It is aided and abetted by the many extrovert characters who emerged from time to time among the fighter units; men whose singular achievements have carved permanent niches in fighter annals. Nevertheless, any objective study of fighter operations throughout the years of warfare indicates unequivocally that the bulk of successes obtained was the result of the accumulative, unpublicised, dogged devotion to duty of the 'unknowns'; the 'many' who gained few, if any, plaudits or awards. They simply 'did their job' – and did it superbly well. It is really to them – the 'silent majority' – and especially the many who 'failed to return', that this story is offered in sincere dedication, and unending gratitude.

Chaz Bowyer
Norwich 1979

1. Ancestry

At midnight on 11 November 1918 – the first evening of peace in more than four years for a war-weary Europe – the Royal Air Force was little more than seven months old. Despite its tender age the Third Service was an extraordinarily healthy 'baby' on that date. It comprised more than 290,000 men and women, had a strength of approximately 3,500 aircraft of every type, and its main operational spearhead could boast a total of 188 first-line squadrons. In non-operational spheres were a further 187 training units. Of the 100 units based along the Western Front in France, 59 squadrons were equipped with fighters; while in the United Kingdom another 16 fighter squadrons were tasked with a Home Defence role.

The world's first independent (of Army or Navy) air service, the RAF was at that moment the world's largest air force. Yet within 15 months of the armistice almost 90 per cent of its personnel had been demobilised, while in Europe, by November 1919, just one RAF squadron, No. 12, was still in existence. If such dismembering of a proud force seemed savage to some, it was in part a natural reaction of a nation sickened by the horrors of a prolonged and ugly war. The fighting was over, the task now was to rebuild from the shreds of a once-peaceful era; to create the 'land fit for heroes' blandly promised by the politicians. In March 1920 the RAF possessed a mere total of 25 squadrons, with eight more in the slow process of re-formation, but the bulk of these were based overseas. In the UK were just seven squadrons, with five others in the nucleus stage. Immediate planning for the 'peace-time' RAF envisaged a total strength of 3,280 officers and 25,000 non-commissioned ranks, while the annual budget allotted to 'rebuilding' the service was set at approximately £15-million for the next five years. This yearly sum may be compared with the £1-million *per day* which had been expended on the air war during 1918, and the 1919–20 annual expenditure of £54-million on demobilising and disbanding the RAF.

In the political euphoria of the immediate post-1918 era, the ruling Coalition Government under Lloyd George adopted a basic assumption that Britain and her empire would not be likely to be involved in any major war for the ensuing ten years. In the prime context of financial estimation for the future, such an hypothesis gave the Treasury a comfortable basis for concluding that no preparation for any such conflict need be instigated. This 'Ten Years' Rule', as it became known, though neither logical nor practical, was then 'stretched' and adhered to by succeeding governments until 1932. The effect on any form of possible re-armament was to be profound. Nevertheless, the matters of naval and military strategy, including the domestic issue of defence of the homeland, were by no means shelved entirely. Based on another pure hypothesis that the only possible future aggressor would be France – the only major European country still capable of maintaining strong military and naval forces – the defence of the United Kingdom was considered to be completely safe in the hands of the Army and, especially, Britain's traditional first-line defence, the Royal Navy.

Exponents of the urgent need to build a strong aerial defence force, amongst them Hugh Trenchard, the Chief of the Air Staff, received a crumb of comfort from the governmental decision in early 1922 to provide for a metropolitan air force of 14 bomber and nine fighter squadrons for home defence; the higher proportion of bomber units reflecting the contemporary Air Ministry's view that offence was the finest defence. At the end of the same year, however, the existing coalition was replaced by a Conservative government, led initially by Bonar Law, then Stanley Baldwin. The new leaders quickly reached the conclusion that the existing disparity between French and British air strengths was 'menacing', requiring a prompt solution. Thus, on 20 June 1923, the Cabinet adopted a fresh scheme of expansion for the RAF intended to provide initially a metropolitan air force comprised of 52 squadrons – 394 bombers and 204 fighters as first-line establishment. Despite the warning of his Secretary of State for Air, Sir Samuel Hoare, that such a figure could not be achieved for at least five years, Baldwin calmly announced that this new establishment was 'to be created with as little delay as possible'. This expansion programme got off to an ostensibly good start, nevertheless, and within two years 25 of the promised 52 squadrons were declared to be in existence. What was not emphasised was that of the 52 squadrons envisaged – 35 bomber and 17 fighter – 13 were to be non-regular units. Of these latter six were to be Auxiliary Air Force (AAF) squadrons, raised and maintained by local County Associations, while seven would be Special Reserve (SR) squadrons.

Much of the '52 Squadron Scheme' for home defence was a direct outcome of a report from a committee headed by Major-General C. F. Romer in 1924. From this committee came various recommendations which were eventually adopted, including the start of recruitment for an Observer Corps which would become a network for reporting all aircraft movements in vital defence areas. Another recommendation was that a new RAF command be created, titled Air Defence of Great Britain (ADGB), ultimately responsible for the control and direction of all operations by bombers, fighters, anti-aircraft guns, searchlights *et al*. The ADGB came into official existence from the beginning of 1925, and its first Air Officer Commanding-in-Chief (AOC-in-C) was Air Marshal Sir John Salmond, who had his temporary headquarters in the Air Ministry in London. Salmond inherited no sinecure. Already bedevilled by the ponderous need to channel all command decisions through both Army and RAF channels, he arrived only months before a fresh governmental revision of the promised 52-squadrons' scheme. In November 1925 a committee headed by Lord Birkenhead recommended that, due to improving political atmospheric conditions between England and France, the completion of that scheme could safely be modified or even suspended '. . . in the interests of goodwill and economy.' A new Conservative government seized upon this opinion and decided that the scheme's completion date could now be stretched until 1936.

The immediate effect upon the RAF's expansion programme was that only six squadrons were added to the home defences within the following three years, by which time a total of 31 squadrons (of the promised 52) had been inaugurated. Indeed, in the following four years, i.e. by 1932, just eleven more squadrons came into being – ten short of the expected complement. If Salmond was forced to accept the prolonged delay in overall equipment, he could at least organise his command to the best possible effect. In mid-1926 ADGB headquarters was moved from Air Ministry to Uxbridge, and the command was reorganised into two main zones; the Wessex Bombing Area (for regular bomber units) and a Fighting Area (for fighter squadrons). The

15

AAF and SR squadrons, formed from 1925, were designated No. 1 Air Defence Group in 1927 and added to Defence Command. At the beginning of 1930, however, Hugh Trenchard finally resigned his lengthy tenure as the Chief of Air Staff, and was succeeded in that post by John Salmond.

From the late 1920s until 1934 additional equipment and finance for the RAF (and the other armed services) was restricted partly by the disastrous economic depression which affected trade and industry throughout the world, and hardly less by the continuing idealistic hopes of the politicians for a permanent peace; epitomised by the various disarmament conferences and proposals mooted in this period. In such a climate of international crises allocation of money for additional armed strength was unpopular, even dangerous from the narrow, blinkered political viewpoint. Finally, and almost reluctantly, the British Cabinet, convinced that the latest international disarmament conference being held at Geneva would again fail, appointed a committee under Sir Maurice Hankey in November 1933. Its task was to advise on how best to counter the 'worst deficiencies' in both national and imperial defences. This committee submitted its findings in February 1934, amongst which was the reasoned conclusion that the 'ultimate potential enemy' would be Nazi Germany. It was a view backed by the General Staff who believed that Germany might be ready for a major conflict by 1938, or at latest 1939. British intelligence had already gathered ample evidence of Hitler's 'secret' Luftwaffe, built in overt defiance of the restrictive Versailles Treaty, and had warned senior government members of the Luftwaffe's probable strength in the near future.

By the close of 1934 the Luftwaffe had at least 22 first-line squadrons of bombers and fighters in service, with an escalating back-up production programme; some 560 quasi-operational aircraft. This figure was to be doubled as quickly as possible if long-term planning was to be completed on schedule. Such a figure was a rough parallel with the contemporary figure for RAF aircraft based in Britain; a fact which led to Winston Churchill attacking the government's sloth in expanding the RAF, by stating that by 1937 the Luftwaffe would be twice the size of the RAF numerically. Though exaggerated, Churchill's dire predictions played a part in persuading ministers that the RAF must be strengthened rapidly. After much deliberation the government decided in 1935 to adopt a suggested 'Scheme C' programme of expansion. The essence of this scheme made provision for a UK-based force of 70 bombers and 35 fighter squadrons; the whole build-up to be completed, in stages, by 1942 at latest. The continuing bias in favour of bombers reflected the contemporary view that future aerial warfare would be primarily a bomber-versus-bomber battle of attrition, with fighters employed in the main to guard the bomber bases from attack.

'Scheme C' immediately presented a prospect of administrative and operational control difficulties under the existing overall RAF organisation. Accordingly the service was drastically re-organised with the creation of four new commands; Bomber, Coastal, Fighter and Training. The existing ADGB was dissolved, and RAF Fighter Command came into being with effect from 14 July 1936, on which date its first AOC-in-C, Sir Hugh C. T. Dowding, took up his appointment on arrival at the future command headquarters at Bentley Priory, Stanmore. Dowding's initial command comprised four main internal formations; Nos. 11 and 12 (Fighter) Groups, No. 22 (Army Co-operation) Group – for administrative purposes only, and the civilian-manned Observer Corps. Destined to continue in command of the RAF's fighter forces for the next four and a half years, including Fighter Command's 'finest hour' – the 1940 Battle of Britain – Hugh Dowding was, at shallow acquaintance, an unlikely selection to command a fighting formation containing many of the most extrovert, youthful and individualistic pilots of the RAF. Only in retrospect is it now firmly acknowledged that probably no finer choice could have been made from Dowding's contemporaries for such a vital post. Totally honest, utterly professional, and wholly dedicated to his responsibilities, Dowding, despite an austere outward appearance, could almost have been chosen for his role by destiny.

Although born in Scotland on 24 April 1882, Hugh Caswall Tremenheere Dowding was from a family with deep roots in England's south-west country. Educated at Winchester College, he was there a contemporary of another Wykehamist who later gained high rank and distinction, Field Marshal Earl Wavell. Entering the Woolwich Military Academy in September 1899, Dowding was then commissioned in the Garrison Artillery the following year. By early 1914 he had reached the rank of Captain and obtained a pilot's certificate in the Royal Flying Corps. In this latter capacity he was attached to the RFC from the outbreak of war in August 1914 and eventually saw active flying service in France, rising in rank by 1918 to Brigadier-General in the

RAF. Granted a permanent commission in the post-1918 RAF as a Group Captain, Dowding settled down to what may be regarded as a reasonably normal Service career; spells of overseas service interlaced with various senior staff appointments. By 1929 he had been promoted to Air Vice-Marshal, and at the end of that year returned from duty in Palestine to become Air Officer Commanding (AOC) RAF Inland Area, the fighter Group of the ADGB. His appointment lasted less than a year, and he was next appointed to the Air Council as Air Member for Supply and Research. It was a task he was to continue for the following six years, during which period his far-sighted and down-to-earth policies were to have huge bearing upon the state of Britain's air defences by the outbreak of war in 1939 with Hitler's Germany.

Shortly after the RAF High Speed Flight had secured for Britain permanent possession of the coveted Schneider Trophy in 1931, Air Ministry circles were favouring the idea of a further form of maritime air speed trophy in order to continue research into high-speed aircraft, apart from the matter of British prestige. Dowding, strongly opposed to such a suggestion because he was convinced that such research had no bearing on the real need for modern, fast, heavily armed fighters, proposed instead that private tenders should be invited from Hawkers and Supermarine for two such high-speed fighter designs for eventual RAF equipment. The ultimate results of his proposal were the Hawker Hurricane and Supermarine Spitfire fighters. By January 1935 Dowding's office was relieved of the problems of pure supply, and he became Air Member for Research and Development, leaving him free to concentrate on modernising the equipment of Britain's air defences. Almost his first task, and certainly his most significant, was to put the full weight of his office and personal enthusiasm behind the development of a new device – radio direction finding (RDF), which in later years became more widely titled as Radar. A civilian scientist, Robert Watson-Watt of the National Physical Laboratory, demonstrated in February 1935 the possibility of detecting the approach and course of an aircraft by means of transmitting a radio wave pulse at the aircraft and receiving an 'echo' pulse in return; thereby enabling the aircraft's approximate range and direction to be calculated. With Dowding's backing, Watson-Watt's experiments resulted in the first RDF stations being approved for construction in 1936, guarding (initially) the eastern approaches to the Thames Estuary. In the event a 'chain' of 20 such

RDF stations, with their 250-feet high masts, was approved to be built quickly; the nucleus of a much longer chain of watchdog RDF units stretching around England's southern and eastern coastlines, all operational by early 1940. To control and direct these stations, Watson-Watt was appointed overall director, based at Bawdsey Manor on the Suffolk coast for central control.

On taking up his new appointment as AOC-in-C, Fighter Command, Hugh Dowding began as he was to continue – modestly, quietly, without fuss or pomp. His actual arrival at Bentley Priory has been recorded in some detail:[1]

> True to character from the first, Dowding arrived at the gate sharp at nine o'clock in the morning. Equally true to character, he was both unexpected and unaccompanied, and the guard only let him in after that solemn inspection of a pass that goes by the name of Security. No staff had yet arrived, and there was only a holding party under the command of the Camp Commandant, but as he was away for the day on business, the honours were done by Sergeant Cornthwaite, the NCO in charge of the Orderly Room. Cornthwaite was not the sort of man to get flustered over a sudden visitation of this kind, but he was relieved to learn that the lack of a formal greeting suited Dowding perfectly, and that the Air Marshal would be content to look quietly around the premises under his guidance. Together they explored the Priory and grounds. When the tour was over, the new Commander-in-Chief selected a room looking south that contained some office furniture, and told Cornthwaite to put his name on the door.

Dowding's command presented a disquieting picture in the contexts of pure numbers and, particularly, modernity in fighter designs. Of the 18 fighter squadrons available for immediate operations in Britain in mid-1936, four were equipped with the obsolescent Bristol Bulldog, five with two-seat Hawker Demons, six with Gloster Gauntlets, and the remaining three with the sleek Hawker Fury I. All were biplanes, only two of which – Fury and Gauntlet – were capable of exceeding 200 mph in level flight. Immediate future replacements envisaged were also biplanes, Gloster Gladiators and Hawker Fury IIs. With one exception, all relied on a twin-gun fire-power of rifle calibre, little advanced in design from their 1918 predecessors. In the 17 years since the close of the 'Great War', the only real progress in design and concept of the RAF's first-line fighters had been in aero engines and a myriad of minor items relating to safety and reliability. Pure fighter armament had

---

[1] *Fighter Command* by Peter Wykeham; Putnam, 1960.

virtually stagnated, overlooking the basic purpose of all military operational aircraft as vehicles for the carriage of offensive weaponry.

Fortunately, salvation in the shape of new, metal-constructed, high-speed, heavily-armed monoplane fighters was already in embryo stage. On 6 November 1935, K5083, the prototype Hawker Hurricane, had made its initial test flight, and on 3 June 1936 the Air Ministry had confirmed a production contract for 600 of the eight-gun monoplanes. Only weeks earlier, on 5 March 1936, another prototype monoplane fighter, K5054, made its first flight from Eastleigh Airport – sire of the now-legendary Supermarine Spitfire. On 3 July followed an initial production order for 310 Spitfires for the RAF. Under the latest RAF expansion plan, 'Scheme F', 500 Hurricanes and 300 Spitfires were expected to be in service by March 1939.

If the capacity of contemporary first-line fighter aircraft in the RAF in 1936 was doubtful in terms of repulsing any determined aerial assault, the quality of the fighter pilots was unchallenged. Thoroughly trained in their craft, highly professional – if sometimes unorthodox – in their attitude to their 'job', the peacetime fighter 'boys' had few, if any, peers. Nevertheless, they were bound somewhat rigidly to outdated concepts of tactical thinking superimposed by higher authorities whose practical knowledge of 'modern' aerial warfare was almost nil. Few senior RAF officers flew regularly in the mock-operational exercises that were religiously practised annually; most were mentally leashed to 1918 standards of combat tactics. This outmoded philosophy was part-reflected in the contemporary fetish for drill-square standards of air formation flying. Such 'pretty' and precise patterns of flying had great value in instilling a tight discipline into the pure practice of flying, and unquestionably offered a thrilling spectacle to the layman public audiences which yearly thronged to watch the RAF Displays at Hendon. As pure practice for their real purpose, air fighting, the contemporary fighter pilots learned little of real value beyond the essential lesson of teamwork. Individual initiative was rarely permitted full rein of expression; safety and strict adherence to the 'book of rules' pervaded most facets of any junior RAF officer's existence, thereby stifling genuine and serious attempts to 'up-date' tactical thinking.

2. Spreading Wings

By 1936 the fighter pilot in the RAF was very much the 'glamour boy' of the Service – at least, in the layman's mind. As the inheritor of a 1914–18 aura of the dashing, extrovert 'ace', he retained the charisma of such legendary figures as Albert Ball, Mannock, McCudden and a hundred others. As such he represented the ultimate goal of a thousand schoolboys' ambitions, nurtured by a flood of post-1918 books and magazines featuring the factual exploits of World War One aviators, and the fictional feats of Biggles and his entourage. The fighter pilot was also, to a large extent, the secret envy of his RAF counterparts flying lumbering bombers or staid army co-operation aircraft. A majority of newly-fledged RAF pilots, on graduation from flying schools, opted first for postings to fighter squadrons; eagerly hoping to join the community of the RAF's 'sharpest end'.

Those relative few who succeeded in such a goal were quickly inculcated into a brotherhood encompassed by the contemporary sleek, silver-skinned biplanes, gaily decorated with traditional unit heraldry. Once having joined his first fighter squadron, the newcomer was immediately made aware that he had, without question, been privileged to have been included in the ranks of *the* finest squadron in the RAF. It was then made crystal clear to him that he was expected to uphold the unit's high reputation in all circumstances. He had thus entered a community where sheer professionalism held top priority; expressed in an unceasing striving for perfection in every facet of the daily round. Though pursued in the healthiest of competitive atmospheres, rivalry twixt fighter squadrons was intense; not simply in flying performance and achievement, but in every possible facet of appearance, attitude, even speech. To don a flying overall carrying the cloth badge of a particular fighter squadron was an honour akin to admittance to a masonic enclave. Such an honour had to be 'earned' worthily and upheld in all matters. Unwritten codes of conduct were strictly observed, even at the expense, occasionally, of the written 'rules' laid down in King's Regulations. The squadron came *first* – indeed, *was* first in all considerations. Such attitudes were virtually an extension of the British public school system of conduct; a reflection of the British love of small communities and, to a much lesser extent, fascination with 'secret' societies. Such an attitude is almost wholly associated with maturing adolescence; akin to the muscle-testing capers of young cubs in any pride of lions, daring their elders and savouring the sheer joy of unknown danger in the maturing process.

If such inter-squadron rivalry was keen within units of the regular-serving RAF, it was doubly so between pilots of the more recently created Auxiliary Air Force (AAF) and their 'regular' counterparts. Created officially in 1924, the AAF had been envisaged by Hugh Trenchard originally as an élite formation to be organised on a territorial basis throughout the United Kingdom, and supported by local county associations. A total of 20 AAF squadrons was to be the ultimate objective, but all were to be distinctly separate from the RAF. In other words, the AAF was an *addition* to Britain's air strength, not merely a form of reserve for replenishment of the RAF's regular units. From its inception the AAF's dominating force was *esprit de corps*; a jealously, fiercely guarded pride in identity which was eventually to produce some of the most outstanding air crews of World War Two. Deliberate flouting of regular RAF customs was paramount among the highly individualistic members of the AAF; as witnessed by 601 Squadron's habit of wearing bright red socks with uniform. This same unit regularly displayed a notice outside its dispersal at annual camps: 'AAF ONLY. Tradesmen, RAF etc., entrance at rear.' Such apparent frivolities masked a unity and incredible spirit among AAF crews which found expression in immaculate flying precision and a dedication to flying unsurpassed in any other comparable force.

For all the social advantages and status level of being a fighter pilot in the mid-1930s, however, little opportunity was given to the squadrons to practise realistically for their ultimate function – air combat and defence. Financial restrictions imposed on all RAF activities and equipment were particularly evident in the context of pure armament. Practice in the use of 'live' ammunition for firing was severely limited; usually only at the annual two weeks' detachment to an armament practice camp in some remote area of Britain. Opportunities for attempting interception of 'invading' bomber forces were mainly confined to the yearly 'war games', wherein both 'invader' and defender were given rigidly-planned roles and confined to copy-book tactical parameters of movement. Such inflexible thinking by the organising hierarchy smacked strongly of a fairy-land philosophy, suggesting that under actual war conditions individual initiative had no place, and that pre-set fighting tactics – and strategy – would be rigidly adhered to by both the aggressor and the attacked. Adaptability, flexibility, spontaneity in the light of immediate circumstances – all were frowned upon, even mildly discouraged.

The foregoing generalisations may seem harsh, especially with the golden advantage of hindsight, yet a basic fault lay in the inherited system and background of outdated tactical thinking. If an individual commander and the occasional very senior RAF officer thought in more modern terms, he was inevitably faced with long-established mores in a tightly bureaucratic organisation, which itself was totally subservient to the whims of its political 'masters' of the particular moment. By 1936, too, progressive RAF leaders at all levels were only just being given the opportunity to break out from the previous 18 years of neglect and lethargy in Service matters enforced by succeeding governments. New equipment, 'modern' designs in aircraft, increasing financial budgets, expanding recruitment in personnel, even a huge programme for mass production of aircraft and the building of many new RAF stations – all these were only beginning to be inaugurated, albeit in indecent haste. Such items gave promise of far superior 'ironmongery' and material facilities, but could not in themselves automatically revise firmly-rooted abstracts such as tactical appraisal or strategic policies.

Combat tactics for RAF fighters in the period leading up to 1939 were in essence merely an extension of parade-ground drill manoeuvres. Known by the inherited title of Fighting Area Attacks, these specified air manoeuvres were neatly numbered in variations designed to cope with every predicted combat situation. All were based on the concept of neat, tidy and tight formation flying, whereby 'Vics' of three fighters in an arrowhead formation were the foundation elements. In practice this meant that the Vic leader issued appropriate orders for the particular FAA to be employed in whatever situation presented itself, but his two wing men necessarily concentrated primarily on holding strict station with their leader, leaving no time to prepare fully for the

23

actual moment of engagement with the target. Such drill square precision looked fine on a blackboard – it was useless in achieving its ostensible purpose. To add to the lack of realism, during the annual air exercises 'enemy' bombers invariably flew on pre-determined courses and altitudes already known to their 'interceptors'; thereby nullifying the hope of true practical testing of the aerial defences. Moreover, the bombers were seldom, if ever, escorted by 'enemy' fighters, leaving defenders with a free field of manoeuvre in attacks.

This well-worn pattern of 'war practice' was rudely shattered in the 1937 annual air exercises, when the 'invading' bomber forces included some of the latest Bristol Blenheim I monoplanes. Intercepting fighters found the bombers – but were unable to overtake them, having to suffer the humiliation of watching powerless as their 'opponents' calmly flew away at a speed higher than the fighters' best. Clearly the era of the twin-gunned, open-cockpit biplane fighter was over. Even if the existing interceptors had proved capable of matching a modern bomber's performance, the chances of that fighter's obsolete armament inflicting any real damage were, to say the least, doubtful. Increasing aircraft speeds meant that any target would remain in a fighter pilot's gunsight for only fleeting seconds, and the rate of fire of existing machine guns in 1936 meant that, effectively, less weight of hitting power could reach the target. Modifications of such guns to deliver a higher weight of ammunition within the time available could only be an interim measure; while to design and produce an entirely new gun would take many years. The obvious solution – though still a form of improvisation – was to increase the number of guns carried by a fighter. Just such a measure had already been mooted by Squadron Leader Ralph Sorley of the Research and Development Department in respect of an Air Ministry Specification F5/34, issued in January 1935. This called for a monoplane fighter of high speed, capable of destroying a bomber with just two seconds' gunfire. In its original form the specification called for four, possibly six machine guns; but at a slightly later date Sorley pleaded for this number to be raised to eight, wing-mounted guns of .303-inch calibre. The contemporary AOC-in-C, Air Defence of Great Britain, ACM Sir Robert Brooke-Popham, expressed his personal view that '. . . eight guns was going a bit too far. I should have been content with four.' He also added that these should be fitted into the cockpit area, and further expressed his opposition to enclosed cockpits.

Fortunately, Brooke-Popham's views were over-ridden and the

specification was issued. It called for an enclosed cockpit, retractable undercarriage, and – most important – eight wing-mounted Browning machine guns, each supplied with approximately 300 rounds of ammunition; sufficient for a total of 15 seconds firing. The responses by the firms of Hawker and Vickers Supermarine were to be the Hurricane and Spitfire respectively.

Like many other classic aircraft eventually used by the RAF, the Hawker Hurricane was originally conceived as a private venture by the firm's chief designer Sydney Camm. In October 1933, privately convinced that the biplane had had its day, Camm began design of a monoplane fighter. The completed design was submitted to Air Ministry on 4 September 1934, but progress continued while awaiting official response. On 21 February 1935 the Air Ministry cautiously issued a contract for the construction of one 'high speed monoplane' (the type was not officially titled Hurricane until 27 June 1936). This prototype, carrying the official serial number K5083, made its first flight on 6 November 1935 from Brooklands and proved to be virtually viceless, extremely manoeuvrable, and capable of speeds well in excess of 300 mph. The following June saw the Air Ministry place its first production contract, for 600 Hurricanes, and the first of these, L1547, made its initial air test on 12 October 1937. The Hurricane eventually entered RAF service 15 months later by re-equipping 111 Squadron at Northolt.

The Supermarine Spitfire – arguably the most aesthetically pleasing fighter design of all time – was the creation of Reginald J. Mitchell, designer of the Schneider Trophy winning floatplanes. The prototype 'Spit', K5054, made its first-ever flight from Eastleigh airport on 5 March 1936, and was quickly ordered into production. The first RAF unit to re-equip with Spitfires was 19 Squadron at Duxford in August 1938. Slightly smaller, more slender than the rugged Hurricane, the production Spitfire was faster by some 30 mph, but a shade less manoeuvrable. It, too, housed a battery of eight Brownings in its sleek elliptical wings.

Though such up-dated fighters were firmly in prospect, the UK fighter squadrons of 1936–8 were still equipped with obsolescent biplanes. In 1937 at least 19 squadrons were flying Gloster Gauntlets; two-bay, open cockpit fighters with the usual two-gun armament and a top speed, fully-loaded, of 230 mph. The Gauntlet's intended replacement was another biplane and stablemate, the Gloster Gladiator.

Originally built as a private venture, to satisfy the requirements of Air Ministry Specification F7/30, the eventual design made its first flight in 1934, and was immediately ordered into production in slightly modified form. Nevertheless, the first three production machines were not produced until early 1937 for the RAF, and 72 Squadron received its first nine examples at Tangmere in February of that year. Serving alongside the Gauntlets and early Gladiators were Hawker Fury IIs, the ultimate Hawker biplane fighters in RAF service. All these 'interceptors' were designed for daylight operations – the need for any form of specialised night fighter had hardly even been considered; this despite the overwhelming pre-occupation of the RAF hierarchy with finding means of combating any enemy bomber forces.

The Hurricane and the Spitfire were by no means the only monoplane fighter projects put forward from the mid-1930s. On 11 August 1937 the prototype Boulton Paul Defiant made its first testing flight; a two-seat fighter intended specifically to deal with invading bomber formations. Its basic conception was, however, outdated, having no forward armament for the pilot, and relying entirely on a four-gun, power-operated BP turret behind the pilot for offensive armament. On 11 October 1938 came the first flight of a highly unorthodox monoplane single-seat fighter, the Westland Whirlwind. Powered by twin engines, the Whirlwind carried a battery of four 20mm cannons in its slender nose. Other projected single-seat monoplane fighters during this period included the Gloster F5/34, Bristol Type 146, and the highly original, slab-sided Martin-Baker MB1; none of which earned a full production contract in view of the existing Hurricane and Spitfire mass orders.

Though much emphasis was necessarily laid upon the future production of truly updated fighters for Britain's aerial defences, these were but the 'sharp end' of a vast effort to prepare a support organisation fully capable of using the squadrons to the best possible advantage in war. The advent and future promise of RDF location and prediction had already led to Hugh Dowding requesting a chain of RDF warning stations around the vital approaches to London in the south and east coastal zones. In immediate back-up to the invisible RDF 'eyes' were the Observer Corps' observation units, who could physically plot the direction, approximate heights, speeds and strengths of any airborne formation. The combined details were passed direct to Fighter Command where the information was 'translated' onto a table-map of the UK. These data were then passed by telephone to a Group Operations

Room, where they could be superimposed on another table-map, this time of simply that Group's operational area. Thus briefed, the Group Controller could alert and despatch the most appropriately-located squadrons within his Group to intercept the enemy formations. In the beginning Fighter Command possessed two main areas to defend, each side of a line running east–west through Bedford. Of these No. 11 Group was tasked with all defence of the area south of that line, while a new Group, No. 12, was formed to cover the UK north of the same dividing line. Within each Group were specified Sectors, each surrounding a particular fighter station designated as the Sector Station. It was an uncomplicated delegation of levels of specific responsibility which, on paper, posed few problems in administration. In the event even these divisions proved too cumbersome for one Command headquarters to control singly, and further fighter Groups were inaugurated, subdividing the existing Group areas into more manageable zones of control.

With practice, and in the light of the expanding strength of the command, this basic system of reporting and control was continuously modified and improved. In November 1938 another facet of defence was placed under Dowding's aegis; RAF Balloon Command was formed at Stanmore, and the location details for the various 'barrages' were planned at Bentley Priory. Just four months later a further responsibility loaded upon Dowding's shoulders was the Anti-Aircraft Command, which formed as a corps separately from its former Army control. This ever-increasing volume of administrative and operational control for Dowding was happily in the highly capable hands of his Senior Air Staff Officer (SASO), Air Vice-Marshal Keith Rodney Park. An ex-World War One fighter 'ace', the tall, slim New Zealander had vast experience – and personal enthusiasm – for fighter operations, and as Dowding's second-in-command, Park was able to ease much of the vast responsibility piled piecemeal upon his commander. In early 1940 Park was to become commander of the vital No. 11 Group and then guide its fortunes throughout the critical months of the Battle of Britain; but long before that time he had played a major part in ensuring that Fighter Command was in the best possible state of organisation and equipment for its wartime tasks.

Having finally been forced to the conclusion that any lasting peace in Europe was a remote possibility, and therefore compelled to make good the omissions of a decade and more of failure to maintain a viable armed defence for Britain, the governmental ministries were, by 1938, engaged in an undignified scramble to bolster the existing armed services, particularly in regard to the RAF. Further impetus to this expansion came in September 1938 with the Munich Crisis. Poised perilously on the verge of war with Germany, the British Prime Minister, Neville Chamberlain, managed to appease the German leaders – mainly by being a party to the 'surrender' of Czechoslovakia – and returned to England proclaiming 'Peace in our time'. Though well informed of the RAF's inability to defend Britain if war was declared at that time, Chamberlain's appeasement ploy was not primarily made for that reason. Nevertheless, the shock of Munich, and the eventual 'extra year of grace' gained by the Munich 'surrender' gave huge relief to Hugh Dowding, who knew better than anyone how unprepared was his contemporary Command for any full-scale aerial defence of Britain. His fighter force comprised 29 squadrons, nearly all of which were still equipped with ageing biplanes. In addition no official manning establishment had yet been made for the vital Operations Rooms; while the civilian Observer Corps – so necessary in the general pre-warning system – had yet to be included in any mobilisation scheme should war come. Another subject of vital importance was the provision of all-weather runways for the fighter airfields; almost all existing stations were still grass-covered and thereby dependent on weather conditions. In this context Dowding met stiff opposition from the Air Staff, whose disapproval was based on the opinion of an Army officer responsible for a system of camouflaging aerodromes. Runways of concrete or similar materials would 'spoil the camouflage'!

Nor was this the only aspect of Command needs to be opposed by chairborne Air Staff 'experts'. When Dowding asked at one 1938 conference that bullet-proof windscreens should be fitted to Hurricanes and Spitfires, the Air Staff immediate reaction was pure amusement. Dowding retorted sharply, 'If Chicago gangsters can have bullet-proof glass in their cars, I can't see any reason why my pilots should not have the same!' The chief obstacle in Dowding's prolonged battles with Whitehall was one of RAF policy. Until Munich the RAF was virtually unshaken from the original Trenchard doctrine of offence being the finest form of defence; hence any purely defensive measures, such as Fighter Command, had tended to become of lesser priority to the need for a strong Bomber Command. After Munich, however, priorities became reversed, and Dowding's constant pressure for adequate squadrons of first-line fighters received closer attention. His chief and over-riding concern in this context was to obtain a firm commitment from the Air Staff on the minimum number of front-line squadrons necessary for the defence of the United Kingdom. It was to be his prime concern throughout his tenure of command, and the reason for his almost constant battles with both the Air Staff and a succession of Cabinet ministers. Dowding had ample reason for being concerned about an adequate strength for Fighter Command. The 1935 'Scheme C' expansion programme had promised at least 35 fighter squadrons; while further revisions ultimately estimated a need for a minimum of 53 squadrons by 1939. Yet on assuming command in 1936 Dowding had 15 regular and three AAF squadrons; and two years later could only muster 24 regular and six AAF units – every squadron being biplane-equipped. These latter would have been Britain's defending force had Munich resulted in all-out war.

Equally important to Dowding were his estimated reserves in both men and machines. The various expansion schemes of the late 1930s made large provision for training pilots – approximately 3800 per year – while at the close of 1936 the RAF Volunteer Reserve was created to provide training for a further 800 pilots annually. In 1935, in anticipation of such a training programme, five fresh Flying Training Schools (FTS) were opened (Nos. 7–11) and 13 civil flying training schools were co-opted. In addition nine Armament Training Camps were to be opened as soon as suitable sites could be agreed and purchased by the Air Ministry. Throughout Britain in 1937, at least 30 new aerodromes were opened, though nearly all were to have only hutted temporary accommodation initially; the main building priority being hangars and other technical accommodation. Notwithstanding all these burgeoning expansions, Dowding, too experienced in dealings with Service hierarchy and politicians to be complacent about glowing promises for the future, continued to press for the necessary squadrons and other essential equipment – RDF, personnel *et al* – envisaged in his overall plans for defending Britain.

While fully occupied in building the vast network of UK air defences, Hugh Dowding was also to be bedevilled by a succession of shifts in a personal vein. Early in 1936, prior to his appointment as AOC-in-C, Fighter Command, Dowding had been told by the existing Chief of Air Staff, Edward Ellington, that he would succeed Ellington as CAS; then on 3 February 1937 informed by Ellington privately that in fact the

Secretary of State for Air had selected Cyril Newall as the next CAS instead. Though personally disappointed, Dowding put aside any feelings of injustice – he was, after all, the senior officer of the RAF active list at that time – and merely expressed his wish to continue in his present post. In July 1938, however, he received a letter from the new CAS, Newall, telling Dowding that his services would not be required after the end of June 1939; or as an Air Ministry letter dated August 4th put it, '. . . unable to offer you further employment in the RAF after June 1939'. Between Newall's letter and the official confirmation missive, Dowding's successor at Fighter Command, Air Vice-Marshal Christopher Courtney, was notified that he would take up his appointment on 1 July 1939. Hugh Dowding accepted this notification of his retirement date quietly, then continued to press forward the many plans for his Command.

In February 1939 Dowding was surprised to receive a telephone call from Newall, in which the CAS referred to a recent newspaper announcement of the impending change of command, but then inferred that Dowding would continue in his present post until at least the end of 1939. Having already made his plans for a June retirement, Dowding wrote to Newall, formally requesting firm confirmation of the CAS's actual intentions; only to get a reply which ended in a request that Dowding defer his retirement until March 1940. Dowding patiently agreed to this new date, mainly because he remained anxious to see his Command's organisation brought to the highest possible state of efficiency before letting go the reins of control. On 30 March 1940 – just 24 hours before Dowding was due officially to leave the RAF – he received yet another jolt to his plans; a letter from Newall requesting that he remain at the helm of Fighter Command until 14 July 1940.

At that period Dowding was firmly convinced that it could only be months, possibly weeks, before all his years of planning for the aerial defences of the United Kingdom would be fully tested in action. To be replaced at such a moment – to 'swap horses in mid-stream' – was unthinkable; hence he willingly agreed to this latest date for his civilian 'bowler-hatting'. Even then he was not to be left in peace. On July 5th, in response to a telephone conversation with Newall requesting to be told the name of his successor – only ten days before his ostensible retirement, Dowding had yet to be given this information – he received another written request to re-postpone his retirement date until the end of October 1940. It was the fifth 'retiring date' offered to him since 1937 – it was not to be his last. Even allowing for hindsight, and knowledge of the myriad of pressures placed upon the Air Ministry at that particular period, it remains an astonishing fact that the commander of Britain's first-line defences was so treated at a moment in history when this country stood on the brink of possible massive armed invasion. As will be seen, his later treatment by these same Whitehall pundits was to plumb even greater depths of unvarnished discourtesy and downright ingratitude.

Although Hugh Dowding was to bear the foregoing string of uncertainties for his personal future, his over-riding concern in early 1939 was the existing state of his Command's operational material and organisation. The September 1938 political crisis – whatever else it may have achieved – at least offered a momentary breathing space from actual war, but to all but the obtuse it had given grim warning of the apparently inevitable conflict to come. Clearly, Hitler's Germany was not going to be content with its latest '*Lebensraum*' acquisitions in territory; particularly when Czechoslovakia had been given to the Germans without a murmur of opposition from the other leading European countries. Hitler's Luftwaffe seemed strong, due to an unprecedented campaign of propaganda by the German authorities, and in the lack of accurate details available to him, Dowding was forced to regard the given strength of his potential opponents as reasonable fact. For nearly three years he had fought steadfastly against Service and political obstacles to obtain the right aircraft, men, facilities *et al* for Fighter Command. In a private summary of events recorded by Dowding in early 1939, he noted,

> I can say without fear of contradiction that since I have held my present post I have dealt with or am in the process of dealing with a number of vital matters which generations of Air Staff have neglected for the past fifteen years . . . this work has had to be carried out against the inertia of the Air Staff, a statement which I can abundantly prove if necessary.[1]

These were not the words of a boastful man, but the carefully considered opinion of a highly professional airman, dedicated to his Service, and with his heart and soul totally occupied by his given tasks. Above all things Dowding was a realist, and his immense foresight, coupled with meticulous planning, was to produce a ground organisation for

[1] *Dowding & the Battle of Britain* by R. C. Wright; Macdonald, 1969.

Fighter Command by 1940 that withstood the cruellest testing under war conditions and continued to function. Added to this perspicacity was Dowding's immediate and deep grasp of virtually all the new technical facets of that embryo organisation – RDF, armament, air rocketry, even cannons for aircraft; all came within his aegis of research and development at some stage. Never one to shrink from unpleasant facts, he also foresaw that under wartime conditions of any air assault on England, his precious fighter squadrons would inevitably be depleted in strength in any battle of attrition, and therefore laid down plans for rapid interchanges of war-weary units and fresh squadrons between the far north of England and Scotland and the units in the 'forward zones' of southern England. And at every opportunity he continued to press his superiors in the Air Staff and government for more and better aircraft, men and vital equipment; a battle he was to fight almost to the last days of his RAF service.

Some of that modern equipment, particularly the eight-gun Hawker Hurricanes and Supermarine Spitfires, had already begun to filter through to the first-line fighter squadrons by 1939; though only relatively slowly and in small quantities. An interim stop-gap replacement for some biplane-equipped units was an adaptation of the twin-engined Bristol Blenheim I bomber. Modified to accept a four-machine gun pack under its belly, fired by the pilot, this Blenheim version was labelled as Mk 1F. In the first week of August 1939 the annual air exercises were held, despite the critical European political situation, and all sections of the UK-based RAF received a modicum of realistic testing under 'wartime' conditions. These included an impressively accurate recording and reporting of virtually all air movements by Dowding's Observer Corps and small RDF chain – a portent for the future. Just three weeks later, on September 1st, Germany attacked Poland and set Europe ablaze.

On that fateful date RAF Fighter Command's overall strength in aircraft was still well below the estimated 53 fighter squadrons' minimum considered necessary for the defence of Britain in the CAS's most recent assessment. Its true strength on 1 September 1939 stood at 37 squadrons, 14 of which were hastily mobilised Auxiliary Air Force 'non-regular' units. Of all these, 17 squadrons had Hurricanes, 12 were equipped with Spitfires, and no less than six were flying the stop-gap Blenheim 1F 'fighters'. Between them the 37 squadrons held the following totals of aircraft:

Hurricane	347	(400)
Spitfire	187	(270)
Blenheim 1F	111	(111)
Gladiators	76	(218)
Gauntlet	26	(100)

The bracketed figures here were the total aircraft of each type held on overall RAF strength that day. Thus of a complete 'stock' of 1,099 fighters, the front-line squadrons actually had 747 machines. The proportion of outdated or 'interim' fighters gave added emphasis to Hugh Dowding's three years' struggle with the powers-to-be for up-to-date and numerically adequate equipment for his squadrons – and is an overt illustration of how badly he had been served by his 'masters'.

As the last hours of peace approached Dowding's thinly-scattered fighter squadrons were at a high pitch of alertness and anticipation; eager and ready to repulse the first sign of any German onslaught. The vast majority of pilots were young, superbly trained to pre-1939 standards of flying skill though woefully lacking in hard practice for actual combat conditions. Relatively few of the pilots in the Spitfire and Hurricane units had even fired 'live' ammunition from their guns; a state which was to last until May 1940 in certain squadrons! All were inculcated with the parade-ground mentality of the outdated Fighting Area Attacks for combat tactical manoeuvres, though a minority privately held that such were, at least, questionable for actual fighting. Most of the junior pilots had grown up in an era when the exploits of the almost legendary fighting 'aces' of the 1914–18 war were being published widely. Men like 'Mick' Mannock, 'Jimmy' McCudden, Albert Ball, and the romantic German 'knights of the air' epitomised by Manfred von Richthofen, the 'Red Knight of Germany', and the incredibly courageous Werner Voss. Such men had helped to formulate the 'ground rules' of aerial combat, and their example and prowess served as shining pinnacles to embryo RAF fighter pilots of the 1930s.

Yet among the highly individual exploits of those doughty fighters there had been some who had applied an almost uncanny foresight to the whole business of air combat, particularly Mannock and von Richthofen, each of whom instigated the first truly successful fighting 'teams'. Both men, apart from exemplifying individual courage and achievement, welded the units under their command into co-ordinated fighting combinations; in effect becoming thereby the prototype Wing

Leaders which were to be 'introduced' into the RAF's fighter field more than 20 years later. Their immediate predecessors, men like Lanoe Hawker, VC, DSO and Oswald Boelcke, the 'Father of German fighters', and a hundred others, had pointed the way as squadron or *staffel* commanders who first taught the basic principle of teamwork at internal unit level, but it was not until late 1917 that the creed of inter-unit co-operation and planned mutual support became fully implemented for pure fighter combat.

Why this basic tenet of aerial warfare, fully tested and proven in the crucible of war, should then have been virtually ignored throughout the post-1918 RAF training is difficult to understand. Certainly, during the 1920s, the fighter arm of the RAF had been badly neglected and relegated to a much lesser priority in strategical thinking than the lumbering bomber. Nevertheless, many of the senior officers at all levels in the peacetime RAF had been men who 'won their spurs' in fighters during World War One, and were – in varying degrees – in positions where their views and experience might have exerted some influence. By 1939 a majority of fighter squadron commanders were men who had never known war, and whose background was almost entirely shaped by the peacetime era of Service bureaucracy, training, and fairly rigid adherence to the 'book'. Their individual quality as officers, leaders, and professional pilots was high, as was to be fully proved in the acid trial of combat; but long-held habits and obedience to higher authority often bred rigid thinking processes and a distinct hesitance to change such habits rapidly. Tragically, many such squadron commanders who failed to release their minds from the bonds of blind obedience were among the earliest casualties of 1939–40; often in circumstances of their own making in which younger pilots, faithfully following their leader, were also dragged into an unnecessary oblivion.

Any fault lay not with the individuals concerned but in the inherited system of training and practice for fighter combat, whereby singular examples of personal initiative and reasoned thinking on the part of junior officers were too often discouraged, even forbidden, by unimaginative career officers at higher levels in the promotion pyramid. Fortunately for the RAF, not all pre-1939 pilots of very junior rank were convinced of the efficacy of the official tactics imposed. One such was Flying Officer A. G. Malan, a South African, who was a Flight Commander in 74 Squadron in 1938–9. In the November 1938 competition for the Sir Philip Sassoon Trophy for fighter combat tactics, Malan ignored the text-book and led his men according to his personal ideas on how air fighting should be done. Though flying Gloster Gauntlets, the oldest aircraft designs at the competition, Malan's Flight won the trophy. In doing so they displeased certain of the judges, who ordered the 74 Squadron team to repeat their manoeuvres before finally agreeing to award the prize.

Malan's rooted objections to rigid 'book' tactics were to continue when, in 1940–1, he became the acknowledged top-scoring fighter of the RAF, and virtually a legend among his peers for his superb qualities of leadership. To Malan a fighter aircraft was simply a 'flying gun', designed for the sole purpose of destroying enemy aircraft, and not merely a vehicle in which to indulge a passion for 'pretty flying'. His opinion merely echoed the words of his famous predecessor of 1918 in 74 Squadron, 'Mick' Mannock, VC, DSO, MC, who had taught his men, 'Good flying never yet killed a Hun. You just get on with sighting your guns and practice spotting Huns. Then shoot them down before they shoot you'.

The spirit of the 1939 fighter pilot was universally one of aggression, of the true offensive outlook so necessary in broad terms of all fighting. Paradoxically, Hugh Dowding's prime, over-riding concern was that of *defence*, and his whole efforts were always channelled into what he firmly regarded as the real purpose of Fighter Command at that period – the protection and defence of Britain against any and every form of aerial assault. That was his 'portfolio' in office, and he never once forgot it. It was an awesome responsibility for any single commander, however experienced the man or well equipped his available forces; but in the summer of 1939 Dowding's command was by no means equipped to its requisite level. As his able 'lieutenant' Keith Park remarked, the personal 'conflict' between Dowding and the Air Ministry in his constant attempt to strengthen his forces, '. . . began long before the war started in 1939, when the Air Ministry failed to supply the C-in-C of Fighter Command with the squadrons, radar and other equipment which he had been promised for the effective air defence of Great Britain'.[1]

As events moved irrevocably towards war in the closing days of August 1939, Dowding and his staff at Bentley Priory worked incredible hours into each night, preparing for the inevitable. On the various grass-covered airfields of his command – only six fighter stations at that

---

[1] Quoted in *Dowding & the Battle of Britain* by R. C. Wright; Macdonald, 1969.

moment possessed concrete runways – the pilots waited impatiently for the 'balloon to go up'; waiting by their dispersed Spitfires, Hurricanes and Blenheims in flying gear, eager for the fray, excitedly or languidly – according to individual codes of behaviour – talking of the prospects of war. Emotions inwardly were mixed. The more extrovert debated tactics, manoeuvres and the relative merits of their own aircraft and the Luftwaffe's Messerschmitts, Heinkels, Dorniers and Junkers. Many other pilots, however, were virtually silent, each pondering his private reactions when the true test of courage and skill came in combat; whether the stirring 'butterflies' in his stomach would vanish once action was joined. Few, if any, thought seriously in terms of being killed; it only happened to 'others'. The warm sun set on the last evening of peace on September 2nd, leaving them still wondering . . . and waiting.

3. Debacle

As the clipped, nasal voice of the Prime Minister, Neville Chamberlain, announced that 'a state of war now exists with Germany' on Sunday morning, 3 September 1939, the peoples of Britain and her empire received the news with mixed emotions. Chamberlain's private disillusionment with such a climax to his many idealistic hopes for a workable peace with Hitler was reflected in the minds of the high proportion of men and women to whom stark memories of the horror and slaughter of the 1914–18 conflict were still relatively fresh. Added to such dismay was an apprehension about Germany's possible first move; generally considered to be most likely an immediate, massive aerial bombing assault on England's capital city and other population centres. Despite the governmental sloth and virtual public lack of interest in rebuilding a strong Royal Air Force after 1918, the British tax-paying civilian had inevitably become vaguely aware of the potential threat of modern air power. Newspapers and other media had dramatised blatantly the recent examples of air bombing during the Spanish Civil War – the razing of Guernica and other cities, with their high toll of civilian lives. More thoughtful readers of these accounts realised that many of the aircraft responsible were German, flown by crews of the Luftwaffe's *Kondor Legion* 'detachment'; gathering first-hand practical experience of the effectiveness of modern air warfare which might now be used against Britain.

On the eve of war, the possibility of an overwhelming bomber assault on Britain appeared to British leaders to be wholly within the scope of Hitler's Luftwaffe. Intelligence reports about the strength of Germany's air arm varied. One estimate – quoted in official publications for many years after 1945 – gave a precise total of 4,161 first-line aircraft on 3 September 1939; while an official publication by America's West

Point Academy in 1945 stated a strength of '. . . approximately 7,000 first-line machines'. The true figure, extracted from the daily strength reports of the Luftwaffe's Quarter-Master General's office, was a *total* strength of 4,704 aircraft, but of these less than half – 2,069 – could be classified as bomber or 'attack' machines. At his Bentley Priory head-quarters Hugh Dowding could only accept the latest intelligence esti-mate available and plan accordingly. Even allowing for the lowest estimated figure, he was left with the bald knowledge that his fighter pilots might find themselves facing odds of five, ten or even more to every single RAF fighter, should any such blanket bombing force set out against Britain. His overall defence policy was based, by higher direction, on the assumption that German bombers would be based in Germany, thus obviating the added threat of any fighter escort. Dowding privately worried about the future position should Germany obtain bases further west or north-east. If the Luftwaffe crews were able to operate from Belgium, Holland or northern France, their effective destructive range would be increased automatically, and they could to some extent be shepherded by strong fighter escorts; thereby present-ing Britain's defenders with a dual problem of how best to thwart the bombers *and* fighters.

Dowding was satisfied that Fighter Command's basic organisation was the right one, however large or mixed the opposition might be. His chief anxieties, as always, were about the pure quantitative strength and updated quality of his front-line units. The foundations he had worked tirelessly to establish were firm, though as yet incomplete, and would improve in efficiency under actual war conditions. Yet he still desperately needed sufficient men and machines to guarantee that organisation's true effectiveness. Possessing only 70 per cent of the promised 'minimum' number of squadrons considered vitally neces-sary for any defence of Britain, Dowding's slender resources were diminished almost immediately upon the declaration of war, when four of his squadrons, Nos. 1, 73, 85 and 87, were despatched to France as direct tactical air support for the army's British Expeditionary Force (BEF). Though he had been aware of this pre-planned decision to attach fighter squadrons to the BEF, Dowding had been under the firm impression that these units would only be withdrawn from Fighter Command *after* it had achieved a 53-squadrons' strength; from units *added* to that minimum figure needed to defend the homeland. As if such a ready depletion of his command was not enough, Dowding was also instructed to bring a further six squadrons to a 'mobile state' in readiness for a possible further addition to the BEF's air support formations.

Replacements for these gaps in his defending force were not readily available, either in aircraft or – particularly – trained fighter pilots. The hasty 1936–9 expansion schemes envisaged thousands of both in the immediate future, but Dowding, ever a realist, was primarily concerned with his present situation. 'Pie in the sky' was never an attractive train of thought for Dowding; long, bitter experience with a succession of political and Service chiefs had taught him the hollow value of promises on paper. His immediate reaction to this reduction in strength was to write to the Air Staff, complaining firmly about the matter, and pointing out the obvious further weakening of his resources should any more squadrons be taken away from his command. He also reminded them of their past promises, and emphasised that such detachments to France would also necessitate allocation of reserve aircraft and pilots to replace normal 'wastage' expected in any war operations; reserves he had been depending on for reinforcement of his already-understrength command in Britain. Dowding was quite aware that the policy of sending large armed support for the French was mainly a political one, but was solely concerned with what he regarded as the true priority – the aerial defence of the United Kingdom.

The first 'test' of that defence came within minutes of Chamberlain's sober speech, when an unidentified single aircraft was plotted as approaching London from the direction of the Continent. At 11.15 am the London air-raid sirens moaned out the first of 1224 more dirges to be heard in the city throughout the following years, warning the population of an approaching air assault. At Bentley Priory the 'hostile aircraft' was quickly established as a French machine carrying two officers to join an Allied mission in London and landing at Croydon; hence no interception orders were issued. Nevertheless, several southern fighter stations ordered pairs of fighters into the air simply to patrol the local area. This principle that all unidentified aircraft were to be regarded and treated initially as 'hostiles' was one adhered to by Fighter Command controllers throughout the war. The edgy alertness of the defence forces again proved 'over-enthusiastic' on September 6th, when a searchlight crew on Mersea Island reported an incoming 'raid' of German aircraft approaching the Thames Estuary. This false alarm escalated, with anti-aircraft guns at Chatham opening fire blindly at unseen 'targets', and 11 Group controllers ordered fighters from Hornchurch and North Weald to take off and 'intercept'. The arrival over Southend of these latter merely added to an increasing confusion on the RDF screens, resulting in even more fighters being sent off. Within the hour all the defending fighters had returned to their bases, having seen nothing of the reported 'enemy', and the 'Battle of Barking Creek', as this fiasco became titled, entered the annals of Fighter Command as its last serious error in the radar reporting and identification system.

As the first weeks of war lengthened into months, and the expected bombing assault failed to materialise, the British population relaxed mentally; while Dowding and his fellow Service chiefs continued to prepare for the immediate future. In France his fighter squadrons saw little action and therefore required little in the way of replacements or additional strength, thus easing Dowding's immediate anxiety about further drainage upon his resources. Nevertheless, he continued to plague the Air Staff with requests for a firm commitment on the number of squadrons he could rely on for the metropolitan defences. The response remained vague. Priority of effort in Whitehall was concerned with the BEF in France, building up a reasonable facsimile of the 1918 form of land warfare with entrenched lines, base depots and all the paraphernalia of a static army waiting for action. In the air above the 'western Front' the RAF and French Armée de l'Air faithfully pursued a policy of pure reconnaissance, with an occasional and rare clash with the Luftwaffe. As a bitterly cold winter settled upon the scene the prospect of direct action for the Allied forces faded even further, and the popular press dubbed the period as the 'Phoney War' and exacerbated a growing tendency for jingoism and euphoria in Britain; an ill-considered 'campaign' of poorly constructed propaganda which tended to lull the British civilian population into a sense of false security.

In the interim Fighter Command had been truly 'blooded' in action over British soil. The first engagement came early in the morning of 16 October 1939 when a German reconnaissance aircraft was reported over the naval anchorage at the Firth of Forth. A 'Scramble' order was given to 602 Squadron AAF based at Drem, and Blue Section (three Spitfires led by Flight Lieutenant George Pinkerton) intercepted the lone bomber, attacked it but then lost their target in cloud.[1] At 1400

[1] Reported as a Heinkel 111, but actually a Junkers 88 from KG30 based at Sylt.

hours the same day 602 was again despatched to intercept incoming German bombers, this time in company with three Spitfires from 603 Squadron AAF, led by Squadron Leader Andrew Farquhar, also based at Drem. The enemy formation comprised nine Junkers 88s from 1/KG 30, led by Hauptmann Helmut Pohle, which had set out to bomb HMS *Hood* in the Firth of Forth. In the subsequent brief action two Junkers were shot down, one by each of the Spitfire units, both into the sea. On October 28th both AAF units again shared in a victory, when a Heinkel III was brought down on the Lammermuir Hills – the first German aircraft to be brought down on British soil (as opposed to in Britain's territorial waters) during World War Two.

One aspect of the encounter on October 16th was the after-combat treatment given to the dead and wounded German crews. Those killed were given full military honours at their funeral, while the survivors were visited in hospital by the RAF fighter pilots involved; a continuation of the 1914–18 chivalry tradition for an 'honourable foe'. This 'gentlemanly' attitude to the Luftwaffe, though characteristic of the average Briton of that period, was to be swiftly dispelled within the following year, with very few individual exceptions. The war had yet to be regarded – by the British – as a *total* war, involving both civilian and Serviceman entirely; the British tax-payer was still steeped in a centuries-old euphoria of reliance entirely upon its paid, professional Servicemen to protect the country and fight its battles. Occasional raids by small formations of Luftwaffe reconnaissance bombers continued in late October and November 1939, and on November 20th a Vic of three Spitfires of 74 Squadron, based at Rochford, intercepted a lone Heinkel 111 near Southend and shot it into the sea – the first victory by an England-based fighter unit. Also serving in 74 Squadron at this time was Pilot Officer the Hon. Derek Hugh Dowding, son of the AOC-in-C, Fighter Command, who had joined 74 from Cranwell in August 1939, and was to fight in the Battle of Britain in 1940.

Such spasmodic encounters with the Luftwaffe over Britain gave good opportunities for Fighter Command's reporting system, and resulted on most occasions in victories for the eager Spitfire defenders. On 9 February 1940, Andrew Farquhar was again in action over the Firth of Forth, when he shot down a Heinkel 111 which crash-landed at North Berwick, an action which led to the award of a Distinguished Flying Cross (DFC) to Farquhar on February 26th. Four days before HM King George VI pinned the cross on Farquhar's tunic at Drem, however, he had claimed a third victim, another He 111 which crashed at St Abbs Head. In this combat Farquhar had been accompanied by Fg Off G. V. Proudman flying Spitfire L1007, an aircraft fitted with 20mm cannons, and after Farquhar's initial attack had put the Heinkel's engines out of action, he ordered Proudman in to test the effect of cannons, watching Proudman's markmanship chew large chunks out of the bomber's fuselage. It was a portent for future RAF fighter armament, though the testing of and problems of using cannons in fighters were to be prolonged and difficult in the following year. In all these, and other, isolated fighter actions, British-based Spitfires and Hurricanes had encountered only German bombers; none had seen or engaged Luftwaffe fighters. Thus the pre-1939 FAA attacks had been employed by the RAF pilots with success, which was precisely the type of targets – i.e. unescorted bombers – for which such tactics had been evolved originally. By February 1940 the Luftwaffe had no air bases on the continent within reasonable fighter range of Britain, hence the lack of escorts for the various bomber and reconnaissance sorties launched.

'Phoney War' or not, the build-up of forces in France led to France virtually demanding additional strengthening of the BEF during the winter of 1939–40, and Hugh Dowding was instructed to despatch two more of his precious fighter squadrons to the continent; two AAF units, 607 and 615, both flying Gloster Gladiators, leaving Croydon on November 15th to join the four Hurricane units already in France. At least Dowding was able to select which units he would send, and therefore kept his few Spitfire squadrons in England and Scotland. This was perhaps fortuitous, because the Spitfire's narrow-track undercarriage would have created many problems on the mud and grass airfields being used by the BEF's Hurricanes and Gladiators. This insistence by the French for stronger RAF fighter support – it was to be a constant cry from Paris right up until the final capitulation of France in June 1940 – is difficult to understand in the pure context of aerial strength already available for operations along the so-termed Western Front. The French Armée de l'Air, by April 1940, possessed some 550 first-line fighters; while the six RAF squadrons could produce only about 60 readily serviceable Hurricanes and Gladiators on any given day. If the French Cabinet was seeking some sort of parity in numbers, it would have meant literally despatching the whole of Dowding's Fighter Command to Europe; a force originated solely for metropolitan defence, not 'in the field' direct tactical support of a landed army.

The combat capability of those RAF fighter pilots already based in France was sharpened in occasional aerial clashes throughout the winter of 1939–40. The first confirmed aerial victory by an RAF fighter on the Western Front came on 30 October 1939 when Pilot Officer P. W. O. 'Boy' Mould of 1 Squadron, based at Vassincourt, shot down a Dornier bomber a few miles west of Toul. On November 2nd, 73 Squadron recorded its first victory when a New Zealand pilot, Flying Officer Edgar J. Kain, caught another Dornier at the unusually high altitude of 27,000 ft and destroyed it. 'Cobber' Kain was soon to become the RAF's first 'ace' of World War Two, i.e. being credited with five victories. These were, however, isolated instances; by the New Year the RAF in France had only claimed some 20 aerial victories overall. Not all the fighters' lack of successes were due to the relatively small Luftwaffe activity. Several Hurricane squadrons were beset by a spate of gun stoppages due entirely to the use of the thirty-year-old ammunition with which their armouries had been issued; while the majority of Hurricanes were still fitted with two-blade, fixed pitch propellers, thereby inhibiting performance. This latter situation was gradually being resolved during November-December 1939 by fresh aircraft arriving from Britain, each fitted with variable-pitch propellers – Kain's victory on November 2nd was in such a machine – and early in 1940, 1 Squadron, for example, received a fresh batch of Hurricanes, all fitted with either de Havilland variable-pitch or Rotol constant-speed propellers.

Though actual combat was relatively rare over the Western Front, the normal attrition in aircraft operating under 'field' conditions made it necessary for replacements to be provided readily from Britain, thereby making a further steady drain on Dowding's resources. Another worry for the commander of Britain's air defences was the flow to France of trained pilots, all regular-serving officers and senior NCOs due to the lack of wartime-trained pilots as yet. If not 'blooded' in combat, such men were at least reasonably experienced in every other facet of flying fighters, and would normally be regarded as the hard-core nucleus of Flight and squadron commanders for future freshly-formed fighter squadrons as Dowding's command gradually expanded to its requisite strength. Even with a drastically reduced period of training for pilots who had joined the RAF immediately upon the outbreak of war, it would be mid-1940 before any significant numbers of new pilots would be available to replace the regular personnel. It could be argued that the more 'unblooded' pilots who could be detached to France for experience, the better for the future strength of Fighter Command; but Dowding's foremost concern – as ever – was with the pure defence of Britain. The French campaign was not his real concern, beyond necessarily supporting the units from his command already based there in support of the army's BEF.

On 9 April 1940 Germany launched an invasion of Norway, having already occupied neutral Denmark, and thereby provided the Luftwaffe with suitable advanced airfields for operations over Norway in advance. The initial effect on Fighter Command was a further reduction in its immediate first-line strength, when in early May, two fighter squadrons – 46 (Hurricanes) and 263 (Gladiators) – were despatched to Norway for air support to the army and naval forces there. For the following month these two units fought overwhelming odds in extraordinarily difficult circumstances with great gallantry and courage, but the outcome was virtually a foregone conclusion. The Gladiators were literally wiped out, while on June 8th the Hurricanes of 46 Squadron were flown aboard the aircraft carrier HMS *Glorious* for return to England. Less than twelve hours later the *Glorious* was sunk by a barrage of gunfire from the German raiders *Scharnhorst* and *Gneisenau*, and with her the full complement of 46's Hurricanes, and all but two of the unit's pilots.

Even while the Norwegian fiasco was under way, German forces commenced their devastating *blitzkrieg* against the Low Countries on 10 May 1940. On the morning of that fateful day the Luftwaffe's total first-line aircraft strength available was 2,750; of which just over 1,200 were fighters of the latest types. Of the rest, all but 42 were bombers or dive-bombers. Against this daunting array of strength, the RAF could muster just six fighter squadrons. Within forty-eight hours Fighter Command in England had sent four more fighter units to France – 3, 79, 501 and 504 Squadrons – each of whom were in action within an hour or two of actually landing on the Continent. On May 13th, the fourth day of the *blitzkrieg*, a further 32 Hurricane aircraft and pilots were sent to France, and still the French government demanded more to be flung into the battle. At this point Dowding's command had almost a third of its total strength in France, including about 40 per cent of its fighter pilots.

On the evening of May 10th, as the German *blitzkrieg* rolled forward inexorably, Winston Churchill became the new British Prime Minister in a coalition government. As his new Secretary of State for Air, Churchill appointed an old colleague, Sir Archibald Sinclair. Churchill, the ever-unpredictable politician, had little opinion of generals and other Service leaders in broad terms, though paradoxically always considered himself perfectly capable of directing a war strategy. Moreover, his opinions of individuals were always subjective; his memory was long and clear when any particular individual 'crossed' him, usually resulting in a bleak future for any such 'opponent'. On assuming office, however, Churchill was faced with a situation in France which cut deeply into his personal emotional regard for that country, and the escalating, urgent demands from the French premier for more fighter squadrons to be sent to the battle-zone stirred almost undeniable response in Churchill's heart. Only five days later, the French premier had telephoned Churchill, declaring, 'We have been defeated. We are beaten; we have lost the battle.' That same day the Dutch resistance to the German onslaught collapsed. It was sombre news, and Churchill called a Cabinet meeting to discuss the critical situation; in particular yet another request from the French Government for more RAF fighter squadrons.

In attendance at that Cabinet meeting was Hugh Dowding. Alarmed by the increasing loss of his precious fighters to what he already regarded as a lost cause in the French struggle – up to May 13th he had lost over 200 Hurricanes apart from 32 more which had been despatched on that date – Dowding took a most unusual step. He applied through the Air Ministry's normal channels, asking to be allowed to appear before the Cabinet to state his case for the retention of his fighters in Britain. He no longer had complete faith in the Air Ministry fully supporting his case firmly enough to prevent Churchill's continuing acquiescence to French demands. To his personal surprise, Dowding was invited to attend such a meeting. At 10 Downing Street, he was shown into the Cabinet Room and given a seat away from the main table, while the preliminary business of the meeting was discussed. When the subject of the French demands appeared on the agenda, Dowding was asked to sit a few places to the right of Churchill. The Prime Minister then spoke of the military situation in France, expanding in his normal rhetorical manner on the various implications involved. Dowding then rose and in clear, factual, unemotional terms made his case for sending no further fighters to France. He could foresee clearly the inevitable aftermath of a French defeat; he stressed the absolute urgency for retaining every possible means of defending Britain from any subsequent assault by Germany.

Sensing that his words and facts were simply not making any depth of impression on Churchill and the other people present, Dowding then walked to Churchill's chair and placed on the table before the Prime Minister a simple graph he had prepared at Bentley Priory that morning. It was a factual statement of the losses already incurred extended in pure logical manner to indicate the immediate future position of Fighter Command should this rate continue. As he placed it in front of Churchill, Dowding quietly commented, 'If the present wastage continues for another fortnight we shall not have a single Hurricane left in France *or in this country*.' Dowding returned to his seat in the utter silence which followed, while Churchill sat glaring at the graph. It brooked no argument. Dowding had been forced to fight his case alone; the Chief of Air Staff, Newall, and other Air Ministry representatives present took no part in the discussion. In doing so, Dowding had clearly incurred Churchill's displeasure, but so strongly did Dowding feel on this issue that he felt impelled to 'beard Churchill in his den'. He left the meeting shortly afterwards to return to Bentley Priory, with the understanding that his plea had been accepted.

Although understandably relieved to know that the Cabinet had, ostensibly, agreed with his views, Dowding's long experience of politicians still left certain doubts in his mind as to whether his request would indeed be ratified. It was, after all, primarily a political rather than military question, and Dowding's lifetime distrust of political assent led him to take one more decisive step in his private battle with higher authority. His doubts were crystallised in a letter addressed to the Under Secretary of State for Air, dated 16 May 1940, which Dowding composed immediately upon his return to his office. It requested, in formal terms, what Dowding himself desperately needed to have confirmed officially; '. . . how much longer the drain (*on his fighters*) was going on, and I had to ask for a figure at which they would shut the stable door and say no more squadrons would be sent to France.' Dowding's letter, typed on two sheets of officially-titled foolscap paper, was to be one of the most significant documents of World War Two, and today holds a place of honour, framed, in the RAF College, Cranwell. It read:

> I have the honour to refer to the very serious calls which have recently been made upon the Home Defence Fighter Units in an attempt to stem the

German invasion on the Continent. I hope and believe that our Armies may yet be victorious in France and Belgium, but we have to face the possibility that they may be defeated.

In this case I presume that there is no-one who will deny that England should fight on, even though the remainder of the Continent of Europe is dominated by the Germans.

For this purpose it is necessary to retain some minimum fighter strength in this country and I must request that the Air Council will inform me what they consider this minimum strength to be, in order that I may make my dispositions accordingly. I would remind the Air Council that the last estimate which they made as to the force necessary to defend this country was 52 Squadrons, and my strength has now been reduced to the equivalent of 36 Squadrons.

Once a decision has been reached as to the limit on which the Air Council and the Cabinet are prepared to stake the existence of the country, it should be made clear to the Allied Commanders on the Continent that not a single aeroplane from Fighter Command beyond the limit will be sent across the Channel, no matter how desperate the situation may become.

It will, of course, be remembered that the estimate of 52 Squadrons was based on the assumption that the attack would come from the eastwards except in so far as the defences might be outflanked in flight. We have now to face the possibility that attacks may come from Spain or even from the North coast of France. The result is that our line is very much extended at the same time as our resources are reduced.

I must point out that within the last few days the equivalent of 10 Squadrons have been sent to France, that the Hurricane Squadrons remaining in this country are seriously depleted, and that the more Squadrons which are sent to France the higher will be the wastage and the more insistent the demands for reinforcements.

I must therefore request that as a matter of paramount urgency the Air Ministry will consider and decide what level of strength is to be left to the Fighter Command for the defences of this country, and will assure me that when this level has been reached, not one fighter will be sent across the Channel however urgent and insistent the appeals for help may be. I believe that, if an adequate fighter force is kept in this country, if the fleet remains in being, and if Home Forces are suitably organised to resist invasion, we should be able to carry on the war single handed for some time, if not indefinitely. But, if the Home Defence Force is drained away in desperate attempts to remedy the situation in France, defeat in France will involve the final, complete and irremediable defeat of this country.

Dowding's reservations about the eventual outcome of his meeting with Churchill's Cabinet were, in the event, well founded. Even as he was en route back to Bentley Priory the ministers changed their decision, and approved the move of four more fighter squadrons to France; the orders for this move being sent to Air Ministry for immediate implementation by the Deputy CAS, Sholto Douglas. Douglas 'interpreted' this order for four squadrons in terms of eight Flights, thereby leaving – in his view – the 'nucleus of the eight squadrons' on which he assumed Dowding could easily rebuild further units. It was not only muddled thinking on Douglas's part, but contrary to Dowding's way of thinking. He had neither time, personnel nor resources available to 'reconstitute' new squadrons, therefore the 'nucleus squadrons' simply became less effective for their prime purpose. Within 24 hours a further order – this time direct from Churchill in Paris – required a further six squadrons to be sent to France, despite the obvious lack of even remotely suitable airfields or facilities available by then to accommodate six first-line fighter units in France. Yet again Churchill had allowed personal emotion and a curious lack of understanding of the necessities of modern warfare to over-ride any objective, statesmanlike view of the contemporary situation.

When Churchill's latest order reached the Air Staff, Cyril Newall, the Chief of Air Staff, who had failed to back Dowding at the crucial Cabinet meeting of May 15th, now took a firm 'stand', especially in the light of Dowding's letter of May 16th. Instead of sending the requested six squadrons to France, he ordered arrangements for six units to be moved to forward airfields around the southern coast of England, from where they could operate over French territory, yet return to their English bases at the close of each day. On Churchill's return from Paris he presided over another War Cabinet meeting called to consider the latest situation in France, and had his first sight of Dowding's letter of May 16th. Finally, on May 19th, Churchill recorded his decision that 'No more squadrons of fighters will leave the country whatever the need of France.' In postwar years, when writing his personal version of those momentous days, Churchill was to record, 'Air Chief Marshal Dowding, at the head of our metropolitan Fighter Command, had declared to me that with twenty-five squadrons he could defend the Island against the whole might of the German Air Force, but that with less he would be overpowered.' It can only be speculation now as to why Churchill should have chosen to place such an inaccurate statement on record, for Dowding had never had any opportunity to discuss the question of the strength of his command with Churchill before the vital Cabinet discussion of May 15th, and at no time had he ever expressed a view that a mere 25 squadrons would suffice to defend Britain against the Luftwaffe. Regrettably Churchill's written version continues to be quoted as 'gospel' by latter-day historians even in most recent years, thereby giving a totally false impression of the events of mid-May 1940.

While Dowding fought his lone battle to preserve a sufficient strength in his command for the – to him – inevitable battle to come, his few squadrons in France had been fighting against vastly superior odds in a grim, losing struggle to stem the tide of Luftwaffe aircraft battering the Allied forces and supporting the German ground advances. From shortly after dawn on May 10th the Hurricanes had been in constant action, flying five, six, even seven sorties each day with little respite between sorties. In the main the fighters were called upon for escorts to the various hastily-mounted bombing raids by the Battles and Blenheims of the BEF's air component formations, but the Hurricanes were too few in number to offer anything but a token aid in this context. Too often a single formation of eight, or even fewer, Hurricanes set out to rendezvous with an RAF bombing force, only to be swamped by a horde of Messerschmitt Bf 109s even before the projected rendezvous could be made. Combat was fierce and savagely swift; casualties on both sides were high, with the RAF pilots generally giving better than they received in terms of 'victories'. Yet the outcome was virtually a foregone conclusion – sheer weight of numbers prevailed, while all RAF units quickly found themselves living a gipsy mode of life, shifting airfields and bases as the battle progressed westwards and northwards.

The details of that daily, hourly conflict are not strictly part of the story of Fighter Command, but apart from the significance of the eventual massive losses in both pilots and fighter aircraft – which patently had an enormous importance to Dowding – the actual tactics used generally by the RAF fighter pilots in France are of significant interest. Roland Beamont, later to rise to Wing Commander, DSO, DFC, joined 87 Squadron (Hurricanes) at Lille Vendeville in October 1939, having come directly from the 11 Group Fighter Pool at St Athan, with a total of 130 flying hours in his log book, of which just 15 were on Hurricanes. As such he virtually represented the type of young fighter pilot then emerging from the latest training syllabuses in the RAF. Speaking of his own experiences from 10 May 1940, Beamont recorded:

My third combat was a classic example of the weakness of inflexibility. We were now operating full-time from the grass field at Lille Marque and had been ordered off at three-squadron strength to patrol the ground battle area at Valenciennes at 10,000 feet. We made a fine sight as 36 Hurricanes formed up in the late afternoon sun in three squadron boxes, line-astern, four sections of Vic-Threes to a squadron. I was flying No. 2 in the right-hand section of 87 Squadron, leading the Wing, and it made one feel quite brave looking back at so many friendly fighters. And then without fuss or drama, about ten Messerschmitt 109s appeared above our left rear flank of our formation out of some high cloud. The Wing leader turned in towards them as fast as a big formation could be wheeled, but the 109s abandoned close drill and, pulling their turn tight, dived one after the other on to the tail sections of the Wing. Their guns streamed smoke and one by one, four Hurricanes fell away. None of us fired a shot – some never even saw it happen – and the enemy disengaged, while we continued to give a massive impression of combat strength over the battle area with four less Hurricanes than when we started. We had had more than three times the strength of the enemy on this occasion and had been soundly beaten tactically by a much smaller unit, led with flexibility and resolution.

The Battle of France was soon over but the authorities were slow to react to facts and change the rules, and change came about the hard way by squadrons learning from experience and adapting themselves. Nevertheless, there were still some squadrons going into action in the beginning of the Battle of Britain in 'standard Fighter Command attacks', and many in the inflexible three-sections Vic formation. In 87 Squadron we had modified our tactics to an initial turn in towards the enemy when sighted, followed by flexible exploitation of the subsequent situation – in other words, every man for himself. We still flew in three Vics of three, but in extended battle formation with wing men weaving for cross reference, and at no time did we practise close No. 2 cover, or the basic 'Finger-Four' formation flown by the Germans and adopted by the RAF tardily at the end of the battle.[1]

The pace of the fighting over the Western Front was intensive until the close of the battle. A few examples of individual squadrons' prowess epitomise the determination and courage of the Hurricane pilots as they clashed with almost frightening odds. The Auxiliaries of 501 Squadron were in action within an hour of arrival in France, and during its first 48 hours had claimed 18 victories for the loss of two pilots. Two weeks later the 'week-end fliers' were still in the heat of combat when 13 Hurricanes tackled 24 Heinkels and their 20 Messerschmitt escorts; claiming a total of 15 Luftwaffe aircraft either destroyed or probably destroyed. In the other Hurricane squadrons the story was much the same. From dawn on May 10th until May 24th, the

[1] *Hurricane at War* by Chaz Bowyer; Ian Allan Ltd, 1974.

original pilots of 1 Squadron, led by 'Bull' Halahan, claimed over 100 victories – officially a minimum of 87 – for the loss of three pilots, before the survivors were repatriated to England and replaced by fresh pilots. Another of the initial four squadrons to go to France at the outbreak of war, 87, claimed some 80 victories in ten days of furious fighting in May 1940, but lost nine pilots killed in action, with five others wounded.

Before the final collapse of France, the German *blitzkrieg* had cost the BEF's air components and Fighter Command a total of 477 fighter aircraft; but the most grievous losses were the many pilots killed in action, men who had become veterans in mere weeks of action, and whose experience was then lost for ever to the future command's fighting squadrons. Men like the Australian Leslie Clisby of 1 Squadron who, unofficially, ran up a tally of 19 victories before his death; and the New Zealander Edgar 'Cobber' Kain, DFC of 73 Squadron, who became the first RAF fighter pilot to achieve five-victory 'acedom' and then died in a simple flying accident after his seventeenth victory, on the very morning he was due to leave France for England. Fighter aircraft could be replaced with reasonable ease in mid-1940 – the factories were already geared to produce approximately 400 new machines per month – but nothing could immediately fill the void of trained, experienced pilots.

While the Hurricane squadrons maintained their all-out effort to stem the German onslaught, the position of the BEF grew rapidly precarious. Constantly forced to retreat by the speed and strength of the German thrusts, the British and French armies were inexorably pushed towards the Channel coastline. With the distinct possibility of the loss of the entire BEF should the pitch of fighting continue, the order came from London to instigate Operation Dynamo – a general evacuation of the BEF, centred around the coastal town of Dunkirk – commencing on May 26th. Aerial protection for the Dunkirk evacuation – which would patently become a top priority bombing target for Luftwaffe bombers – was the prime responsibility of Keith Park, now AOC of 11 Group, Fighter Command. At his disposal were, at most, 200 fighters in 16 squadrons, based around the south-eastern corner of England. His only 'reserves' were the remaining units of Fighter Command already protecting the Midlands and Northern Britain; squadrons which Dowding was not prepared immediately to throw into the wasteful campaign in France, having always his premier regard for the immediate future need for a strong defence for Britain itself.

Park's tactical use of his relatively few squadrons was later to be heavily criticised by, among others, the Admiralty who, being responsible for providing the shipping required to 'lift off' the BEF from Dunkirk's beaches, expected 'continuous air cover' from the RAF throughout. Such continuity in air presence was simply beyond the capability of Park's squadrons, most of which were based at least 60 miles from the beach-head. Instead, Park chose to despatch single squadrons on a form of patrol 'rotation' above the evacuation area; this latter to include at least ten miles inland from the beaches in order to tackle any German bombing formation approaching the area. Personally, Park would have preferred to send stronger formations at longer intervals, in order to achieve more significant results in combat. He acknowledged that the sheer numerical superiority of the Luftwaffe would mean that some bombers must reach the evacuation zone, but felt that single squadrons could hardly repel even a worthy proportion of such attacks. It was perhaps predictable that those many soldiers who eventually reached England via Dunkirk were scathing in their complaints about a 'lack of air cover' over the beaches. The huge effort made by Park's squadrons was either too high in the sky, or too far inland for the weary and exhausted infantry having to endure bombing attacks along the Dunkirk shoreline to appreciate. Certainly, those crews of the Luftwaffe attempting to seal off the surrounded BEF would not have agreed with the view that the RAF was 'absent'; as II Air Corps' war diary gives witness in its account for May 27th, when 23 German aircraft were lost along with 64 air crew members killed. As Major Werner Kreipe of III/KG2 reported, 'The enemy fighters pounced on our tightly knit formation with the fury of maniacs.'

It was during this period that Park's precious Spitfire squadrons got their first real taste of combat with full formations of the Luftwaffe; while many pilots who were later to become leading fighter 'aces' were to be 'blooded' in action. From Hornchurch, Flight Lieutenant Adolph 'Sailor' Malan, leading a Vic-three patrol of Spitfires, scored his first victories – a Heinkel 111 and a Junkers 88 – on May 21st; then early next day shared in the destruction of another Ju 88. His report on the latter engagement was couched in *de rigueur* wording of the period:

I was leading three sections off Dover at 12,000 feet when I sighted a Ju 88 steering NW in a clearing in cloud. Formed line astern with Red Section and cut enemy aircraft off from cloud. He dived for sea very steeply at 400 mph IAS (Indicated Air Speed) and jettisoned four bombs. I delivered No. 1

attack at 250 yards' range. After second two-seconds' burst rear gunner stopped firing from top blister. E/A (Enemy Aircraft) took avoiding action by skidding and turning. I saw incendiary enter port engine and all round fuselage whilst white vapour was emitted from both motors. At commencement of action IAS was 280 mph, but after my fifth burst speed suddenly reduced and as my windscreen was covered in white vapour I broke off to port and observed results of action. No. 3, whose R/T had failed, then attacked from 200 yards and expended all his ammunition and broke off. No. 2 then attacked but after his first burst E/A suddenly lost height as though both engines had stopped, and broke up. There was nothing left after two seconds, except the dinghy. Searched for crew but found none.

On May 23rd another Hornchurch-based Spitfire pilot had his first taste of combat, and in the course of two patrols that day shot down three German fighters. During the following two years Robert Stanford Tuck was to rise to Wing Commander, DSO, DFC and achieve a tally of 30 victories before being shot down by flak during an offensive sweep over German-occupied territory and becoming a prisoner of war. Yet another future fighting leader of huge repute, Douglas Bader, the 'legless ace', then a Flight commander with 222 Squadron based at Hornchurch, claimed the first of a long string of victories over Dunkirk on June 1st, shooting down a Messerschmitt Bf 109. Such men were to become the virtual 'spine' of Fighter Command during the coming year of combat; all three were pre-1939 trained pilots of relatively large flying experience who now completed their 'training' by putting into practice their years of 'theory'. As Malan's combat report illustrated, however, the actual tactical approach to fighting was still tied to peace-time thinking; automatic adherence to the 'pretty' copy-book Fighting Area drills and manoeuvres. Individually, each man had serious doubts about such methods, but none were yet in a sufficiently senior position to influence overall thinking on the subject; they could only follow orders.

When Operation Dynamo was completed on June 4th, Dowding took stock of the situation in relation to his command's immediate strength and potential. For the following two weeks RAF fighters, in diminishing strength, continued operations in and over France, but on June 18th the last remnants returned to England. From May 10th until the end of Dynamo, a total of 432 Hurricanes (mainly) and Spitfires had been 'expended' – the rough equivalent of at least 20 squadrons – apart from the almost irreplaceable pilots in many of these. There is little doubt that of the 1,284 aircraft also lost by the Luftwaffe, a high proportion had been lost to RAF action. On June 1st Dowding could count a total of 446 operationally-fit aircraft, of which 331 were Hurricanes and Spitfires. Actual fighter production for the month of June 1940 was planned to be 292, but in the event the factories provided a total of 446 machines. In July this total was increased to 496.

Across the Channel the Luftwaffe settled into its new bases and airfields. The recent campaigns had taken a heavy toll in aircraft, crews and immediate replacement resources; while the operational crews needed rest and recuperation before they could be fit for any further extended intensive operational effort. Though a series of, mainly, reconnaissance flights continued to be made over southern England after the collapse of France, the bulk of the German units stationed along the northern French coastline kicked their heels, waiting for the signal to resume. The procrastination in pursuing the war over England was due mainly to an air of some confusion in intent at the highest levels of command in Berlin. One school of thought, abetted by Hitler, considered that Britain might well sue for peace now that she stood alone, facing a victorious *Wehrmacht*. In truth, the sheer speed of the German victory in the West had come as a surprise to the German general staffs; they were only partly prepared for any continuation of the war to Britain itself. It was not until July 2nd that Hitler finally approved a directive to his High Command to commence preparations for a possible 'landing operation against England'. Two weeks later, in the absence of any response to his hopes for a peaceful settlement with London, Hitler confirmed his intention to invade England, stating that, 'Since England, in spite of her hopeless military situation, shows no sign of being ready to come to an understanding, I have decided to prepare a landing operation against England and, if necessary, to carry it out.'

The projected target date for completion of these preparations was set for mid-August, 1940, and on July 21st the head of the Luftwaffe, Hermann Göring, conferred with his senior air commanders at his home, Karinhall, announcing his plans for the 'final phase' of operations against England.[1] The available strength of the three *Luftflotten* detailed for the subjugation of British aerial defences, on July 20th,

[1] The term 'England' was virtually always used by the Germans when referring to Britain as a whole.

comprised totals of 1610 bombers (all types) and 1155 fighters; though aircraft actually serviceable for immediate operations on that same date were 944 bombers and 824 fighters. Against this awesome aerial might – though obviously Dowding had no precise figures for the Luftwaffe's actual strength at that moment – Fighter Command comprised a total of little more than 600 serviceable fighters, a proportion of which were outdated types, like the Boulton Paul Defiant two-seat 'turret fighter' and the rehashed Bristol Blenheim 1F 'fighter'. These were spread thinly along the whole length of Britain among four Groups; 11 Group with 19 squadrons defending the vital south-eastern areas of England, 12 Group with 14 squadrons to defend the Midlands, 13 Group with 12 squadrons for the protection of northern England and the whole of Scotland, while the newly-formed 10 Group with seven squadrons was tasked with the defence of south-west England and Wales. These 52 squadrons – the total considered vitally necessary to defend Britain in 1939 against a Luftwaffe *based in Germany only* – were now expected to provide an adequate shield against a German air force with bases stretching along the whole coastline of Europe and in Norway; some of the newly acquired French airfields being situated within 100 miles bombing range of London, the capital city.

Many past published accounts of the aerial war in early 1940 have tended to create an impression that after the final evacuation of the BEF from Dunkirk there came virtually a lull in air operations for Fighter Command and the Luftwaffe, thereby permitting Hugh Dowding to take advantage of this 'respite', and to build up his defences for the forthcoming battle over south-east England. In fact, nothing could be further from the truth. While it is true that the Luftwaffe eased in the intensity of its operational effort, due to the necessity for regrouping, refurbishing and recuperation after its French campaign *et al*, and by July was deliberately reserving itself for the expected major effort which would be required to precede Hitler's intended invasion of England, German bombers and reconnaissance aircraft continued to operate over the Channel almost daily. Their targets were the vital shipping convoys supplying Britain with materials with which to continue prosecution of her war. These convoys, braving the narrow confines of a channel virtually under the noses of the enemy, were legitimate objectives and easily reached by the Dorniers and Junkers based in northern France. The British Admiralty, clearly unable to commit large naval escorts in such narrow, vulnerable waters, logically demanded aerial protection from the RAF for the shipping, specifically from Fighter Command.

The responsibility for provision of this fighter 'umbrella' fell, yet again, on the capable shoulders of the 11 Group commander, Keith Park, who proceeded to detail small Flights of (usually) six aircraft to patrol above any convoy as it entered the narrows of Dover. The existing radar defence chain could forewarn Group headquarters of any sizeable German formation heading towards a convoy from French bases, hence reinforcement fighters could be despatched in reasonably quick time when necessary. Throughout the remaining days of June these patrols, and other Fighter Command units stationed much further north, clashed occasionally with isolated German raids of a minor nature; yet the command was still desperately trying to regain a full operational status before the expected aerial storm. The survivors of the French debacle were, in the main, in need of almost total refurbishment in men and machines, while many of the veteran pilots of that savage campaign were quietly 'rested' in instructional posts or other 'backwater' occupations – at least, for the moment. Their experience of combat with the Luftwaffe was badly needed for inculcation of the as-yet untried pilots in the command, many of whom had yet to fire a gun 'in anger'. Apart from the need to 'salt' the first-line squadrons with such veterans as Flight and squadron commanders where feasible, Dowding's immediate concern remained the question of a steady flow of trained pilots to man the new fighters being issued from factory floors. A combing of the other RAF commands, and the Fleet Air Arm, produced a small number of such men, ostensibly competent in the role; while he could also begin to create a handful of units from the 'pool' of refugee pilots who had fled Nazi domination in Czechoslovakia Poland, Belgium, France and other countries. At dawn on 1 July 1940 Fighter Command's Order of Battle showed a total first-line strength of 57 squadrons – though of these, six were actually non-operational for various reasons. Manning these units was a gross total of 1,103 fighter pilots; 11 Group having 553, 12 Group 228, and 13 Group a total of 322. Bearing in mind the six 'non-operational' units, this meant that Britain's immediate fighter defence on that day lay in the hands of less than a thousand young men.

The general mood of those pilots could be fairly described as buoyant. The more experienced element had by then recovered to a great extent from their harrowing experiences in France or over the

Dunkirk beaches, and were ready for the 'next round'; while the inexperienced in combat – the majority – were keyed to a pitch of anticipation. In every dispersal hut there was an air of quiet confidence, composed partly of complete faith in their aircraft, and in their training. Added to these was the unconscious, boundless self-confidence of youth; that peak of physical and mental ability which feels it can tackle anything and still win through. Within weeks this latter facet was to be severely tested to its limits as individual pilots watched close friends blasted to oblivion or sent to a fiery grave. Only then came the horrifying thought that they were not immortal; that death offered no favours in its selection.

4. So Few

The date given for the start of the Battle of Britain varies widely according to which published and official accounts are consulted; some German sources even virtually denying that any such defined battle per se occurred. It could certainly be reasonably claimed that the 'Battle' really started on one of two dates; June 4th, when the Dunkirk evacuation of the BEF was – officially – completed, or possibly July 1st, when German troops completed initial occupation of the Channel island of Guernsey, unopposed, and thus captured their first section of the sovereign territory of the British Isles. Nevertheless, the official qualification for award of the 'Battle of Britain Star' – a gilt rose emblem worn centrally upon the medal ribbon of the 1939–42 Star (later amended to become the 1939–45 Star) – was to have been an aircrew member of stipulated squadrons in Fighter Command, who flew at least one operational sortie between 0001 hours on 10 July 1940 and 2359 hours on 31 October 1940.

This rather arbitrary selection of dates hardly takes into account the 'pre-Battle' combats fought so fiercely and at no little cost. Nor does it give sufficient importance to the significance of the 'opening rounds' of the aerial struggle immediately preceding those bureaucratically-selected parameters. The closing week of June and first days of July 1940 saw the Luftwaffe mainly concerned with an unco-ordinated variety of operations over southern England, both by day and by night, but the principal daytime sorties were directed against the many Allied merchant shipping convoys threading their way through the Channel waters towards the Thames Estuary. The intention was primarily a form of aerial blockade of Britain to starve her of the essential resources needed for continuance of the war. Hitler was still hopeful that Britain would conclude her part in the war by accepting peace terms, and as yet

58

he was not fully prepared to undertake any serious offensive operations directly against the island. Such air raids as were flown against Britain, from both French and Norwegian bases, were either in the form of single Dorniers or Junkers 88s attempting daylight reconnaissances, or fairly strong formations of bombers, heavily escorted by Messerschmitt Bf 109 fighters, intent on sinking merchant shipping in the narrow Channel. Almost none of these operated unscathed and were intercepted by Dowding's fighters, albeit usually in relatively small numbers. Yet the first nine days of July saw frequent despatch of the defenders which clashed each time with superior numbers around the southern coast. The outcome was that in those nine days the Spitfire and Hurricane pilots claimed at least 56 victims,[1] but lost throughout Fighter Command totals of 28 aircraft and, more seriously, 23 aircrew members either killed or wounded. It may well appear ironic that none of the latter were later to be considered 'qualified' to receive the gilt 'Battle of Britain Rosette' . . .

These early clashes though necessarily intercepted and – in the main – repulsed, were patently probing sorties as far as Dowding and Keith Park were concerned. Dowding's foremost concern was with the expected bombing onslaught to come; pure peripheral actions, and especially fighter-versus-fighter combat were therefore in his eyes wasteful of effort and expenditure in casualties among his fighter squadrons. He recognised the need for engaging enemy fighter escorts in order to get at the bombers these were protecting, but emphasised his view that the priority targets, always, should be the bombers. This policy accorded with the *raison d'être* of Fighter Command under Dowding's terms of reference, and remained his first tactical principle throughout the battle.

On the German side the limited operational range of the Messerschmitt Bf 109 – the only single-seat fighter type used by the Luftwaffe during the 1940 operations over Britain – even when based close to the Channel, led to serious restrictions. The hope was to draw up RAF fighters into a pure fighter battle of attrition and thereby achieve a clear sky for the planned bomber assault. Yet German fighter units stationed in the Pas de Calais and Cotentin peninsula areas could only count upon an operational fighting radius, in round figures, of perhaps

---

[1] This figure is derived from actual losses recorded in Luftwaffe documents; RAF claims were rather higher.

125 miles, barely sufficient to reach London's suburbs. By denying the Luftwaffe fighter arm its hoped-for fighter battle, Dowding's policy of 'reserving' his main effort for repulsing the bomber formations proved to be correct. This was later admitted by Adolf Galland, one of the Luftwaffe's brilliant fighting leaders on the 'Channel Front' during that fateful summer. He has recorded:

> Our fighter formations took off. The first air battles took place as expected and according to plan. Because of German superiority these attacks, had they been continued, would certainly have achieved the attempted goal, but the British fighters were recalled from the area long before this goal was reached. The weakened squadrons of the RAF left their bases near the coast and used them only for emergency landings or to refuel. Concentrated in a belt around London in readiness for our bomber attacks, they thus evaded the attack *in* the air in order to counter more effectively the attack *from* the air which would logically follow. The German fighters found themselves in a similar predicament to a dog on a chain which wants to attack the foe, but cannot harm him because of his limited orbit. As long as the enemy kept well back, our task could not be accomplished.[1]

Galland's comment was perhaps an over-generalisation, but it contained the essence of the difference in aim and purpose between the two air forces' employment of their respective fighter arms. RAF Fighter Command, in 1940, had become what Dowding had steadily built it up to be – a *defence* force to counter almost any form of attack upon the United Kingdom. The Luftwaffe's *jagdstaffeln* and *geschwadern*, on the other hand, were principally intended as adjuncts to the bomber arm and/or ground forces in direct tactical support for any offensive operations. As such the German fighters had no intrinsic *fighter* role except as shepherd dogs to the flocks of slower Dorniers, Heinkels and Junkers, and remained thus until at least the closing stages of the battle over Britain. The '*Freijagd*' – 'Free Chase' – tactics pursued during the opening stages of the anti-England aerial assault were quickly forbidden by higher authority, and replaced by direct orders from the Luftwaffe supremo, Göring, for fighters to stay close to their bomber charges.

Apart from the obvious restriction upon the initiative and freedom of the fighter pilots, such 'apron strings' left the Bf 109 pilots with, at best, some 20 minutes' fighting time over any target area before the red warning lights on their dashboards indicating critically low fuel states

[1] *The First & the Last* by Adolf Galland; Methuen, 1955.

forced them to disengage and attempt to recross the Channel. The dilemma of the eager German fighter pilots detailed for such a frustrating role is partly summed up by a comment by Hellmuth Ostermann of *Staffel* III of *Jagdgeschwader* 54:

We clung to the bomber formations in pairs – and it was a damned awkward feeling. From below we looked up at the bright blue bellies of the Tommy planes. Mostly they waited there till our bombers made their turn. Then they would swoop down, pull briefly out, fire their guns and at once dive down. All we could do was to shoot off short nuisance bursts while at the same time watching out that there was no one nibbling at our tails. Often we pulled madly on the stick till the ailerons shook, but were then unable to turn round quickly enough and could only watch as the Tommies knocked hell out of one of the bombers.

Faithfully attempting to fulfil their appointed task of literal close escort to the bombers, in late September JG54 was to lose 12 Bf 109s in a single sortie due to starved fuel tanks; five of these scraping forced landings on French beaches and the remaining seven having to ditch in the Channel.

Despite the superior numerical odds facing them, the fighter pilots under Dowding's overall command were to have certain distinct advantages over their German counterparts during the battle. In terms of aircraft the Messerschmitt Bf 109 was superior to the Hurricane in many respects, and in several lesser ways to the Spitfire. As a combat machine the Bf 109 was well-tailored for its designed role. The main German weaknesses lay in their bomber designs. The Heinkel 111, Dornier 17, and to a lesser extent the Junkers 88, were all too slow, too poorly armed, and too cumbersome in manoeuvre to carry out unescorted sorties successfully against the fast, eight-gun British fighters. The Junkers 87 dive-bomber – 'Stuka' – which had earned something of a notorious reputation for its deadly precision bombing during the *blitzkrieg* tactical wars in Europe, proved to be disastrous for its crews when met by determined fighter opposition over England. Another utter failure was the much-boosted Messerschmitt Bf 110 two-seat *Zerstörer* – 'Destroyer' – fighter. Intended as a long-range escort fighter to the bomber, in combat the Bf 110 quickly proved an encumbrance to the other escorts of Bf 109s – indeed, at one stage had to be virtually 'escorted' themselves. Later in the war, modified Bf 110s were to find an important niche in the nightfighter roles in defence of Germany against the ever-increasing RAF and USAAF bomber offensive against the

Reich; but during the daylight battles of 1940 its crews were to suffer disproportionately high casualty rates.

Psychologically, Dowding's men had one great advantage over the German crews; they were fighting above their own homeland and defending in British skies. In the event of having to abandon his Spitfire or Hurricane, an RAF pilot knew he was over friendly territory or, at worst, descending into British coastal waters where his chances of retrieval were reasonably good. For the German crews, once they left the French shore they were in hostile skies every inch of the way to and from base; liable to be attacked at any juncture and facing inevitable capture if their aircraft was forced down on land or off-shore. Added to such hazards were the constant worries about fuel; every mile of further penetration into British skies meant steady depletion of their limited capability to return across the dreaded Channel waters. No operational German aircraft in 1940 had been designed for long-range, deep penetration, sustained bombing operations, or for extended fighter escort and combat capability so far from base. The overall concept during the build-up of the Luftwaffe had been as tactical support for the army's ground strategy; not as a separate *air* force to be used as a third arm in its own right.

The greatest advantage for Fighter Command lay in its pre-intelligence system and organisation. By February 1940 a thin chain of 29 radar 'listening' posts had been constructed along the southern and eastern coastlines of Britain. Each was linked directly to a control centre in Bentley Priory, from which information could be passed to Groups and Sectors for translation into immediate reaction by intercepting fighter squadrons. By July 1940 this thin chain contained 51 such radar posts: 30 of these being Chain Home Low (CHL) stations designed to search for low-flying aircraft. Backing up this radar 'shield' was the Observer Corps[1] with its wide network of visual and telephonic outposts throughout Britain. When mobilised on the outbreak of war the Corps comprised 32 centres, more than a thousand posts, manned by approximately 30,000 observers. The vast majority of its personnel were unpaid volunteers, working shifts on a part-time basis to their regular employment.

Thus any German formation setting out for Britain was capable of being detected many miles from the coastline, and appropriate defence

[1] In April 1941 the Corps was granted the 'Royal' prefix.

measures were set in motion by Fighter Command and its ancillaries. RAF fighter squadrons could be 'scrambled' for interception, with in-the-air instructions being steadily passed by radio giving approximate size, location, direction of approach, and – though less accurately – estimation of altitude of the German formations. This seemingly baffling ability of RAF fighters to appear from nowhere in the right place confused German crews in the early stages of the battle. As operations intensified, and German crews realised that their opponents had some form of pre-warning and control, this confusion changed to a constant apprehension which tore at the edges of their confidence once over English territory. Even later, as the German intelligence and propaganda machines issued optimistic figures for what seemed to be the virtual destruction of Fighter Command as a fighting entity, the German crews continued to meet large and fierce opposition from Spitfires and Hurricanes which – they had been assured – simply did not exist in such numbers.

This latter 'phenomenon' was a result of Dowding's immense foresight in establishing a rotation system for combat-area squadrons to be 'exchanged' at regular intervals – or when sheer necessity dictated it – for 'fresh' or rested units based further north and west, away from the vital fighting zone in south-east England. It was also partly the result of an almost unprecedented effort made by the factories and civilian repair centres who between them produced an increasingly heavy stream of new or repaired aircraft, night and day during the battle. At squadron level a similar round-the-clock maintenance devotion by the anonymous and unpublicised ground crews provided elementary 'first-aid' repair to bullet-riven and cannon-slashed aircraft, so that 'their' pilots could continue to fight. The patient, dogged and unceasing efforts of those un-named 'erks' was to play a huge part in the eventual victory by the frontline squadrons; a share worthily earned in the plaudits which is seldom emphasised and too often overlooked or simply taken for granted by latter-day historians.

This then was the background to the opening of the legendary Battle of Britain. On the one hand a numerically superior and confident Luftwaffe, based within bombing and fighting range of south and east England, eager and ready to pursue the war into English skies. Facing them was a defence system built up carefully, if slowly, over four years under Hugh Dowding's personal guidance and direction; smaller in numbers than Dowding would have wished, yet of unquestioned quality in men and machines, and backed by a resolute network of radar and Observer Corps pre-warning systems, and an aircraft production and repair organisation prepared to work incessantly to provide the necessary 'tools' for that defence. Of Dowding's fighter pilots, a minority had already seen combat either in France and/or above the Dunkirk evacuation area. The bulk were a mixture of pre-1939 regular officers and senior NCOs, some of relatively senior rank; while the remainder were recently-joined, quickly trained men with no fighting experience at all, and only a barely requisite number of flying hours on Spitfires or Hurricanes in their log books. Here and there was a thin selection of hastily 'converted' pilots from all other RAF and Fleet Air Arm units and commands, with a sprinkling of refugee European-trained pilots – Poles, Czechs, Belgians *et al* – many of whom had already seen fierce action over their now-defeated homelands before fleeing to England in order to continue their wars. Whatever their background or experience, few – if any – lacked confidence in their machines, or their ability to cope with anything Göring might choose to fling against them. This air of confidence and an almost grim determination was one reflected throughout the British population at that point in the war; the so-termed 'Dunkirk Spirit' of mutual, willing support and co-ordinated aim and purpose found in any community facing and sharing a common peril.

The actual Battle for Britain evolved into fairly distinct phases, though the exact parameters of each phase are still quoted as of different dates according to which source one consults. The official British dating was given later in the qualifying limits for the award of a Battle of Britain gilt rose emblem, i.e. July 10th to October 31st inclusive overall, split down into five significant stages; significant in that each stage provided a distinct shift in emphasis in the Luftwaffe's primary aims, and thus changed the nature of the necessary measures to be taken by Dowding and Park as far as they were able to ascertain such changes. Adolf Galland, who fought throughout the 1940 air battles, is specific in his breakdown of the battle from the German viewpoint. He, too, divided the struggle into five parts of an overall plan for the preparation and then execution of an invasion of English soil. The first part covered the attacks on Allied shipping in the Channel, ending by July 24th; stage two was a pure fighter-versus-fighter phase during which the Luftwaffe attempted to destroy Fighter Command in the air, between July 24th and August 7th. His third phase, commencing on

1 *Bristol Bulldogs of B Flight, 3 Squadron, in a neat echelon. Squadron marking was a green fuselage band, and Flight marking yellow wheel discs.*

2 *Gloster Gauntlet of 46 Squadron at Kenley, May 1937, with 'red arrow' unit markings. Pilot was Ian 'Widge' Gleed, who as a Wing Commander, DSO, DFC, was killed in action in North Africa in 1943.*

3 (Left) Hawker Fury IIs of 25(F) Squadron in immaculate formation.

4 (Below, left) Gloster Gladiator of 73 Squadron in pre-1938 finish. As the RAF's ultimate biplane fighter, the Gladiator gave sterling service in World War Two.

5 (Below) Bentley Priory – Fighter Command's headquarters, from where the Battle of Britain was directed. The building was destroyed in a fire, early 1979.

6 *(Left) Hugh Dowding (centre) with Group Captain Nichols (left) and ACM Sir Guy Garrod (right) at a 1949 annual dinner of the RAF Reserve Club, London.*

7 *(Below, left) Keith Park, the New Zealander who commanded 11 Group throughout the Battle of Britain, and, as Dowding's 'right-hand man', was part-architect of the eventual victory.*

8 *(Below) Hawker Hurricane fighters under mass production at the beginning of 1939.*

9 *(Above) Spitfire I, P9450, with Jeffrey Quill at the controls, on air test in April 1940. This particular Spitfire saw combat in 64 Squadron and was missing in action on 5 December 1940.*

10 *(Below) The first German aircraft brought down on British soil in World War Two. Heinkel 111, shot down by Flying Officer Archie McKellar, 602 Squadron, Auxiliary Air Force at Lammermuir, Scotland, on 28 October 1939.*

11 *(Top, right) Chain Home (CH) radar, 1940. Three towers at left are transmitters; those on right, receivers.*

12 *(Right) The nerve-centre of Fighter Command – the underground Operations Room at Bentley Priory in 1940.*

13 (Over the page) Warrior's return –
Pilot Officer A. G. Lewis, DFC, of 85
Squadron, climbs out of his Hurricane,
late 1940.

August 8th, was the switch in tactics to an intensified assault on Fighter Command's base airfields south of London. Then, on September 7th, the whole emphasis of the Luftwaffe's campaign changed to an all-out daylight onslaught against, principally, the British capital city, London, and its associated docks and industries; though even here it was still hoped to draw up Fighter Command into a battle of fighter attrition. This phase – according to Galland – lasted until October 20th; thereafter all main efforts were directed into a night bombing assault on Britain's major cities and population centres, and industrial complexes, with German fighters virtually relegated to use as hit-and-run 'nuisance' raiders along the coastal areas of England's southern shores.

To the ordinary RAF fighter pilot in a first-line squadron in July 1940, an awareness of an impending crisis in the air war was only vaguely comprehended. Recent events in France, culminating in the Dunkirk evacuations of the BEF, had been so rapid that there had been little time in which to re-evaluate the immediate future prospects. His daily concern was mundane – a serviceable aircraft to fly, plenty of flying practice when time permitted, and the daily domestic comforts and pleasures. Life on an RAF fighter squadron was surprisingly uncomplicated; its purpose was clear and simple to all involved, and everything else was subverted towards that single aim. The real war – at least, for the many unblooded pilots – had yet to erupt. All were keen to 'prove' themselves in action, even eager to join combat, with that semi-serious, semi-curious anticipation of being fully 'tested' which every novitiate feels when on the verge of an unprecedented experience in life. Yet when that action finally came it was to be only a matter of weeks, even days, before such youngsters – those who survived their baptism of fire – were exhausted, weary, emotionally drained and 'aged' in outlook, and secretly thankful for any rest from the incessant flying, fighting and killing.

The general tactical methods employed by Fighter Command were outlined in a tactical memorandum (No. 8, dated June 1940), which in spite of certain statements therein illustrated how relatively little had been learned – at least, by higher RAF command – from the admittedly brief fighting experiences of those fighter pilots who had fought the Luftwaffe over France in May–June. Tactical formations were still allied to the rigid pre-1939 Vics of three aircraft in arrow-head formations; whereas the Luftwaffe, profiting wisely from its Kondor Legion's

65

experience in the Spanish Civil War, operated its fighters in double pairs, each pair being a fighting unit, self-protecting. Nevertheless, slight modification of the RAF's peacetime obsession with tidy, drill-square formation flying was evident; the Vics of three were now to be looser and layered in altitude, with one Vic led by an experienced pilot acting as rear guard; weaving a figure-of-eight pattern above and behind the main formation to obviate surprise attacks and thereby act as a pre-warning buffer should the squadron be jumped from higher altitude. These official instructions were not to be amended until after the daytime battles had petered out in November. The same memorandum No. 8 emphasised boldly that '. . . it must be constantly borne in mind that our aim is THE DESTRUCTION OF ENEMY BOMBERS, and that action against fighters is only a means to an end.' This prime principle lay behind Dowding's and Keith Park's unceasing endeavours during the ensuing months.

Of the battle itself, exhaustively detailed accounts of the day-to-day progress have been published in a mini-mountain of books, periodicals, magazines, journals and articles over the past 40 years. To avoid mere repetition of well-established facts in a form of pure historical chronology here, selection of a particular day, Sunday, September 15th, will to a large degree exemplify the type and forms of combat experienced throughout the struggle by both the RAF and their opponents. That day saw virtually the climax of effort by both factions, the turning point of the battle in Dowding's favour. It is, appropriately, the date on which commemorative functions have continued to be held throughout the British Commonwealth ever since 1940. As an illustrative twenty-four-hour-period of the Battle of Britain, September 15th was not the most successful in the context of enemy aircraft actually destroyed; nor was it the hardest day's actual combat for the RAF in terms of odds or casualties. It did, however, provide the RAF, and incidentally the British population, with a heartening boost to morale. Certainly, in moral terms, September 15th gave the Luftwaffe its most crushing defeat to date.

That fateful Sunday dawned in light misty weather which promised yet another fine sunny day. It found Fighter Command in relatively better fettle than had been the case for several weeks. The savage in-fighting of the August clashes had imposed almost intolerable strains upon pilots and resources; indeed, had brought the command to within the verge of possible break-down in back-up organisation and necessary replacements for the rising toll of casualties. Throughout the latter weeks of August, and the first six days of September, Göring and his field commanders had concentrated almost wholly on direct assault against Fighter Command's machines and bases; then, on September 7th, had switched to massive daytime raids against London and the civil population centres. This extraordinary decision by Göring, at the height of a slowly gaining air offensive, gave Fighter Command – relatively speaking – some measure of relief. Dowding's efforts could now be channelled into providing a bulwark of straightforward aerial defensive tactics to protect the capital; a simplification of means and methods which entirely suited his main purpose. The intensity of air combat was no less fierce, but after September 7th the command's ground organisation revived, improved and strengthened daily as the weight of interference lifted.

In the first-line squadrons, most pilots had seen less exhaustive action during the previous six days, and some had even enjoyed several long periods of virtual rest, beyond being readily available by their aircraft at the base airfields. There had even been time on some units for a few precious inculcation training flights for freshly-arrived 'sprog' pilots straight from the flying schools – a luxury unheard of during the crucial days of August and early September. In direct contrast the bomber and fighter crews of the Luftwaffe were rapidly reaching a stage of disillusionment with their commanders' tactical decisions, and morale was slipping inexorably. Constant assurances from the German intelligence and propaganda machinery that RAF Fighter Command was down to its '. . . last 50 Spitfires' were blatantly ridiculous as the bombers over England continued to meet squadron after squadron of eager, thrusting Spitfires and Hurricanes. On this day the German crews were to experience massive shocks as they clashed with some of the biggest concentrations of British fighters to be met during the whole battle.

In the early hours of daylight on September 15th the Luftwaffe's *Luftflotten* 2 and 3 despatched several individual reconnaissance sorties over the south-eastern areas of England; while Park ordered a series of light coastal patrols by Section or Flight strengths, with several full squadrons on the ground being held at full Readiness state, from 0700 hours onwards. Though vectored onto some of the isolated German recce aircraft, only one victim, a Heinkel 111, was claimed as destroyed. Park's controllers in 11 Group were, however, more concerned with the obvious possibility of a follow-up heavy bomber assault; the weather conditions were right, and those early reconnaissance probes added weight to such a prediction. Their fears were justified at 1050 hours when a radar report from the Rye Chain Home station gave warning of a build-up of German aircraft over the French coast, some 10 miles south-east of Boulogne. As this plot increased in density, Park ordered all 11 Group squadrons to full Readiness, and also warned the neighbouring 10 and 12 Groups of the incoming raid.

High above the Calais and Boulogne area some 70 Dorniers from KG3 and KG2, with a heavy fighter escort of Messerschmitt Bf 109s from JG53 and other *geschwadern*, slowly wheeled into tactical formation. The previous system of individual units joining formation en route to England had already proved to be expensive in casualties long before any target could be reached; hence the pre-building of formation over 'friendly' territory. This tacit compliment to the effectiveness of RAF fighter defences also incurred a glaring tactical error – the lack of the surprise element. British radar was automatically given relatively good pre-warning of any such impending assault; thus Fighter Command could be alerted in good time and have its first-line units in 11 Group airborne and waiting. This was the case on this morning. As the radar plot indicated movement northwards, Park sent up eleven squadrons at short intervals, while 12 Group, commanded by Trafford Leigh-Mallory, despatched his '12 Group Wing' – five squadrons based at Duxford, and led as an entity by the legless Douglas Bader. All indications pointed to London being the principal target for the Luftwaffe, and Park arranged a 'carpet' of interception along the presumed flight path of the incoming raiders.

The vanguard of KG3's Dorniers met their first fighters shortly after 1130 hours as they crossed the southern coast of Kent near Dungeness, when some 20 Spitfires pounced on the leading sections and began to hack at the awesome bomber array. These were from 72 and 92 Squadrons, covering the Canterbury-Dover-Dungeness zone. They were the first of five pairs of squadrons Park planned to despatch at appropriate times, with 253 and 501 Squadrons patrolling over the Maidstone area, and 229 and the Poles of 303 Squadrons orbiting just south of Biggin Hill. Further north, waiting to go, were 17, 73, 257 and 604 Squadrons, joined by 609 Squadron from Middle Wallop which was moved to cover the Brooklands-Windsor approach along the western edge of London. From Duxford were to come 12 Group's 'Balbo' of five squadrons, Nos. 19, 302, 310, 242 and 611, commanded by 'Tin-legs' Bader. The ability of Park to concentrate all his squadrons in this manner was due in no small measure to the German planning for that day's attack on London. Their usual ploy of sending advance feint and/or 'dummy' raids to confuse and disseminate the RAF opposition was not employed; leaving Park with a clear, almost unconfused picture of things to come. His overall intention for Spitfire units to smother and engage the Luftwaffe fighter escort 'umbrella', thus leaving the Hurricanes to batter the bombers directly, did not work out entirely to pattern. Once engaged, the fighting became a mixed bag dictated by opportunity and circumstance.

Stepped up in layers from 15,000 to 26,000 feet, the German bomber force presented a formidable display of Teutonic might to the Spitfire pilots who first encountered them. At 20,000 feet over Canterbury Cathedral, Tony Bartley of 92 Squadron looked down from his Spitfire cockpit at one huge gaggle of bombers 3,000 feet below, noted the darting minnow-like Messerschmitt escort, and breathed in awed wonder, 'Jeepers, where the hell do we start on this lot?' Seconds later ten Spitfires of 72 Squadron slid into cohort and the two squadrons plunged together upon the black-crossed host below. The initial impact of the 20 fighters, with their combined battery of 160 machine guns, scattered the lumbering Dorniers and Heinkels in all directions, as each German crew sought safety. A few immediately jettisoned their bomb loads wildly and turned for the coast, others closed up for mutual protection from their gunners' crossfire. A few reeled drunkenly out of the mêlée, one spuming smoke from its starboard engine, another trailing pieces of a shattered aileron and engine cowling. As the core of the battle moved north-westwards, the Dorniers of KG3 continued their intention of reaching London, whatever the cost. Near Maidstone fresh assaults came from a pair of Hurricane squadrons, again breaking the tight, arrow-headed German formations and picking off individual bombers as these raced away. Only minutes later four more Hurricane units joined the fray, diving headlong into the centre of the Dornier stream and weaving Messerschmitts. One Belgian pilot, Georges Doutrepont, in a 229 Squadron Hurricane, tackled 25 Messerschmitts single-handed in an attempt to divert them from the bombers, but died as his shattered aircraft plunged into Staplehurst railway station; while over Biggin Hill the Canadians from 1 RCAF Squadron were thoroughly bounced by a gaggle of Bf 109s and lost two pilots before they had time to react. Elsewhere the gunners in the Dorniers claimed half a dozen victims among their attackers.

At noon the main bombing formations reached the city of London – and immediately received a hammer blow as the five-squadron Duxford Wing descended upon them. The shock of being confronted with a fresh force of some 60 defenders was the final blow to any intention of accurate, co-ordinated bombing. As each bomber sought salvation, the bombs were released haphazardly over a wide area of the city; two of these falling in the grounds of Buckingham Palace but failing to explode. The latter Dornier was almost immediately sent down to explode in the forecourt of nearby Victoria railway station. As Bader's Wing slashed its way through the huge sprawling mass of German aircraft, the bulk of the bombers raced southwards over Kent, accompanied where possible by the remnants of their fighter escorts; the latter already conscious of the red warning lights blinking in their cockpits, indicating minimum fuel states. The fleeing mini-armada found no respite when clear of London, as Park sent in four more squadrons to harry and maul the retreating Luftwaffe. By 1300 hours the RAF fighters were back at bases, being refuelled and re-armed swiftly, while the jubilant pilots excitedly exchanged accounts of their own part in what Bader described as '. . . the finest shambles I've ever been in'. Further south dozens of German bomber crews were nursing battered and sieved aircraft across the coldly inviting waters of the hated 'Kanal' (Channel) attempting to reach 'friendly' territory. Many carried dead or wounded crew members, while all were haunted by the myriad sights of close comrades blown to oblivion or disappearing into the English countryside, trailing flame and smoke. Above all was the indelible impression created by the non-stop mauling they had received from almost 300 of the RAF's 'last 50 fighters'. In the words of Oberst Johannes Fink, courageous leader of *Kampfgeschwader* Nr 2, 'No man could be asked to bear more tension, mental or physical.'

The undoubted success of the RAF fighters lay in the simple fact that, with good pre-warning, they had been in the right place, at the right time, and in force. However, in putting up literally every squadron at his disposal by noon, Park had left himself with no immediate reserves had the Germans followed this first large assault with an equally strong bomber force almost immediately. Such a second force had indeed been planned and if it had been despatched in succession would have reached London mainly without strong RAF opposition, because Park's men were on the ground refuelling. Instead this second wave, comprised of some 150 Dorniers and Heinkels from KG2, KG53 and KG76, supported by Bf 109s from the crack JG26 (led by Adolf Galland) and JG54 (Hannes Trautloft), were only beginning to join up in initial formation over France at the same time as the RAF's fighters were completing their turn-round at base. Thus when the massive second wave approached London minutes before 1400 hours, Park's squadrons were already airborne or about to take off, and were in full available strength despite the morning's casualties. Thus over Kent, before they reached the London outskirts, the Luftwaffe's latest attempt to destroy England's capital was swamped by some 170 fighters. The highly experienced German fighter pilots on this mission gave better protection to their charges than was possible earlier in the day; but as the main bomber stream arrived over London they were again faced with sudden and huge opposition as the Duxford Wing of five squadrons, along with eight other units from 10 and 11 Groups, battered all semblance of cohesion out of the German formations with heart-stopping head-on attacks and then savage, close-in combat.

Typical in many respects of the multitude of individual exploits during that afternoon battle was a lone sortie flown by Group Captain Stanley Vincent, station commander at Northolt and the 'home' of 303 Polish Squadron. Though 43 years old – he had been a fighter pilot with 60 Squadron in 1916–17 – Vincent was determined to play an active part in his latest war. Taking off alone in a Hurricane, he climbed to 19,000 feet over Biggin Hill and spotted 18 Dorniers from KG76, escorted by some 20 Bf 109s coming towards him. There seemed to be no other RAF fighters around, so Vincent promptly made a head-on attack on the leading section of six Dorniers, splashing ball and incendiary ammunition along the length of the bombers' line-astern formation. On breaking away, he saw five of this section continuing northwards, while 13 bombers turned about and retreated south. Closing on the latter, Vincent proceeded to use up his remaining ammunition and saw at least one Dornier drop out, losing height and speed. By then Vincent's wing guns were empty and he returned to base. Elsewhere, other individual attacks assumed dramatic proportions. Mike Cooper-Slipper of 605 Squadron, in a damaged Hurricane, calmly rammed a Dornier, ripping away the Hurricane's port wing, but he baled out uninjured; while Pilot Officer Stephenson of 607 Squadron charged a closely-formated pair of Dorniers from head-on, delivered a

'left and right hook' by jinking his Hurricane's wings into contact with
each bomber, then took to his parachute safely, having sent down two
enemies without firing a shot. Shortly after 1400 hours 'Ginger' Lacey
of 501 Squadron – a veteran of France and the summer battles, with
some 15 victories already credited – ran head on into a formation of a
dozen Bf 109s. Dipping the nose of his Hurricane, Lacey pulled off a
tight loop, blasted the rear Messerschmitt and watched it fall vertically
in flames. He next sank a burst into a second Bf 109 which jerked out of
formation spuming a white stream of glycol. The remaining ten Germans finally realised what was happening and attempted to avenge
their lost comrades, but Lacey dived away hard and escaped their
attentions. Before the day was out he was to claim a third Bf 109 and a
Heinkel.

Even as the shattered German formations fled south they were
harried and savaged by more fighters from both 10 and 11 Groups,
some Spitfires even attacking well over the Channel before their diminishing fuel forced their return to England. While these bombers wearily
attempted to reach base, a force of 27 Heinkel 111s from KG55, based
at Villacoublay, feinted an attack on Southampton but then attacked
the naval base at Portland, though with little effect. Shortly after a force
of Messerschmitt Bf 109s and two-seat Bf 110s slid over the Kent coast
as a form of diversion, but were virtually ignored by the RAF fighters.
Even as KG55's Heinkels disappeared south, the radar screens gave
warning of yet another force shortly after 1700 hours. These were 18
Bf 110 fighters, some fitted up as bombers, from *Erprobungsgruppe* 210,
which made a fast, low attack on the Woolston aircraft works near
Southampton which produced Spitfires (though this fact seems to have
not been realised by German Intelligence at the time). Heavy anti-
aircraft fire upset the bomb-aiming and little damage was accomplished, while the RAF fighters sent up to intercept arrived too late to
inflict any losses. It was the final bombing effort during daylight hours
of September 15th.

As the last RAF fighters let down and rolled to their dispersals,
combat claims for the day's fighting were hastily totted up, and that
evening the BBC radio services announced to the world that a total of
185 German aircraft had been shot down – the highest daily total claim
of the battle. On the German side official confirmation was granted for
totals of 51 Spitfires and 26 Hurricanes brought down. The British
nation thrilled to this huge claim by Fighter Command, but in the light

of more careful analysis the true figures were eventually found to be no more than 60 German aircraft actually shot down; though this figure did not take into account the dozens of others which barely struggled home with shattered controls, leaking fuel tanks, and dead or wounded crew members. Of the RAF's losses, 26 fighters were lost, though 13 of their pilots were retrieved safely to fight again another day. Such exaggerated claims by both sides were perfectly comprehensible in the white-heat of almost non-stop combat over an area as large as southern England. The actual figures are relatively unimportant; what really mattered was the significance of the day's operations in the overall planning at German high command levels. Even to the obtuse, it was patent that the RAF's fighter arm was by no means destroyed; indeed, to judge by after-flight reactions from the bomber and fighter crews, that fighter opposition had heavily increased both in quantity and fierceness of opposition. Clearly the projected pre-invasion necessity to 'clear the English skies' with Göring's vaunted Luftwaffe had yet to be accomplished. Göring's original promise to German Service chiefs to destroy Fighter Command in 'four to five days' was blatantly a fantasy of vain-glorious imagination.

In the face of such an unpalatable conclusion, Hitler issued a personal order on September 17th that Operation Sea-Lion – the invasion of Britain – was to be postponed until further notice; while four days later the massive concentration of invasion barges and vessels housed along the Channel ports and harbours began to be dispersed. It was this decision by Hitler, in the light of the events of September 15th particularly, that gives especial emphasis to the importance of the *effect* of Fighter Command's unquestioned victory that day upon the whole battle. Nevertheless, it was by no means a clear-cut victory in overall context as far as contemporary RAF commanders were concerned. The fighting and raiding were to continue until early November, though on a gradually diminishing scale, and Dowding's problems remained as urgent as before. Until the Luftwaffe's night bombing 'blitz' campaign became the prime problem from November until the following spring, Fighter Command continued its daytime defensive measures at a high key. During the last two weeks of September combat continued to be joined fiercely, with relatively heavy casualty rates being suffered by both protagonists; but whereas the Luftwaffe incurred unacceptably high losses in both aircraft and, especially, many seasoned and almost irreplaceable unit commanders, to little military advantage, the RAF's fighter force steadily increased its strength and resources. The days of high density daylight bombing raids were a thing of the past by October, being mainly replaced by the use of Messerschmitt Bf 109s and Bf 110s and the fast Junkers 88s as bombers on hit-and-run style attacks. Despite the widespread damage and civilian casualties these latter caused, results were relatively minor in the context of Göring's original intentions, and could only be classified as a form of petulant nuisance value.

In human and material terms the Battle of Britain had been grievous for Fighter Command. Accepting the arbitrary parameters of the battle *per se* as being from July 10th to October 31st inclusive, a total of 3,080 pilots had served at some period, however brief, in the command's front-line strength; though it should be borne in mind that at any given date the actual total available for operations varied between some 1300 and 1700. Of this overall total, 481 men were killed or listed as 'Missing', while a further 422 received serious wounds or injuries during this period. Between them they had destroyed at least 1733 German aircraft, and damaged a further 643 in various degrees of severity. The command's own losses in aircraft destroyed or written-off due to battle damage amounted to 1140. Due to the magnificent efforts of the aircraft industry and repair organisations, the wastage in aircraft alone was not the most vital factor. The most tragic loss was of so many pilots, many of them pre-1939 trained men with huge potential as the future field commanders of the RAF − a brilliant potential now denied to the Service. In balance, at least partially, was the emergence of many other pilots who in later years were to become outstanding fighter leaders; men like Adolph 'Sailor' Malan, the South African commander of 74 'Tiger' Squadron, 'Hawkeye' Wells, Norman Ryder, the New Zealander 'Al' Deere and Colin Gray, Brian 'Kingpin' Kingcome, 'Johnny' Kent, and dozens of others of equal character.

Although this mini-galaxy of 'aces' became well-known to the hero-hungry British public of the period, it should be stressed that the largest measure of the ultimate victory had been due to the unheralded prowess of the vast 'silent majority' of fighter pilots on the squadrons; unpublicised men and boys whose steady, dogged 'devotion to duty' had provided the rock foundation for the final nullification of Göring's grandiose dreams and schemes. Equal tribute is overdue to the men and women of the ground crews and support organisation. On the dispersals and in the hangars a mini-army of mainly peacetime-trained fitters, mechanics and aircrafthands – male and, to a lesser degree, female – worked virtually without pause every day and night through-out the battle; repairing, servicing, improvising, provisioning, prepar-ing the aircraft before and after combat – always striving to give 'their' pilots a combat-worthy 'kite' wherever humanly possible. Trade demarcation lines were unknown, working hours a matter of necessity rather than literal, motivation or incentive merely matters of consci-ence and the corporate brotherhood-in-arms mood which prevailed. In the radar posts and controllers' cellars a similar spirit of dedication to the task was clearly evident among the WAAFs, airmen, officers of all levels, many of whom continued at their posts despite devastating bombing raids or strafing. Their composite courage and example illustrated the determination and purpose of Fighter Command during that fateful high summer.

Having paid rightful tribute to the men and women of the com-mand's ground services, it must nevertheless be to the fighter pilots themselves – the 'Few' as Winston Churchill was to immortalise them in yet another of his carefully dramatic phrases – that the true accolade of triumph must be given. They were almost wholly a company of young men, many having yet to attain the contemporary legal definition of maturity of 21 years' age; standing on the brink of adult life, at the peak of physical and mental ability. Each was a volunteer – there were no 'pressed men' in the ranks of the RAF's aircrews – and thus each had willingly laid his life 'on the line' in the defence of his heritage and birthright. Yet such was the general mood that any such attributed noble motivation would have merely provoked embarrassed humour. They preferred a mask of frivolity and gaiety in the presence of 'outsiders'; accentuating the imperturbability and languid approach to all dangers so long associated in foreign eyes with the British national character. If beneath this veneer of coolness lurked a natural fear of death or mutilation, it was seldom permitted to surface in company. A dry, incisive note of grim humour often penetrated the 'business in hand'; as when the Canadian John Kent was leading a section of six Hurricanes and reported sighting a German bomber formation of 100-plus to his controller, hoping for reinforcement before tackling the awesome array of enemy aircraft. The response from the controller was carefully laconic, 'Understand you are only six. Be very careful.'

If some squadrons lived an extrovert life out of the cockpit, it was the natural extension of the 'short life and a gay one' attitude of men committed to a recognised life and death struggle in which the future was a misty mirror. Life was reduced to the immediate necessities; tomorrow was too far away to be worried about. Once strapped into his bucket seat, a pilot became an agent of destruction, finely trained, instinctively aggressive, committed to the kill. This restless urge to get to grips with the enemy was one shared by almost every Spitfire or Hurricane pilot; a quality to be found in all élite fighting men throughout the annals of warfare. Such a spirit, added to the knowledge that they were fighting literally to preserve the sanctity of Britain and its people's freedom, gave the RAF fighter pilots a psychological edge over their German opponents. Undaunted by overwhelming odds, fighting to the limits of physical and mental endurance, and ever ready to return to the fray, the pilots of Fighter Command ensured the freedom of a nation in the bright blue arena of the skies over England in the summer of 1940.

5. Dark of Moon

At 20 minutes past midnight on 18 June 1940, a Spitfire I, K9953, took off from Rochford airfield. At the controls was Flight Lieutenant Adolph Malan, DFC, of 74 Squadron. His subsequent combat report recorded:

> During an air raid in the locality of Southend various E/A (enemy aircraft) were observed and held by searchlights for prolonged periods. On request from squadron I was allowed to take off with one Spitfire. I climbed towards E/A which was making for coast and held in searchlight beams at 8,000 ft. I positioned myself astern and opened fire at 200 yards and closed to 50 yards with one burst. Observed bullets entering E/A and had my windscreen covered in oil. Broke off to the left and immediately below as E/A spiralled out of beam. Climbed to 12,000 ft towards another E/A held by the searchlights on a northerly course. Opened fire at 250 yards, taking good care not to overshoot this time. Gave five two-second bursts and observed bullets entering all over E/A with slight deflection as he was turning to port. E/A emitted heavy smoke and I observed one parachute open very close. E/A went down in spiral dive. Searchlights and I followed him right down until he crashed in flames near Chelmsford. As I approached target in each case, I flashed a succession of dots on downward recognition light before moving in to attack. I did not notice AA fire after I had done this. When following second E/A down, I switched on navigation lights for short time to help establish identity. Gave letter of period only once when returning at 3,000 ft from Chelmsford, when one searchlight searched for me. Cine camera gun in action.

Both Malan's victims, Heinkel 111s, were confirmed as destroyed, yet the whole nature of Malan's lone patrol exemplified the state of Fighter Command's lack of co-ordinated defences against the night bomber, even at this stage of the war. During 1916–18, when Britain endured a succession of night and day bombing forays from Zeppelins,

Gothas and other heavy bomber aircraft, a Home Defence system had been devised in co-operation with the army's anti-aircraft guns' defences, balloon 'aprons', searchlights and sound detectors. The UK-based RFC, RNAS and, later, RAF squadrons were specifically tasked with a night 'fighter' role; though few of their aircraft were of sufficient performance to even reach any high-flying raider in time to intercept, let alone destroy. By a combination of good fortune, determination and sheer luck, a number of German raiders were brought down, but the heavy casualty toll among the Zeppelins and Gothas due to other causes – weather, mechanical failure, and pure accidents – was far more significant in causing these raids to cease, than anything inaugurated by the British Home Defence system.

Nevertheless, the rudiments – and necessity – for an effective aerial defence against a nocturnal enemy had been realised and attempted. Indeed, by mid-1918 a squadron of Sopwith F.1 Camel fighters, No. 151, had even been sent to France, tasked with an *offensive* nightfighter role – the pioneers of the RAF's night 'intruders' of World War Two. With the signing of the Armistice in November 1918, and the consequent euphoria of 'peace in our time', the RAF became a mere shadow of its former self in sheer quantity, and its very existence as a separate Service threatened by the machinations of Army, Admiralty and political factions in Whitehall's corridors of power. The survival of Britain's Third Service, due in no small measure to the obstinacy and determination of Sir Hugh Trenchard, its first Chief of Air Staff, is well recorded in many published accounts of the period. With a miserly annual budget, Trenchard concentrated on building a firm foundation for the future RAF upon which, he hoped, further realistic expansion could then be accomplished in due time. Thus Trenchard's initial priorities were channelled into the provision of training establishments and ground equipment, with little finance remaining for the improvement of existing aircraft designs, or experimentation in the 'minor' facets of aerial strength.

With an emphasis on development of the RAF's bomber force, the fighter arm inevitably suffered in the context of progress in modern designs and appropriate equipment. Those few fighter squadrons based in the UK throughout the 1920s and early 1930s were classified as 'interceptors'; this being considered their obvious role for metropolitan defence against any would-be aerial aggressor. The concept was, however, based almost entirely on the firm belief that any such aggression would arrive in daylight hours in the main; thus fighter tactics and esoteric equipment were designed entirely for daytime combat. Considering the attention being paid to the bomber in the RAF, it may appear paradoxical that some form of 'antidote' for interception of a night raider was hardly given consideration by the Air Ministry. Yet few RAF bomber crews were given training or practice in night flying or operations; a lack of experience equally reflected in the fighter squadrons.

This is not to imply that the need for night fighters had not been appreciated by certain individual aircraft manufacturers or, indeed, particular members of the Air Ministry or Air Staff. The over-riding need for simple economy in financial outlay from an annual Air Estimate of niggardly proportions dominated re-equipment within the RAF until the mid-1930s. Such 'luxuries' as ample monies for fresh aircraft designed for 'one-off' operational roles could not be seriously considered. In the pure context of the night fighter role, the only feasible method of possible interception until the advent of radar comprised a combination of loose co-operation between fighters, searchlights, anti-aircraft guns and the archaic sound-detectors then available; a system which had not advanced in efficiency since 1918. Actual location of any night-flying bomber relied mainly on visual identification – and a generous measure of pure luck.

The full history of radar has no place in this particular text, and is amply recorded elsewhere in a host of authoritative accounts. Its eventual adaptation to the needs of RAF Fighter Command is, of course, highly relevant. Based on a principle expounded by a German, Christian Hülsmeyer, in his patent dated April 1904, radar – the term did not come into general usage until late 1943 – was not to be fully exploited until the mid-1930s in Britain, when Robert Watson-Watt of the Radio Department of the National Physical Laboratory composed a memorandum on 12 February 1935 to the Air Ministry. In it Watson-Watt set out the general principles of 'radio direction finding' – his term for what became known later as radar – and how a defensive RDF chain could be set up and its results translated into operational use by the RAF. At that time the Air Member for Research and Development was Hugh Dowding, who saw RDF as 'a discovery of the highest importance' and promptly gave his considerable backing to further research and experimentation in the subject. Dowding's foresight envisaged the use of RDF as a defensive belt of prewarning devices for the fighter arm, and urged all possible speed for its development. Thus Dowding was in at the virtual 'birth' of the British efforts in the radar field, and one of its most enthusiastic exponents; an enthusiasm he carried into his appointment as AOC-in-C, Fighter Command in 1936, fostering RDF growth and introduction into his command. This 'tremendous leap forward', as Dowding once described RDF, enabled Fighter Command to withstand the massive Luftwaffe assault during the summer of 1940 by providing essential notice in reasonably accurate terms of every incoming air raid, thereby obviating the need for constant standing patrols in the air which was simply not within the physical capability of the command at that period.

The conception of airborne radar (as opposed to pure ground installations) came in February 1936 when Watson-Watt and his team put forward just such a project for consideration. In August 1937 an experimental airborne transmitter was fitted into an Avro Anson and operated with some success, and by the close of the following year A.I. (Airborne Interception) sets were being contracted for production. By July 1939 air tests had established A.I. as a working item and Dowding himself took part in one such trial as an observer. Again, his deep interest and technical grasp of the essentials led to a shrewd opinion that A.I. could best be utilised in future in twin-engined aircraft with a two-man crew; a sound prediction which was to bear fruit handsomely in later years. The first A.I. Mk 1 sets were installed in three Blenheims of 25 Squadron just prior to the outbreak of war. These early A.I. sets, and the techniques required to obtain any worthwhile results from same, were crude by eventual standards; yet they paved the path to subsequent success. Nevertheless, the progress in design and technique was slow, and during the first year of the war Dowding's night fighters perforce relied on reports of incoming raiders relayed by the ground radar controllers to indicate very approximate locations of the enemy aircraft, followed by simple visual hunting in the night blackness. By April 1940 Fighter Command possessed only six squadrons equipped with A.I. fighters: the Blenheims of Nos. 23, 25, 29, 219, 600 and 604 Squadrons. These aircraft, like the Spitfire, Hurricane and two-seat Defiant, had not been designed for night work, and were thus patently unsuited to the specific needs of such a role. Moreover, the crews allotted to the night interception role were not trained specifically for such a task, being normally trained for general day operations. Only time and experience were to produce the specially trained night fighter

14 *Eric James Brindley Nicolson, the only fighter pilot to be awarded a Victoria Cross during 1939–45. Awarded for his action on 16 August 1940, he later received a DFC for leadership of 27 Squadron in Burma, and was lost in action on 2 May 1945. Seen here with his wife and baby son, late 1940.*

15 *Spitfire of 602 Squadron, AAF, being 'turned round' during the Battle of Britain.*

16 *The victory tally of Robert Stanford Tuck, DFC, in late 1940, marked alongside his Hurricane's cockpit.*

17 *Adolph Gysbert Malan – 'Sailor' – who led 74 'Tiger' Squadron in 1940, and became a legend in RAF fighter annals for his prowess and aggressive leadership.*

18 *'Sailor's Rules' – the ten combat 'musts' expounded by Malan, which became a standard tactical guide for other fighter pilots.*

TEN of MY RULES of AIR FIGHTING.

1 <u>Wait until you see the whites of his eyes.</u>
Fire short bursts of 1 to 2 seconds and only when your sights are definitely 'ON'.

2 Whilst shooting think of nothing else; brace the whole of the body; have both hands on the stick; concentrate on your ring sight.

3 Always keep a sharp lookout. "Keep your finger out"!

4 Height gives <u>You</u> the initiative.

5 Always turn and face the attack.

6 Make your decisions promptly. It is better to act quickly even though your tactics are not the best.

7 Never fly straight and level for more than 30 seconds in the combat area.

8 When diving to attack always leave a proportion of your formation above to act as top guard.

9 INITIATIVE, AGGRESSION, AIR DISCIPLINE, and TEAM WORK are words that MEAN something in Air Fighting.

10 Go in quickly – Punch hard – Get out!

81 GROUP TACTICS C-505.

19 *'Night Fighter' – the superb painting by Eric Kennington of Squadron Leader R. P. Stevens, DSO, DFC, the most successful 'lone' Hurricane night fighter pilot in 1940–1.*

20 *Crews of 604 Squadron, AAF, gathered outside their Officers' Mess, the Pheasant Hotel, on the Andover–Salisbury road. Third from right is John Cunningham, DSO, DFC, with (far right) his navigator, 'Jimmy' Rawnsley, DSO, DFC, DFM.*

21 *Night fighter pilots of 85 Squadron relaxing at dispersal prior to patrol, wearing 'night vision' goggles to accustom their eyes to darkness. Second from right is Squadron Leader Peter Townsend with his pet Alsatian dog, 'Kim'.*

22 *Douglas DB7 'Havoc', an American design used as an 'interim' night fighter. This Havoc belonged to 23 Squadron, based then at Ford.*

23 *Bristol Beaufighter VIF of 307 (Polish) Squadron bringing General Sikorski (C-in-C, Polish Forces) to the squadron base at Exeter in September 1942.*

24 *Chocks away! Beaufighter pilot waves the wheel chocks away prior to a patrol.*

25 *They also served . . . Warrant Officer G. Carpenter and Corporal K. Warren sorting out a 'duff' air vent from a Hurricane IIb of 402 Squadron, RCAF, at Warmwell on 9 February 1942.*

26 *Night shift – the indefatigable 'erks' (ground crews) toiling over a Spitfire V in the early hours of the morning.*

27 *HM King George VI greeting pilots from a Spitfire squadron on 29 April 1942. Each pilot is wearing his flying helmet with oxygen and radio leads attached, and a 'Mae West' life-preserver waistcoat.*

28 *Spitfires of 122 Squadron take-off from Fairlop for a daylight sweep over France, 1942.*

29 *Australian Spitfire pilots of 452 Squadron, RAAF. Fourth from left is Wing Commander Brendan 'Paddy' Finucane, DSO, DFC, at this time a Flight commander.*

crew, in an adequate performance aircraft, fitted with reliable radar equipment; but on the night of 22/23 July 1940 a Blenheim from the Fighter Interception Unit (FIU) based at Tangmere, piloted by Flying Officer G. Ashfield, made contact with a German bomber, a Dornier 17 from KG3, and was able to use its A.I. set to get within firing range behind the raider and then shoot it into the sea off the Sussex coast.

Ashfield's success – the first A.I.-assisted night kill – was significant but untypical of the level of success being achieved by Fighter Command generally at this time. Though the Luftwaffe seldom concentrated more than two dozen bombers against any UK target by night until the start of the heavy night blitz which commenced in early September 1940, the RAF's night interception crews went through many months of utter frustration attempting merely to *locate* any incoming bomber. Added to this frustration was the rising toll in RAF casualties among the night fighter units due to pure flying accidents, as day-trained pilots in day fighters attempted to adapt to the very different conditions of flying by night, in totally unsuitable weather conditions, trying almost desperately to find an elusive target in total blackness. If the general night scene appeared gloomy in every sense of the word, occasional flashes of success were obtained by non-radar fighters; the outstanding individual example being that of a Hurricane pilot of 151 Squadron, Richard Playne Stevens, who eventually ran up a tally of 14 victims, all without the doubtful benefit of radar.

While the A.I. sets were rapidly improved, Fighter Command began to receive its first examples of a new fighter of huge promise, the pugnacious Bristol Beaufighter. First flown on 17 July 1939, the Beaufighter was an inspired 'stop-gap' design, based on the Beaufort torpedo bomber, and initial deliveries reached Fighter Command's FIU at Ford for Service trials by July 1940. Beaufighters, fitted with A.I. Mk IV sets, were then issued to 29, 25, 219, 600 and 604 Squadrons before November, replacing outdated Blenheims, and the first Beaufighter kill came on the night of 19 November 1940 when Squadron Leader John Cunningham and Sergeant J. Phillipson of 604 Squadron, in Beaufighter R2098, 'H', caught a Junkers 88 over the Birmingham area and eventually shot it down to crash in Norfolk. Again, this was an isolated success and it was not until the following spring that the Beaufighter crews began to accumulate significant victory tallies; enhanced by the introduction of efficient ground control installations (GCI) in January 1941, which enabled the ground organisation to plot both fighter and quarry upon a Plan Position Indicator (PPI). During the early winter months of 1940–1, however, the Luftwaffe held unquestioned supremacy in the night skies over Britain, sustaining relatively few casualties from the combined night defence organisation under Dowding's overall command. A wide variety of possible – and highly improbable – schemes were devised or projected as additional anti-aircraft 'antidotes' though most of these proved to be totally impractical, heavily expensive, and/or simply the outpourings of vivid imaginations by 'inventors' totally ignorant of the basic requirements of aerial warfare. Meanwhile the pioneering teams of RDF equipment worked incessantly to provide more efficient, workable airborne sets, while the Beaufighter and Blenheim crews continued patiently to test and improve their techniques for air use of the 'black boxes' in their cockpits.

The ineffectual defences guarding London during the bomber blitz of late 1940 were exemplified during one of the particularly heavy raids launched on the night of October 15th/16th. Some 400 German bombers were involved arriving in waves from various approach angles, to be met by a fierce but unpredicted anti-aircraft guns' opposition, with plentiful searchlight activity. In addition, throughout the eight hours duration of the bombing – some German crews actually making two sorties that same night – a total of 41 RAF fighters were airborne, seeking prey. Of the latter only one made a successful contact; a Defiant of 264 Squadron which, by more luck than judgment, happened upon a Heinkel 111 from KGr 126 and shot it down to crash at Ingrave, Essex. A Blenheim of 23 Squadron, equipped with radar, intercepted another bomber near Tunbridge Wells but lost it in the subsequent chase southwards. The anti-aircraft guns' 'barrage' was almost totally ineffective, and was treated with a measure of contempt by most Luftwaffe crews, many of whom remained over their designated target areas for nearly half an hour, leisurely releasing individual bombs at five-minute intervals to add to the boiling confusion below. Another stark illustration of the inability of Fighter Command to cope with a massed raid was the notorious concentrated attack on the cathedral city of Coventry on November 14th/15th. A force of 449 German bombers, with 13 Heinkel 111s from KGr 100 acting as advance 'markers', devastated the city with a deluge of incendiary and high explosive bombs. Despite the bright moonlight that night, only seven of the 119 fighter sorties despatched even sighted a bomber, and none were destroyed, though two raiders were claimed by the anti-aircraft batteries.

If the night fighters could not catch their prey over the target, they might at least revenge themselves upon the Luftwaffe by attempting *offensive* action against the known German airfields on the Continent. Accordingly, the Blenheim crews of 600, 604 and 23 Squadrons began a series of 'intruder' sorties from such forward bases as Manston, attacking German airfields along the French coastal strip and further inland. In doing so they revived a tactic first employed successfully by the Sopwith Camel pilots of 151 Squadron in 1918. If material success was inevitably small, the moral effect of lurking Allied night fighters in their airfield's proximity upon returning German bomber crews was high, adding extra strain and danger to an already strenuous situation. Such intruder operations – made in small numbers and infrequently – were the harbingers of a mounting night fighter offensive by crews of Fighter Command in the later years of the war; an offensive which ultimately spread disorder and a state of near-panic among Luftwaffe air and ground crews during 1944–5.

With the introduction of GCI installations by January 1941 – there were six operational in that month, at Sopley, Durrington, Willesborough, Avebury, Orby and Waldringfield, all covering the southeastern coastline approaches – the night fighter defence became effective. One of the first GCI-cum-Beaufighter radar successes came on January 12th, when John Cunningham and his radar set operator 'Jimmy' Rawnsley contacted a Heinkel 111 and hit it hard with their opening burst of cannon fire. However, failure in the cannon's air pressure system prevented total destruction of the German bomber. That same month brought only three victories, but by March, when six squadrons were operating radar-equipped Beaufighters, the monthly total rose to 22; while in May this tally escalated sharply to 96 victims. By then Hitler's obsession with the destruction of Russia – which he had declared to be the real prime objective as early as June 1940, *before* the start of the Battle of Britain – had caused the bulk of Luftwaffe units to be transferred to the eastern borders of German-occupied Europe, preparatory to the planned offensive eastwards. As a direct result the night blitz against Britain petered out.

On 10 May 1941 London suffered its final large-scale bombing attack of the winter blitz, when the Luftwaffe despatched a total of 541 sorties, which killed 1436 people, injured 1800, destroyed more than

5000 dwellings, and gutted an area of some 700 acres with incendiaries and high explosive. The defences accounted for at least 14 of the raiders. Thereafter the tempo of the German bombing campaign was severely reduced. At dawn on 22 June 1941 Hitler's generals launched 'Operation Barbarossa' – the attack on Russia – supported by virtually 60 per cent of the Luftwaffe's contemporary first-line strength. This almost sudden easing of pressure upon Britain allowed the RAF to mount a restricted offensive by Fighter Command thereafter, supplementing the continuing night offensive carried out by Bomber Command since the start of hostilities. Fighter Command's defensive system had by then increased in strength and efficiency, and by July a total of 17 GCI stations were operational, 'feeding' some 16 squadrons of night fighters apart from other 'one-off' countermeasures' units. These continued in combination to offer effective shields against the continuing small-scale hit-and-run bombing attacks made by French-based Luftwaffe units against south coast targets in England.

For the RAF night fighter crews the air war in the dark had been a long, frustrating saga of exhausting flying with little to show for their prodigious labours until very near the end. Success had come from dogged patience as they wrestled with new-fangled devices, in unfamiliar aircraft, in an arena totally alien to normal human responses. Unlike the relatively 'clean' character of daytime combat, where fighter met opponent in a straightforward struggle for individual superiority with, usually, a clear-cut triumph of victor over vanquished, night fighting was a clandestine, sneak-thief form of mortal combat. In the raven-blackness of a wintry night success went to the devious, resolute hunter who stalked his prey unseen, unheralded – then struck from behind, mercilessly, swiftly. A sudden thrust of cannon shells into an opponent's belly more often than not caught the enemy crew unaware, unprepared, and obliterated men and machine in a crazy kaleidoscope of tumbling, flaming fragments. Chivalry had no place in the night skies; the fatal stab in the back replaced the defiant flourish of a gauntlet. Richard Stevens, the highly successful Hurricane 'lone wolf', once had his wing's leading edge indented by the blood and remains of one of his victims – his order to his ground crew was to leave the grisly souvenir intact. It was his constant reminder of the 'debt' owed by the Luftwaffe for killing his children during the blitz.[1]

[1] Squadron Leader R. P. Stevens, DSO, DFC, was killed in action on 15 December 1941 while flying an intruder operation with 253 Squadron.

The arena of night combat had produced a number of particularly notable and successful pilots and partnerships, chief amongst these being the redoubtable duo of John Cunningham and his 'operator' Jimmy Rawnsley. Cunningham's cool, analytical approach to the complexities of night fighting, combined with a rare skill as a pure pilot, resulted in a mounting personal tally of victories, but also – to Cunningham's acute disgust – widespread publicity in the popular press, being tagged with the sobriquet 'Cat's-Eyes'. Another successful pilot was Roderick Chisholm of 219 Squadron who, after a 'slow' start, gained several victories. Another Beaufighter pilot was Guy Gibson who, on completion of a year's operations with 83 Squadron in Bomber Command, 'wangled' a posting to 29 Squadron in late 1940, and during the following year accumulated three aircraft destroyed, and four others probably destroyed or at least severely damaged, before resuming an outstanding career as a bomber leader. Yet another emerging 'star turn' was John 'Bob' Braham who eventually gained a triple DSO and triple DFC among other awards for his wartime prowess. If such men were well-known to the public via the media, they simply represented many other, unpublicised crews whose dogged perseverance and courage had contributed so greatly to the overall triumph over the night assailants. All had created a firm foundation for later night fighter crews to embellish as the night war gradually moved into the disputed skies above the German Reich in later years.

6. Seek and Destroy

As the crucial daytime Battle for Britain eased into its closing stages, and Göring directed his battered Luftwaffe to seek the shelter of darkness to continue his assault on Britain, Fighter Command – steadily increasing in strength and resources – looked to a fresh future for its operational strategy and tactics. The defensive battle – at least, by day – had been conclusively won; only the night *blitzkrieg* now presented its peculiar problems for the squadrons. The natural reaction was to 'lean forward' – to adopt a fighter offensive into German-occupied Europe; to expand the initial forays undertaken by some squadrons throughout the latter months of 1940, when during the period July 1st to October 31st the command's fighters had flown an overall total of 1321 individual sorties across the Channel. If results had seemed paltry – each air force had lost some 30 aircraft – such operations had the value of forcing the Luftwaffe to retain a defensive fighter force in France, which might otherwise have been used on the eastern front against Russia eventually, or simply added to the continuing battle over England.

By the end of 1940 Fighter Command had mushroomed to an organisation divided into six Groups – Nos. 9, 10, 11, 12, 13 and 14 – covering the whole of the UK. Between them these Groups could muster 71 first-line squadrons and a total of 1467 fighters in operationally-fit condition, with ample pilots to fill the cockpits. With such fresh 'muscle', the command looked eagerly to its new future policy of carrying the air war to the enemy. And to implement this change in outlook, a fresh leader was appointed to Bentley Priory, the contemporary Deputy Chief of Air Staff, Sholto Douglas, who took up his appointment in November 1940. Hugh Dowding, the man whose four and a half years of dedicated and unceasing labours labours as the

head of Fighter Command had resulted in an aerial defence organisation for Britain against which the might of Göring's vaunted Luftwaffe
had crumbled, was quietly shuffled into a backwater post not of his
choosing, and a few months later conveniently retired from regular
RAF service. At the same time Dowding's chief lieutenant, Keith Park,
whose brilliant tactical handling of 11 Group during the battle had
virtually ensured success, was replaced by the jealous and ever-
ambitious former 12 Group commander, Trafford Leigh-Mallory. This
naked 'sacking' of the two chief architects of the 1940 victory was
merely the ultimate step in a somewhat protracted behind-the-scenes
sniping 'campaign' against Dowding engendered by self-seeking individuals in both government and RAF circles; one of the foremost critics
being Leigh-Mallory himself.

Using the well-publicised internal controversy of whether Park's
actual tactical employment of his squadrons in single or paired fighting
units, or Leigh-Mallory's impractical theories for 'big Wings' of four or
five units flying as one fighting formation, was the best method of
defence during the critical months of August and September 1940,
pressure was brought to bear upon Dowding, and – almost peremptor-
ily – he was notified by the Chief of Air Staff that he was to hand over his
command to Sholto Douglas on November 25th. Perhaps more
significantly Dowding, the undisputed victorious commander in the
first pure aerial battle ever, was not even publicly honoured for that
victory in the time-honoured tradition. His only recognition had been
the almost routine award of a KGCB in September 1940, an award
regarded in Service circles as virtually 'normal rations' for any senior
commander of Dowding's stature on the cessation of any lengthy active
appointment, either in war or, even, peacetime. It was, as Peter
Wykeham expressed it, 'the first of the indications that Dowding was
going to escape the plaudits ordinarily extended to a victor, and the
squadrons were to feel the omission as a reflection on themselves'. Even
the manner in which Hugh Dowding was eventually retired from active
service gave evidence of the ill-starred manoeuvring in both political
and RAF hierarchy strata. Against his private wishes, Dowding was
given several unimportant, even pointless appointments before his
final, irrevocable retirement; and it was not until May 1943 that
Dowding learned that his name had been forwarded for the honour of a
Barony. Dowding's 'right hand' during 1940, Park, in the interim, was
relegated to training duties until 1942, when he was appointed AOC,

Malta and immediately applied the same defensive tactics he had used in 1940 with ultimate resounding success for the besieged island.

Such individual facets notwithstanding, the volte-face in Fighter Command policy from defensive to offensive came at a propitious stage in the German onslaught against Britain. Though the night bombing blitz was to continue for many months beyond November 1940, the day battle was conclusively over. Night fighting remained a command responsibility, but was – relatively speaking – a minor part of the fighter war effort. Objectively, too, the change really necessitated a fresh mind at the helm; Dowding's unremitting crusade for an effective air defence organisation had been accomplished, and the basic aspects of that organisation remained the foundation of Britain's air shield for at least a decade after the 1940 'acid testing'. The moment had come now for another leader, one dedicated just as intensely to the philosophy of the offensive. In Air Marshal William Sholto Douglas the Air Ministry had found just such a man. Of stocky, burly build, with an unconscious aura of aggression about him, Douglas had achieved respect and honours as a fighter pilot and leader of fighters during 1914–18, and his subsequent RAF career was marked by a succession of command appointments and steady promotion. His approach to war was non-theoretical; in all things Douglas was essentially a practical exponent. Thus, on taking up his post at Bentley Priory, Douglas's first concern was for the night defence against the escalating German bombing raids. Here his past acquaintance with the development of radar for aircraft was to be of particular importance, and Douglas was well fitted to continue the progress in this field inaugurated and backed by his predecessor, Hugh Dowding. Realising that the full potential of air-borne radar was a long way from being achieved, however, Douglas approved the interim use of day fighters for the night defence, despite their many recognised shortcomings in such a specialised role.

On 20 December 1940, two Spitfires from 66 Squadron left their base at Biggin Hill, crossed the Channel, and strafed the German-occupied airfield at Le Touquet. Seven days later Allan Wright and Tony Mottram of 92 Squadron, also from Biggin Hill, slipped through low cloud cover into France and scoured the Abbeville area, seeking possible targets for their guns. Wright found nothing and returned without firing a shot, but Mottram gleefully shot up a small convoy of German lorries and a staff car, expending all his ammunition before turning for home. These inauspicious sorties were the first pure offensive sorties undertaken by Fighter Command under its new policy of leaning forward into Europe. Such sorties were code-named 'Rhubarbs', but an extension of the main aim was inaugurated on 10 January 1941 when 'Circus' operations commenced; with a single Blenheim bomber unit (114 Squadron) escorted by no less than nine fighter squadrons across the French coast. This latest development had a simple purpose – to draw German fighters up into combat in circumstances favourable to the RAF. This first 'Circus' headed for the Pas de Calais where the bombers released their bombs across an airfield; while the strong fighter 'escort', led by Wing Commander F. V. Beamish, DSO, AFC, found little opposition beyond two lone Messerschmitt Bf 109s, both of which were shot down. Though the prevailing winter weather prevented many such operations, on February 2nd more than 120 Spitfires and Hurricanes were despatched to cover a bomber attack on Boulogne docks, and generally hunt for Luftwaffe fighters. Of the few German fighters seen and engaged, three were claimed as destroyed. The apparent lack of opposition by the Luftwaffe's fighter arm was not due to any faltering in courage among the *jagdgeschwadern*'s crews. Unpractised in pure defensive tactics, and depleted in overall numbers by Hitler's transference of the bulk of units to the eastern zones, the remaining fighter units were at a distinct disadvantage.

The change of policy for Fighter Command brought with it new means and methods for aerial fighting; a re-evaluation of the traditional tactics and a re-assessment of the most effective ways of incorporating such innovations. The out-dated pre-war 'Fighting Area Attacks' of rigidly-held formations in Vics of three aircraft were abandoned, and the RAF 'borrowed' the highly practical methods employed by the Luftwaffe. In future fighters flew in minimum pairs, with a 'leader' or 'No. 1' being protected at all times by his 'wing man', or 'No. 2'; thus the No. 1 was the fighting, killing partner, and his No. 2 kept his leader's tail clear of the opposition and generally covered him in combat. Two such pairs comprised a 'Finger Four' loose formation as the new tactical fighting unit. Such a system offered extreme flexibility and mutual protection to a high degree. The other significant innovation was the adaptation of the 'Big Wing' theory expounded by 12 Group during 1940, whereby four or five squadrons of fighters were grouped, usually on the same base airfield, and led as a Wing by a Wing Leader; the latter being a Wing Commander of proven fighting experience. Among the first such Wing Leaders selected were Douglas Bader and 'Sailor' Malan, who immediately set standards of fighting, tactics and prowess which were to be richly embellished by their successors throughout the war.

New equipment for the revitalised Fighter Command began to reach the operational squadrons early in 1941. The well-tried Spitfire and Hurricane designs were improved and up-rated in both armament and engine performance. The main advance in fire-power came from the installation of 20mm cannons in place of some of the former .303-inch calibre machine gun wing batteries, though initially these were 'mixed', with two or four cannons being supplemented by two or four machine guns. New fighter designs also began Service testing and operational trials; one of these being a stablemate of the doughty Hurricane – the brutish-looking Hawker Typhoon. First flown in prototype form in February 1940, the Typhoon was a fighter destined to undergo lengthy 'teething troubles' on introduction to the RAF, due mainly to its unorthodox and unproven Sabre engine. Produced initially to carry 12 wing-mounted machine guns, it became standardised as a four-20mm cannon armed design, and the first examples were received by the RAF in September 1941. Nos 56 and 609 Squadrons were the first frontline units to test and operate Typhoons in combat conditions, and both units were to experience a catalogue of frustrations and accidents over many months before the 'Tiffie' became fully accepted. Another promising fighter was the sleek, twin-engined, single-seat Westland Whirlwind. With a nose battery of four 20mm cannon, and a maximum speed in excess of 350 mph, the Whirlwind – or 'Crikey' as it became dubbed – first entered RAF service in December 1940 with 263 Squadron, and despite problems with its unique Rolls-Royce Peregrine engines and fast landing speed, proved to be a worthy escort for low-level operations. Only one other unit was equipped, 137 Squadron in September 1941, however, after which production of the type ceased. Meanwhile, at Cranwell, under the tight wraps of security blanking, another prototype made its first flight on 15 May 1941 – and heralded a new era in British aviation. This was the Gloster E.28/39 experimental jet single-seater, powered by a Whittle W1 gas turbine giving 850lb static thrust.

In the continuing night battle against the marauding Luftwaffe bombers over Britain, the Beaufighter was supplemented by a few Hurricanes, Defiants and a recently introduced American twin-engined design, the Douglas Havoc 'fighter', this latter being essentially a variant of the DB Boston bomber. Havocs were principally involved in a makeshift scheme for interception titled Turbinlite; whereby the Havoc was fitted with a powerful searchlight in its nose which, on close interception of an enemy, was intended to illuminate the target. This target was then – theoretically – to be engaged and destroyed by one or two Hurricane fighters which faithfully tagged along with the Havoc. Practice did not make perfect in the case of the Turbinlite units, and the general idea was dropped once the radar-equipped Beaufighter squadrons began gaining considerable successes. In any case, from June 1941 until the following winter, the Luftwaffe bombers seldom raided in any great numbers, due to the opening phases of Germany's offensive into Russia.

The increasing strength of Fighter Command's daylight offensive enjoyed little great success in the summer of 1941. The 'Circus' style of operation involved complex planning and intricate co-ordination with the bomber units acting as 'bait' to suck in German fighter opposition, and the command was as yet insufficiently experienced in such matters to ensure worthwhile results. Such German fighter reaction as was met proved to be of a relatively high standard, led by veteran fighter pilots who had fought through the battles of Spain, France and Britain with hardly a break in continuous operational flying. Some of the earliest 'Circus' operations, ill-prepared and insufficiently disciplined, suffered unnecessarily high casualties, and had little to show for their overall efforts at the end of the day. Moreover, while the superb Spitfire and rugged Hurricane had provided an adequate defence barrier during 1940, the 1941 offensive was being fought over France and the Low Countries, requiring greatly improved performance ranges from the RAF's latest variants of those stalwart designs. In Germany the principal fighter, the Messerschmitt Bf 109, had also been improved as the Bf 109F version, which maintained a slight edge over the latest Mark V Spitfire variant, and completely outclassed the Hurricane I and Mk IIs now in service. Recognising the relatively inferior performance of the Hurricane at high altitude, the RAF henceforth utilised the type as a low-level strafer and light bomber, in which role the Hurricane came to excel throughout the remaining years of hostilities.

The cost of the 'Circus' operations can be part-illustrated by the tally for six weeks in June–July 1941. In 46 such operations, 123 fighter pilots were declared 'Missing', though the RAF claimed a total of 322 enemy aircraft destroyed. The latter figure was grossly overestimated

91

in fact; it represented a higher figure than the entire Luftwaffe fighter strength available in France at that period. Such RAF losses were doubly tragic in that they included many veteran pilots who, having fought through the French campaign and Battle of Britain, were by early 1941 commanding squadrons or Flights; experienced men like Squadron Leader Mungo-Park of 74 Squadron who was killed on June 27th, and Eric Lock who died over France on August 3rd. Only six days later the legendary 'Tin-Legs' Bader was forced to bale out to captivity. Such men were sorely missed and hard to replace. Opposing them were fighting leaders of seasoned experience; men like Adolf Galland and Hannes Trautloft who marshalled and led their slim resources with guile and great skill. Though the main Luftwaffe fighter still in use was the Bf 109F or G variant, on August 17th Flying Officer Vicki Ortmans, a Belgian pilot with 609 Squadron, returned from a combat with some 20 enemy fighters and was adamant that one of his assailants had been 'a Messerschmitt with a radial engine'. RAF Intelligence, caught off-balance by such a sworn statement, preferred to disbelieve Ortmans' description, but clear evidence of the new fighter came from the camera gun film of an escort fighter to a 'Circus' operation on October 13th. It was the newly-introduced Focke-Wulf 190, a design well superior to any RAF fighter of the period, and one which was to gain a modicum of aerial supremacy over France for many months.

Apart from its continuing responsibility for night defence above the United Kingdom, and the daytime offensive armadas into occupied Europe, Fighter Command also became involved in a third major commitment by mid-1941. This was the concerted efforts of Bomber, Coastal and Fighter Commands to prevent enemy shipping traffic along the English Channel and nearby waters. This traffic was vital for Germany and was invariably heavily escorted by both air cover and flanking flak-ships with heavy armament. Code-named 'Roadsteads', the RAF's anti-shipping strikes involved light and medium bombers for actual bombing or torpedo attacks, with several fighter squadrons in direct escort to smother any enemy fighter and flak opposition. Such a tactic meant zero-height attacks against armoured, well-alerted flak batteries, flying through a murderous lattice-work of tracers and shells to press home a pointblank broadside of cannon fire. Inevitably, casualties were high among the fighters, but the heaviest toll was suffered by the Blenheim bomber crews of No. 2 Group who accumulated frightening losses, yet doggedly returned to the fray day after day.

Their superb heroism – there is no more fitting description of such unstinted valour – was never matched by actual results obtained, however, and the whole principle of the 'Roadstead' type of operation became the crux of much controversy at Command staff levels. For the vital 'escort' role, the fighter units selected comprised, in the main, Hurricane and Whirlwind aircraft, adapted to carry 250lb and 500lb bombs under their wings; though accuracy in low-level bombing by any fighter pilot untrained in such tactics was, to say the least, questionable. These same squadrons often alternated between 'Roadstead' and the continuing 'Circus' operations, thereby providing most pilots in Fighter Command during the latter months of 1941 with almost continuous operational flying in a variety of roles.

By the end of 1941 such expensive – in the casualty/achieved results context – operations were in general disfavour with the Air Staff and the government, and Sholto Douglas was, very reluctantly, forced to preach caution to the Group commanders organising and planning future daylight operations of this nature. At that time Fighter Command could muster 100 squadrons overall – 75 fighters for day work, and the remainder night fighters or intruders. Of this total it should be well marked that 34 were mainly manned by non-British personnel: Polish, Belgian, Czech, French, Canadian, Australian, and even American. Such 'nationalised' squadrons – formed at the behest of ill-advised national governments overseas – were untypical of the general attitude to such matters among most RAF flying crews. As in Bomber Command, a mixed nationality crew strength usually proved the most efficacious, though it must be admitted that in units where the English language was not a common factor, a myriad minor difficulties – mainly technical – ruffled an otherwise smooth-running operational effort.

If such an obvious healthiness in operational strength in pure quantity boded well for Fighter Command's coming year, other factors reduced the potential. With the build-up of Bomber Command slowly filling factory floor space, production of the requisite fighter aircraft reserves to replenish the command fell to a lower priority than that enjoyed in 1940. Moreover, the constant search for better performance machines, and the introduction of fresh designs, cramped the flow of aircraft considerably. In the context of new personnel the RAF was never short of ample numbers of volunteers, eager to qualify as aircrew, particularly as fighter pilots. The pseudo-glamour of the 'ace' fighter

93

pilot still remained in the layman's mind, and a plethora of press publicity merely encouraged and maintained such an image. Nevertheless, the 1941–2 training resources for all air crews was limited though ever-expanding. Even by wartime standards of necessity the training required to produce even a modestly 'qualified' pilot still took time – a minimum of 40 weeks actual training, apart from such non-productive aspects as leave, sickness *et al* – before that pilot joined his first operational unit. Even there the 'sprog' pilot needed to be inculcated into the operational scene carefully, if time and circumstance permitted, before being considered capable of 'earning his flying pay'. As in all things, a *soupçon* of actual operations was worth a gallon of theory, however well expounded.

With the introduction by the Luftwaffe of the sleek Focke-Wulf 190 fighter, RAF fighter pilots found themselves facing an obviously superior adversary to their Spitfire Mk V. With its clear edge in sheer speed, the Fw 190 could engage or disengage in combat at will, while its extremely high manoeuvrability and fast diving capability outpaced anything the RAF could put up against it during late 1941 and the early months of 1942. A partial answer to the Fw 190 came in June 1942, when the first Spitfire Mk IX versions were issued to 64 Squadron. By marrying a Rolls-Royce Merlin 61 engine to a four-bladed propeller, in a 'stretched' nose section, the Mk IX offered maximum speeds in excess of 400 mph. Though merely intended as a 'stop-gap' variant to combat the Fw 190, the Mk IX Spitfire eventually equipped 60 squadrons in the UK alone, and a total of 5739 machines were produced – second only to the Mk V in quantity production of the Spitfire. This race for superiority in aircraft – an inevitable consequence of any war – led to a long line of further developments of the basic Spitfire design; each introduced for some succinct prime role, though often employed in other facets of aerial combat.

The 1941 RAF fighter offensive over Europe had provided Fighter Command with an overall situation exactly in reverse to its role in the previous year. During the Luftwaffe's daylight raiding of the Battle of Britain period, German fighters had been shackled to the bomber formations by Göring's express orders, unable to exploit fully their individual task of pure fighting, and hampered seriously in freedom of action generally. The resulting high casualties hardly justified their devotion to orders. As defenders, fighting above their homeland, the RAF's fighter pilots had a huge moral advantage, added to a role more in keeping with their training and experience. In the summer of 1941 however, Fighter Command found itself in precisely the same circumstances as their former opponents; detailed as relatively close escort to much slower bomber formations, unable to engage in the individual freedom of choice open to the pure fighter. In addition they were seeking combat over enemy-occupied territory, where a crippled aircraft almost inevitably led to the loss of its pilot – whether killed or simply prisoner of war. Only the 'Rhubarb' sweeps offered succinct fighter freedom of selection in targets and combat, unencumbered by the responsibility of bomber crews' safety; yet these were, too often, despatched in too few numbers to have any worthwhile result and incurred unjustifiable high losses. It was, therefore, a period of semi-frustration for Fighter Command. Sholto Douglas had yet to be given the adequate strength in aircraft and men to pursue any significant fighter offensive, and had to be content with maintaining a sharp edge to the natural aggressive nature of his fighting arm.

This is not to imply that RAF fighter pilots had any relatively uneventful existence throughout the year. Restriction in parameters of individual choice of combat may have given rise to a feeling of resentment among the fighter squadrons, but there was no lack of action. The daylight 'Circus' bombing sorties – often two or even three in a single day's operations – brought violent reaction from the Luftwaffe in almost every case. The operational limit of penetration into France for RAF fighters then was little better than 70 miles, thereby limiting the combat zone to a relatively thin strip of sky for the *jagdgeschwadern* to protect. The summer of 1941 comprised months of sunlit, blue-haze days, with air visibility almost unlimited; perfect 'fighter weather' where the glint from a perspex canopy could be noted many miles away, and surprise was usually only possible by a lightning dive out of the white glare of the constant sun. Combat was a brief, savage clash of formations, splintering into a tumbling maelstrom of individual duels and twisting tail-chases, with a spider-web pattern of white contrail plumes from the highest antagonists providing a form of celestial ceiling to the main combat arena far below. Survival necessitated a constantly twisting neck, watching every point of the compass from which the slender head-on silhouette of an enemy fighter might herald swift death; a moment's relaxation in vigilance could be fatal. The clashes were seldom lengthy – a wing-turning jinking for tactical advantage, then the headlong plunge into the swarm of black-crossed

95

opponents, and a subsequent shock of realisation that the sky is empty, with the eeriness of a magician's disappearing trick.

The extremes of contrast in a fighter pilot's life left the newcomer to operations bewildered. Each dawn he woke in a comfortable bed, with the full facilities and semi-luxury of a well-appointed Mess in many cases; an almost gentlemanly form of existence far removed from the grim realities of his calling. Within the hour, however, he might be rolling across the green expanse of his airfield in a fully armed lethal aircraft, crossing the cool waters of the English Channel, and then engaged in a life-and-death struggle wherein every nerve in his body was brought to a peak of sensitive awareness and stressed to the limit. Yet less than an hour later he would be settling onto the same grass field, taxying to a sandbagged dispersal under the guidance of shepherding airmen at each wing-tip, then climbing out of his cockpit to be met by a crowd of his fellow pilots, each excitedly recounting their recent actions. A drive back to the Mess after debriefing by the unit 'Spy' (Intelligence Officer), and relaxation in a deckchair on the Mess lawn, sipping hot sweet tea, with the sweat of combat still moist upon his body. As his nerves gradually loosened their high tension, his brain might begin to recall incidents of the past two hours, flashes of memory which had occurred so fast that the brain had simply recorded for future rationalisation. Vivid mind pictures of a Spitfire above him at an impossible angle, its wings pluming smoke as its cannons belched . . . a Messerschmitt's port wing folding back like a box-lid to crush its pilot's cockpit canopy . . . a flowering gout of flames and black, oily smoke as another Messerschmitt exploded . . . the twisting, forlorn grey-black pillar of burning oil and high octane petrol that denoted a third machine – theirs or ours? – falling from the fight on its last return to earth.

And always the high-pitched babble of voices over his ear-phones . . . 'Ten bandits at three o'clock, Bluetail Leader' . . . 'I see them. Prepare to break on my word. NOW, BREAK!' . . . 'Bluetail Three, watch those two bastards at ten o'clock' . . . 'Got 'em, Smudge' . . . 'Yahoo, got the sod!' . . . 'Watch your tail, Ken' . . . 'Reform all Bluetails' . . . 'Can't, boss. I've four of 'em surrounding me' . . . 'Keep turning, Geoff. I'm coming' . . . 'I'm hit, Bluetail leader. The engine's gone. Baling out. Tell my girl I'm OK' . . . 'All Bluetails. Get out, fast and low' . . . 'Come in Bluetail Four. Where are you Frank?' . . . 'Frank's had it, leader. Sorry' . . . 'All Bluetails. Go home. Don't reform' . . . then a hissing and silence as each man hugged the ground desperately, heading for the Channel and home. The whole fight had lasted maybe ten minutes, yet his shirt is sopping wet with sweat, the perspiration running in rivulets down each arm, his back, his forehead. His heart slips into a lower gear, and the relative quiet begins to let through other familiar sounds of his engine drumming evenly. The English coastal cliffs slide away behind him and 20 minutes later he is over base, slipping into 'finals' and rounding out for a bumpy landing across the undulating grass. In three hours time he'll be away again, back across that Channel, looking for trouble; but until then he relaxes, soaking in the drowsy heat of high summer and the beauty of the surrounding, flowering countryside with its Joseph's coat of myriad colours and perfumes.

Such continuing peaks and troughs of tension and stress, both mental and physical, sapped even the youngest body eventually, though most fighter pilots seldom recognised the warning signs of nature when they reached such a stage. An example of this 'battle fatigue', as it became recognised by the medical authorities later, was Adolph 'Sailor' Malan, DSO, DFC. By August 1941 Malan had been continuously flying operations for nearly two years. His superiors suggested to him that it was time he had a rest. 'It wasn't an order', explained Malan. 'They just asked me how I felt about it. I thought I was all right and refused. Since I'd first been approached I'd more than doubled my score, and I kept thinking; "Just a few more".' Then shortly after Malan led a formation into an attack on a gaggle of Messerschmitts, and admitted afterwards that his tactical approach to the fight had been wrong. 'It's hard to explain, but it was my reflexes, if you like. I knew I'd made a mistake – one I'd not have made if I'd been fresh. You don't get the chance to make such mistakes twice in this game.' He was offered a three-days' week-end at a Kent cottage, and accepted the offer. 'It was queer – and salutary. I heard the birds for the first time, smelt flowers, did a bit of rabbit shooting, looked at the scenery properly, and heard people just talking about everyday things. Suddenly I knew how really clapped-out I was.' On his return from that week-end, Malan was taken off operations and sent to America on a form of publicity-cum-technical tour, along with five other distinguished RAF pilots. It was more than two years before Malan flew on operations again.

7. Aces and Kings

The years 1939–41 for Fighter Command were periods of extremes in emotion and practice. At the beginning of hostilities with Nazi Germany, the RAF generally, in keeping with the national optimistic mood throughout Britain, entered its second declared war with much of the spirit of its 1918 pioneer-members. Air fighting held a pseudo-glamour aura in the public imagination, derived directly from the exploits of the legendary names in World War One aerial combat. This cloak of knightly combat, edged with the gold fringe of chivalry, and embroidered with attitudes akin to the playing fields of any English public school, became a mantle exploited by the popular press and officialdom's propaganda machinery. Such evocative phrases as 'eagles of the skies,' 'knights of the air', and, especially, 'aces' were bandied about with a frequency which caused great – if amused – embarrassment to every RAF fighter pilot. At the outbreak of war the squadrons were manned by serving professional pilots, many of whom were career men, having entered the Service via Halton and/or Cranwell and dedicated their young lives to the RAF. Equally professional in the context of devotion to their prime tasks were the crews of the Auxiliary Air Force squadrons, mobilised for front-line operational service immediately at the start of the war.

The anti-climax of the first two months of 'hostilities' after the keyed-up expectation of immediate combat brought with it a form of euphoria. The fighter pilots were no jot less keen to get to grips with the Luftwaffe, but opportunities were few and far between for the UK-based squadrons. Trained to peacetime standards of flying and 'fighting', only a handful of pilots in Britain had actually fired their wing-guns 'in anger' before the first wartime Christmas. Even in France the Hurricane pilots of the AASF and BEF Air Component had

seldom clashed with an aerial opponent, and those few who had –
Voase-Jeff, Mould, Kain *et al* – found their isolated victories lauded in
headlines. Such over-emphasis on individuals' successes was repugnant to the vast majority of RAF pilots, most of whom were inculcated
with the long-standing unwritten tradition of anonymity within any
British fighting Service. Though privately proud of any achievements
attained by any member of one's own squadron, public praise and
laudation were normally derided, and any unwitting 'victim' of press
popularity usually found himself footing a heavy alcohol bill in his
Mess as internal 'punishment'. . . .

The status of 'ace', though never recognised or acknowledged officially in the RAF at any time, was generally applied to any pilot
credited with at least five confirmed combat victories; an arbitrary
figure derived directly from the French air services of 1914–18, and
abetted by the German and American services. The Air Ministry policy
on such matters excluded official listing of victory totals for individual
pilots, though acknowledgment of such successes often appeared
throughout both world wars in the citations for awards and decorations
published in the *London Gazette*. The term 'ace' was never used by the
RAF internally, even in private conversation – indeed, its only wide
application by RAF men was in the form of sarcasm or near-insult on a
light-hearted plane. This is not to say that individual pride in personal
achievements was entirely outlawed. From 1940 many RAF fighter
pilots decorated their Hurricanes, Spitfires, Typhoons and Tempests
with personal 'scoreboards' of claimed victories, usually in the form of
rows of small white swastikas or similar modest symbols. In addition it
became reasonably common practice to embellish the forward fuselage
with names – usually of a wife, fiancée or favourite girl-friend – added
alongside the cockpit entrance door or panel. The more colourful
adornments and markings applied to many Luftwaffe aircraft, especially the *jagdgeschwadern*, were expressly forbidden in RAF Fighter
Command. From the summer of 1938 – initiated by the Munich Crisis –
RAF fighters had been allocated official camouflage markings overall,
relieved only by a two-letter coding system for identification of individual squadrons. Though the specific letter-codes for each unit were
hastily changed on the outbreak of war in 1939, such a system pertained
throughout World War Two, with few exceptions.

This official frowning upon garish aircraft markings by the Air
Ministry found general approval among the ranks of the fighter

squadrons. When the ground crew of Wing Commander Brendan 'Paddy' Finucane, DSO, DFC once painted 21 swastika symbols in a neat insigne on Finucane's Spitfire fuselage, he angrily told them, 'Wash those off!' Apart from the unspoken reluctance to be branded as a 'line-shooter' by his fellow pilots – perhaps the greatest social stigma any air crew could suffer – there were good practical reasons for preferring 'anonymous' markings. During the Battle of Britain some pilots of 249 Squadron began painting their propeller spinners a bright red colour; to the dismay of one pilot, Tom Neil, DFC, who decried the practice, explaining that when he saw a bright coloured nose in his rear-view mirror he automatically assumed it belonged to a Messerschmitt! Nevertheless, by the close of 1940 it became acceptable on many squadrons for individuals to record their victory tallies below the cockpit, particularly those of some of the higher-scoring pilots like Roland Tuck, Eric Lock and others of similar prowess. The only other insignia to be displayed at that period usually comprised some form of unofficial cartoon or symbol indicating the particular unit to which the pilot belonged.

The introduction of Wing Leaders in early 1941 also introduced an officially-approved new style of individual marking, whereby such pilots were permitted to discard all normal unit codings and replace them with the initials of their own names, thus 'Sailor' Malan's markings were AGM, Ian 'Widge' Gleed's IRG, *et al*. Such a privilege was a jealously-guarded and sought-after 'bonus'. This status marking was soon after claimed by many senior RAF officers for adorning their 'private' transport aircraft. Apart from the mandatory black and white striping applied to all aircraft involved in the D-Day operations in June 1944 and several months thereafter, fighter aircraft retained basic camouflage patterns and squadron code letters until the end of the European war in 1945.

Despite the RAF's unwritten 'code of silence' in relation to publicity for the exploits of individuals – the only real exceptions to this being those airmen awarded a Victoria Cross – the popular press and national media constantly pursued a policy of headlining particularly gallant deeds or outstanding prowess, especially those attributable to fighter pilots. It was a perfectly natural response to the needs of a wartime, hero-hungry nation, and no little compliment to the British government's constant policies of uplifting and maintaining national morale. Civilians, from fifteen-year-old schoolboys to eighty-year-old war veterans, avidly followed the progress of the air war during the early years, and certain individual fighter pilots achieved an unsought national fame – usually to their acute embarrassment. Thus when John Cunningham had achieved several successes in radar-equipped night fighters, the daily newspapers tagged him with the sobriquet 'Cat's-Eyes' – much to his personal disgust. Although such hero-worship gradually became tempered as the war entered its third and fourth years, and more emphasis in the media was given to the work of Bomber Command and other facets, the fighter pilots still retained their inherited air of 'glamour' for the younger generations, and the nicknames given to certain individuals became a permanent associa-tion in the public eye.

By 1942 the very nature of the fighters' war had changed radically. From the desperate defensive battles for survival during 1940, the war had moved round to the offensive, with an ever-increasing penetration into enemy-occupied territories and a consequent stepping-up of the pure fighter-v-fighter form of aerial combat. New names emerged in Fighter Command's ranks as fighting leaders, some of these being men who had fought through the Battle of Britain as junior Pilot Officers or Sergeants and were now commanding Flights or squadrons. Others were wartime-trained pilots whose first blooding in operations had come since the Battle of Britain, and were thus inculcated from the very start of their careers in an atmosphere of offensive – as opposed to defensive – tactical thinking and action. The fighters' day war was now fought by large formations in concert; four, five or more squadrons acting as a cohesive fighting formation, at least, initially. Lone sorties were seldom contemplated, and the fighter Wing had become virtually the minimum strength in which to venture over German-held territory. As the equivalent of Bomber Command's 'Master Bomber', the Wing Leaders needed to be men of deep experience and exceptional charac-ter; flying and fighting as individuals, yet capable of keeping an eye and brain constantly assessing and re-assessing the tactical circumstances and issuing the necessary orders to cope with each developing situa-tion. For some leaders, men in their early twenties, it was an awesome responsibility to place on young shoulders; yet aerial combat made a man a veteran quickly, and many 1941–2 Wing Commanders – the equivalent of an Army regimental Lieutenant-Colonel – were barely past the legal definition of majority in years, but were 'old men' in the deadly battles of the skies. Such youthful veterans were often called upon personally to lead and direct formations of more than a hundred Spitfires, and, virtually with no exception, never failed in their onerous task.

The first-appointed Wing Leaders, Adolph 'Sailor' Malan and Douglas Bader, were soon complemented by other men whose names were to become near-legendary in the fighter arm; Alan Deere, 'Paddy' Finucane, Peter Brothers, Hugh Dundas, 'Jamie' Rankin, 'Kingpin' Kingcome, Denis Crowley-Milling, 'Dickie' Milne and scores of others of equal repute. Each had 'earned' his appointment the hard way by coming into the operational scene as a very junior fighter pilot and surviving his early combat sorties by skill, aggression, instinctive tactical 'know-how' – the hallmarks of the successful fighting man in any context. Pure courage alone was no guarantee of survival, though without it none would have lived very long in the aerial arena. Such prowess had been forged in the white-hot crucible of first-hand combat experience, and was now utilised to nurture the younger, inexperienced pilots, and to prosecute the air war to the greatest possible advantage. Overall co-ordination between Wings and Sectors was necessarily controlled broadly by Group headquarters, but in day to day operations Wing Leaders were given a wide parameter in organising their individual Wings, selecting sortie areas, tactics *et al*; a flexibility in decision-making entrusted to their experienced hands and minds.

As a 'race apart', Wing Leaders came from every walk of life and background, having in common only their fighting and leadership qualities. The regular-serving RAF men, trained at Cranwell, Halton and other Service foundation schools, were supplemented by men from dozens of countries and continents who had eagerly travelled or fled to England to join the struggle against Hitler's Germany. By the end of the war these included men from Canada, Australia, New Zealand, Norway, France, Poland, Belgium, South Africa, Rhodesia, Eire; a polyglot community united by a common cause. As in Bomber Command, a mixture of nationals within any particular squadron often proved to be the finest blend of fighting potential, hence the ready acceptance of any 'foreigner' as a fighting leader. Experience was the criterion for selection and, indeed, approval; accident of birthplace bore little significance.

The years 1941–2 saw Fighter Command expand greatly its background training facilities, thereby providing additional and specialised instruction and practice for all levels of future fighter pilots and leaders. At Tangmere had been formed the original Fighter Interception Unit (FIU) which, in 1940, had given the mighty Beaufighter its first taste of operational use. At Wittering there followed the Air Fighting Development Unit (AFDU), while by 1942 a Fighter Leaders' School had been formed at Aston Down. All were specialised role training units additional to the more normal Operational Training Units (OTUs) tasked with providing a final 'polish' to the elementary preparation of a future fighter pilot. These latter units varied widely in their approach to their prime task, ranging from the 'routine' instruction offered by most to the extreme forms applied at units like 53 OTU at Heston. From May 1941 this OTU was commanded by the fiery Welsh World War One 'ace', Ira Jones, DSO, MC, DFC, MM, whose constant creed of the offensive was exemplified by having the lecture rooms' walls 'decorated' with large photos of crashed Spitfires and even funerals of accident victims who had flouted the rules of basic flying. At one stage Jones even gave personal lectures with a mock coffin on the stage alongside him – a grim warning of the consequences of ill-discipline in aerial combat!

Notwithstanding all these facilities for honing the fighting edge of a prospective fighter pilot's operational potential, no training in the world could adequately replace the impact of actual operational experience. Only on joining his first frontline squadron and sweating through his first frightening sorties across the Channel could any fighter pilot be truly assessed as suitable (or otherwise) for his role in the war. Fortunately, by 1942, squadrons had time available to inculcate 'sprog' pilots in the operational scene; keeping them non-operational for a short period while hard-won lessons were drilled into the newcomer's brain, and his actual flying ability was improved to an acceptable level. Such additional training was vital if the freshman was to slot into the unit's tactics and overall methods; one 'weak link' in an essentially team type of warfare could cause unnecessary casualties – each man in a fighter formation had his essential part to play. By then most squadron and Flight commanders in Fighter Command were hard-bitten veterans with a relative wealth of experience to draw upon when leading their men into battle. They knew only too vividly the emotions and reactions associated with a newcomer's first 'ops', and therefore, in the brief time available, did their utmost to prepare the youngsters for this ordeal of 'first blooding'. Above all other matters was the matter of air discipline. Once airborne and en route to the battle zone, one hundred per cent obedience to briefing orders and commands over the R/T from the leader was paramount. Self-discipline was the ultimate criterion, and woe betide any individual who chose to disobey and thereby disrupt the fighting cohesion of his formation.

Air fighting was no longer the almost piecemeal affair of single squadrons or even lone individuals engaged in solitary combat. The battle arena had become a three- or four-dimensional science; a complexity not unlike three-tier chess, where vast formations replaced the gallant knight or lonely bishop as combat was prepared, sought and engaged in pre-planned moves and onslaughts. Though individual skill and courage remained the prime ingredients, the overall panorama was now controlled, directed, calculated and executed with an almost detached objectivity. Each pilot was simply a pawn in the greater 'game', albeit with the added advantage of an inborn individualism which might cope with the unexpected situation or 'unplanned' circumstances. At no time in the annals of fighter warfare have pilots been mere automata, but the skies were now too full with sudden death for any 'loner' to be permitted complete freedom of action.

However 'scientifically' utilised a fighter pilot may have been by 1942, he remained distinctly mortal, with all the weaknesses and failings of any other human being placed under conditions of extreme stress. If sheer experience softened and blurred the sharpest edges of fear in his mind, a pilot remained subject to perfectly normal reactions in the face of possible death or injury. Brendan 'Paddy' Finucane, DSO, DFC, shortly before his own death in action, was reported as saying, 'I'm always comfortable once I'm in my aircraft. The brain is working fast and when the enemy is met it seems to go like clockwork, weighing up this, rejecting that, sizing up this, accepting that, remembering this, correcting that, considering, acting. You haven't time then to *feel* anything. But your nerves may be suffering – if not from actual fear, then from excitement. I've often come back from a sweep to find my tunic and shirt wet through with perspiration. Of course, it can be bloody hot in the cockpit of a Spitfire with the sun beating down on the transparent roof, but it's the mental strain that really grills you.' His pre-operations' 'butterflies in the stomach' feelings were shared by all pilots, whether they admitted it or not, yet most also mentally relaxed once they were strapped in to their seats and busy with pre-flight cockpit checks. As another successful Spitfire pilot expressed it,

> Once I knew we were detailed for a sortie or sweep, my guts churned uneasily, as if I'd not eaten for 48 hours, until that moment my rigger started strapping the kite to my back. From then on my brain was too damned busy to bother with any thoughts of what might happen to me personally. And I should add that the ground crew were a marvellous boost to my morale at that point; always smiling and ready with a dry joke to keep my spirits up. Too little praise has been given to the real contribution of the erks in the books I've read since the war. Their long hours and utter devotion to both the aircraft and 'their' pilots deserved a medal, though few that I knew ever received any gongs.

This latter comment highlights one vital aspect of Fighter Command – indeed, every RAF command – which is seldom recorded in adequate measure: the doughty and devoted services of all squadron ground crews. On the outbreak of war, virtually all 'erks' – the universal RAF nickname for all ground crews – were regular-serving members of the RAF. A high proportion were men trained initially as Aircraft Apprentices at Halton, Cranwell and other foundation technical training schools originated in the 1919 Trenchard Memorandum for the structure of the peace-time RAF; hence their Service sobriquet of 'Trenchard's Brats'. Others had recently graduated from the newer schools at Cosford, Flowerdown, Eastchurch etc – ex-Boy Entrants *et al*. All were inculcated with an ideal of 'service', whereby mere completion of any task was not adequate; every job was accomplished to the highest possible standard. This attitude was reflected in the skills, organisational capabilities and 'know-how' exhibited throughout the war by such 'ex-Brat' airmen and NCOs on the frontline squadrons; and particularly exemplified by the erks on the fighter squadrons which participated in the Battle of Britain. As the non-commissioned ranks of the RAF rapidly swelled in recruitment from 1940, much of this 'vocational' attitude rubbed off on the 'Hostilities Only' airmen, aided and abetted by the regulars. Similar devoted service was given by members of the Women's Auxiliary Air Force (WAAF), many of whom endured frightening situations during 1940 particularly on the various fighter stations, and their fortitude is all the more remarkable when it is realised that until mid-1941, when the WAAF became legally subject to certain sections of the Air Force Act for purposes of discipline,

punishment etc., *any* WAAF could literally pack her bags and 'desert' –
with no legal restrictions to stop her!

Although the pre-1939 arrangement for allocation of ground crews
within a squadron, whereby specific erks of various technical trades
were usually allotted particular aircraft to maintain constantly, could
not be continued exactly under wartime conditions, the essence of this
'family' spirit did apply at both Flight and Squadron level, with a fierce
pride being engendered throughout all ranks of each unit in its
achievements and prowess. Such an unwritten code of 'belonging' gave
the hard-labouring airmen and airwomen a strong sense of individual
identity and a common purpose; characteristics which were inevitably
diluted or even dissipated later in the war when a fashion for the
creation of Servicing Echelons, comprised of most ground tradesmen
on any unit, virtually 'divorced' the erks from 'their' aircraft and pilots.
An extension of this system was re-introduced into the RAF generally
in the 1960s, under the guise of 'Centralised Servicing', ostensibly to
improve cost-effectiveness and 'efficiency' etc – a move which inevitably depressed morale and, frankly, proved no more efficient (or cost-
effective generally) than the decades-old traditional employment of a
squadron's overall personnel. It has always been something of a mystery to regular serving RAF men that while Air Ministry policy had
always tacitly encouraged 'squadron spirit' among aircrews, it should
quite paradoxically treat the ground crews – who by many standards
are always the rock foundation of a fighting unit – as if they were
non-members of that same unit, and utilise them as merely an 'outside'
labour pool.

8. Side-shows

With the swing to the offensive from early 1941, Fighter Command concentrated mainly on building up its quantitative strength, both in aircraft and, especially, pilots. Although this was Sholto Douglas's prime term of reference for his new command, it was by no means his only task imposed by higher authority. Foremost in its clamour for aerial protection was the Royal Navy in the context of the shipping convoys bearing vital supplies and material to Britain almost daily. Naval authorities pressed vociferously for standing fighter patrols over all convoys in UK coastal waters – the inefficiency and inherent extravagance of which had long been recognised by those more cognisant of aerial tactics. Had any such standing patrols been attempted, the fighters involved would also have been placed at a tactical disadvantage to any enemy air attacks. In the event Douglas was able to convince his 'masters' that the most satisfactory compromise was Fighter Command's existing practice of holding a number of fighters at readiness at stations close to Britain's coastline, able to be despatched at minutes' notice to protect any particular convoy under threat of attack.

Equally loud in its demands for aerial protection was the aircraft industry, a commitment thoroughly appreciated by Douglas in view of his personal aim of strengthening his own Command as soon as practicable. Great pressure from the Ministry of Aircraft Production was applied to Fighter Command to provide local fighter defences for threatened factories, despite Douglas's protest that he simply had insufficient men and machines to include such a piecemeal scattering of his existing strength. Again, a compromise was instigated whereby fighter aircraft were allotted to the various factories, to be flown by the industry's own test pilots; a scheme which was militarily unsound but had the virtue of some morale effect on the factories' work force. As the year progressed this thorny problem of 'local' defence came to be given some priority in respect of Fighter Command's own base airfields. Though given a brief, scanty acquaintance with the basic operation of small arms, few airmen indeed had received even the most basic training in the warlike use of such weapons should this ever be necessary; a fact rammed home starkly by that year's debacle in Crete and the Aegean islands. Faced with the distinct possibility that UK airfields might also be subjected to airborne invasion by parachuted troops, the Army provided a thin screen of trained infantrymen for airfield defence duties initially.

The whole question of 'local defence' responsibilities had been first considered in some detail in 1926, when the principle was established for all three fighting Services to be responsible for defending their own 'areas'. Further negotiations between the War Office and the Air Ministry continued until 1937, when the Air Council finally directed all AOCs-in-C that they were now fully responsible for 'the defence of RAF aerodromes or other establishments against low-flying air attacks, and for local defence against attack by land forces'. Vague provisions were made for the supply of necessary firearms to each station for this purpose, yet when war came in 1939 few stations possessed anything like adequate armament for any such task. During 1940, when the Army was forced to withdraw a large part of the forces 'loaned' to the RAF in order to mount anti-invasion defences, a Directorate of Ground Defence was formed at the Air Ministry on 27 May 1940, tasked with organising and training all defence resources within the aegis of RAF authority, and promptly passed the buck for actual local defences to individual Station commanders. The latter were provided with 'specialist defence officers' to advise and train local personnel on each station. In the words of Sholto Douglas's eventual report, 'Many of the officers appointed by the Air Ministry to fill these posts were past their first youth and lacked the resilience of mind and body required for service in the field';[1] a diplomatic reference to certain 'Station Defence Officers' – their more usual title – whose military thinking was still steeped in Boer War or 1914–18 mental channels.

Airmen reallocated to such defence duties became titled Ground Gunners and, though regarded by other tradesmen initially as 'all

[1] Supplement to the *London Gazette* dated 14 September 1948.

boots and no brains', quickly established for themselves a reputation for dogged courage during the Battle of Britain, manning machine guns and anti-aircraft guns coolly in the face of devastating enemy air attacks on the RAF fighter stations. By the end of 1940, some 35,000 ground gunners were on RAF strength in Britain, and these became the foundation for the eventual single defence organisation titled RAF Regiment, which came into being with effect from 1 February 1942.

If the ground defence of his base airfields was something of a headache for Douglas – and in his Despatch he was to admit that 'many Stations in my Command were far from impregnable throughout those months of 1941 when enemy landings by sea or air were at least a possibility' – it was one of his lesser problems. At the end of February 1941 the defence of shipping in the North-Western approaches was given the highest priority, due to the rapidly mounting threat to Britain's literal life-lines from German long-range aircraft and Karl Dönitz's U-boat fleet. That month saw Fighter Command fly 443 sorties in defence of shipping alone; some eight per cent of its total air defensive effort. In March, the Command mounted 2103 sorties (18 per cent), and in April a total of 7876 sorties, or 49 per cent of its overall effort. All such operational sorties were necessarily limited in range to UK coastal areas, and the protection of shipping in deeper waters was tackled partially by the provision of individual fighters – mainly Hurricanes – for Catapult Aircraft Merchant Ships, or CAM Ships as these were usually referred to briefly. It was at best a slightly desperate measure; once catapulted into action the Hurricane pilot faced several unsavoury choices of survival. He could bale out and hope to be retrieved quickly from the icy-cold ocean; attempt to ditch his aircraft alongside his 'parent' ship; or, if within striking distance, attempt to reach the nearest land. These 'expendable aircraft' – as Winston Churchill termed them – were initially piloted by RAF volunteers and a number of Fleet Air Arm crews simply posted to the new duty.

These various 'diversions' from Fighter Command's prime role merely added to Douglas's worries about obtaining adequate numbers of trained pilots for his squadrons. In December 1940, No. 81 Group had been formed under the command of Air Commodore Stanley Vincent to incorporate the existing Fighter OTUs, and these were increased to a total of eleven. Throughout 1941 the Group completed slightly more than a quarter of a million flying hours, and produced 4242 trained pilots. Though an impressive effort, the output was still insufficient to cope with all the demands being made on the parent Command. While the average fighter squadron was paper-established for at least 26 pilots, the actual strength showed only 22 pilots at most. A steady drain in experienced men flowed to the Middle East campaign areas, while others were being appropriated for Flying Training Command as instructors. Added to the rising toll of casualties in the Command's daylight offensive over France, the general outlook seemed disquieting to Douglas by the summer of that year. Nevertheless, to his relief, by the close of the year the prodigious work of the training system had produced a paper surplus in pilots for the available squadrons in the United Kingdom.

In pure organisation Fighter Command expanded from five Groups and 23 Sectors in November 1940, to six operational Groups and 29 Sectors by spring 1941. In September No. 82 Group was formed to defend certain naval anchorages in Northern Ireland; while in the following year overall coverage of the UK was completed when fighter Sectors were established at Stornoway and Tiree to protect these extremities of Scotland. The healthy growth of the Command might have been greater had not the calls from overseas theatres of war diluted the expansion slightly; exemplified by the despatch of six whole squadrons to the Middle East and a further squadron to Combined Operations by autumn 1941, to be followed by six more units to the Middle East in December, though these were in the event 'diverted' to the Far East instead. Even the build-up of the Command's night fighter arm suffered when the decision was made to send Beaufighters to North Africa, thereby depleting the number of Beaus available to re-equip Douglas's night defence units. In the latter area of operations, it should be noted that nearly 100 radar stations were part of the 1941 constructional programme, and the burden of effort for these high priority matters fell on No. 60 Group which, despite a chronic lack of sufficient technicians for installation, calibration and maintenance, as well as crews of radar operators, proved fully equal to their task. One other aspect of pure defence had also increased, with the balloon barrages totalling 2340 actually flying by December 1941 – nearly twice the total of late 1939.

The original target for fighter strength requested by Sholto Douglas of at least 81 squadrons was actually achieved by early April 1941, including 64 day and 16 day orthodox night units. Nevertheless, of the 64 day squadrons, only 30 were flying Spitfires or Hurricanes; the remainder were equipped with obsolescent types of aircraft unsuitable for up-to-date operational requirements, and no match for the latest German Messerschmitt Bf 109F variants being met in the skies of France. Moreover, the tragic casualties incurred in the battles of France and Britain throughout 1940 had robbed the Command of hundreds of its experienced pilots, many of whom might normally have been expected to be leading squadrons and Wings by 1941, able to shape the air war more favourably for the Allies by virtue of their long, hard experience. Such near-irreplaceable losses, and the greater expansion of the Command's total squadrons, inevitably thinned out the hard-core veteran influence of those who still survived, reducing the average potential of most units. Although hardly a case of 'starting from scratch', it remained true that most RAF fighter pilots in early 1941 were tantamount to being unpractised in the 'sharp end' of their role, having little or no first-hand knowledge or experience of aerial combat. The responsibility thus thrown upon the shoulders of the thin vein of veterans among the squadrons was a heavy one. Opposing them in France were men of vast knowledge of fighter warfare, led by brilliant fighter leaders, flying aircraft mainly superior in most facets to the RAF's Spitfire IIs and Hurricanes.

The opportunities for the fledgling RAF fighter pilots to gain front-line experience were plentiful during the middle months of 1941. With the new creed of the offensive, the introduction of 'Circus' and then 'Rhubarb' (originally code-named 'Mosquito') operations were deliberately intended to draw up German fighter opposition in circumstances calculated to be in favour of the RAF. On June 17th, for example, 18 Blenheim bombers set out to bomb a chemical plant at Bethune, and were accompanied by no less than 22 squadrons of fighters. In October the ageing Hurricane was given a fresh lease of operational life when, in its Mk II versions, it was adapted to become a fast, low-level bomber-fighter – or 'Hurribombers' as these became dubbed. With a high Spitfire top cover, the Hurricanes were sent to attack a wide variety of ground targets along the enemy-occupied coastal regions. It was an unprofitable form of warfare, incurring relatively heavy casualties among the Hurricane pilots, as witness an attack against an alcohol distillation plant on November 8th which resulted in the loss of 16 aircraft and 13 pilots. German anti-aircraft defences were notoriously heavy, accurate and mobile, and it needed a special form of courage for any fighter pilot deliberately to penetrate the frightening lattice-work of flak which invariably greeted him on his tree-top approach to his objective. One Hurricane-bomber pilot, who eventually completed more than 400 hours of fighter operational flying, was 'blooded' on ops in just such a low-level raid, and his reactions were possibly typical of many of his companions.

The target was a batch of concrete block-houses near the French coast which, we were told, housed a crack German infantry defence outfit. We left at two o'clock on the dot and quickly picked up our Spit escorts, then set course out over the Channel in bright sunshine with no cloud cover in sight. The Spits flew very high above us, almost out of sight, while we, with our Hurricanes overloaded with two 500lb HE bombs under the groaning wings, kept as low as possible above the waves in order to stay under any German radar. I was way back in our formation, and nervous of what to expect on this run, my first war sortie in earnest. The hot sun beating on my canopy was making me sweat, though part-fear and excitement probably accounted for most perspiration.

As we approached land-fall, the leader waggled his wings, which was our pre-arranged signal to start climbing so that we could actually bomb in a dive eventually. At that moment the flak started coming up from somewhere on the actual coast in bright necklaces of shiny beads which, as they neared you, suddenly whipped by in silver-grey streaks. Within seconds – or so it seemed to me – the sky was filled with a criss-cross of tracer shells and red-hearted black ugly bursts from the heavier guns below. I was so intent on following the guy in front of me – we'd strung out into the pre-briefed line astern formation for the final attack – that I only noticed the flak out of the corners of my vision. The Hurricane I was following – an Australian pilot also new to ops – started his dive and I eased my nose down, took a very deep breath, and prepared to follow him in to that Dante's inferno of muck being thrown up at us head-on. As the earth got larger in my windscreen the Aussie up front suddenly jumped sideways – the flak had found him and sliced his port wing clean off! He hadn't a hope in hell of getting out, and his Hurricane fell in a crazy parabola of spins and fluttering, lop-sided, until it hit the deck and his bombs exploded. With clear vision now ahead I saw the blockhouses directly ahead, dipped the nose slightly, then jerked the bombs away. The next few seconds were a blur as I jinked my way through and out of the groundfire and headed for quieter air. I'll swear I stopped breathing until I was sure I was clear of that awful flak, then started trembling all over as a sort of relief that it was over set in. Keeping right down on the deck I headed pell-mell for the coast and home sweet home. I came back alone but within the hour most of the other squadron pilots had also returned. Every kite had holes in it somewhere; mine was luckier than most, having just one hole the size of my fist through a wing-tip (I hadn't even felt it hit the Hurricane), plus a few minor slashes and scars here and there. Apart from the Aussie, we'd also lost two other Hurricanes – nobody had seen their fate. It was my introduction to German flak, and right until I finally came off ops I never lost my respect – and fear – of those deadly gunners.

Another 'minor' diversion for Douglas occurred in July–August 1941, when the first efforts were made by the Allied government in London to aid Russia, the latest victim of Hitler's ambitions. Immediately after German troops began invading Russia on June 22nd, Winston Churchill pledged utmost support for the latest unlikely 'ally', and merchant shipping convoys of vital war materials began moving round the North Cape and into the various northern Russian ports. To protect these convoys two new RAF squadrons, 81 and 134, equipped with Hurricanes, were formed as 151 Wing in August and then shipped to Vaenga airfield, 20 miles north of Murmansk. Here the Hurricanes commenced operations against the German invaders, and at the same time began a training programme for Red Air Force pilots to 'convert' them to flying Hurricanes. The Wing remained in Russia until the end of November, when all RAF personnel sailed for Britain, leaving their aircraft behind as the vanguard of (ultimately) nearly 3000 Hurricanes supplied to Russia – the equivalent of almost 20 per cent of *all* Hurricanes ever produced.

If 1941 had been a somewhat diversified and turbulent year for Fighter Command, its major role remained the ever-increasingly strong daylight offensive over enemy territory, attempting to entice the Luftwaffe into combat. The pace and intensity of that air fighting, once joined, is exemplified by the experiences of a Canadian Spitfire squadron pilot on one of his earliest operational sorties. Pilot Officer N. R. D. Dick belonged to 403 Squadron, RCAF, flying Spitfire Vbs from Hornchurch, when on August 19th he was part of a 12-Spitfire patrol from the unit detailed as just one of 15 fighter squadrons escorting six Blenheim bombers to raid a power station at Gosnay, near Bethune in France. Dick's after-report reads;

When at 26,000 feet north of St Omer I sighted 15–20 enemy aircraft heading NW below at 15,000 feet and squadron commander ordered us to attack. Whilst diving I saw an ME 109F attacking Yellow 3 from behind and fired a two-second burst at 400 yards range, but missed and enemy aircraft took evasive action by half-rolling to port . . . I then saw three Me 109Fs in line abreast above flying east at 26,000 feet. I fired a seven-second burst from 250 yards range at centre one and thick black smoke poured from its belly. I saw tracers strike cockpit and fuselage; a further two-second burst

113

was then given at 75 yards range and enemy aircraft blew up and spun down vertically in flames. The other two enemy aircraft then dived away towards the south . . .

When approaching the coast near Gravelines I saw a Spitfire at 1000 feet above me at approximately 18,000 feet being attacked by one Me 109F. I pulled my nose up and fired a four-second burst into his belly at 150 yards range. Shortly after, black smoke and flames came from his belly and he was last seen diving to starboard with flames coming from his belly. I then saw another enemy aircraft below at 15,000 feet and used up the rest of my ammunition with a two-second burst at 350 yards range, but did not see result, although I think I hit his tail. During this time I was attacked on port and starboard sides by two enemy aircraft. My starboard wing tip was struck by three cannon shells and broke off. The port wing was also hit by cannon. On making a left-hand turn I found a cannon shell had struck base of control column, rendering my right aileron useless and being unable to straighten out I used heavy right rudder to pull her up.

When at 6,000 feet I see-sawed for cloud cover and was again attacked from astern; the radiator panel was hit and also my reflector sight, and cockpit filled with white smoke. I yanked emergency cockpit cover, which blew off. On my port side I saw another Me 109F about 1,000 yards away about to attack. I went down in a slow left-hand dive and lost 3,000 feet. As I recovered from dive, I saw enemy aircraft turn for France. I levelled out and found engine failing, so used hand pump and injected fuel to keep going. When 2500 feet over Channel I found myself losing control and on sighting cliffs of Dover I realised I could not make land, and jettisoned my helmet. From 2500 to 2000 feet I called 'MAYDAY' on button D, and at 1800 feet baled out clear from port side of aircraft. My parachute opened easily.

While floating down I inflated my Mae West. On the way down I lost one flying boot and my revolver. As my feet touched the water I tried to release parachute but I missed hitting the release. I was dragged three–four feet below the surface and then managed to release myself. I pulled the dinghy towards me and partially inflated it by giving it one full turn, then being exhausted I hung on to dinghy. When on top of a high wave I saw six–seven Spitfires orbiting above me, and also Rescue boat approaching which reached me about ten minutes later.

Dick's various comments on particular items carried for personal survival *et al* spotlight the variety of impedimenta encumbering the average fighter pilot going to war at this period. A comment on such 'gear' was made by a Hurricane pilot of that era, Flt Lt J. W. Brooks, DFC, DFM, 174 Squadron:

The amount of personal equipment we used to carry on operations was really unbelievable. Apart from our uniform of blue battle-dress, thick white socks, white roll-neck pullover (Navy type), fleece-lined flying boots, three pairs of gloves – one, white silk, then a woollen pair, and over all leather gauntlets which were covered in something like varnish (fire-proofing) – one leather helmet, oxygen face mask, combined with microphone, and heavy goggles; we had a yellow 'Mae West', a pack of escape money, iron ration pack containing glucose, barley sugar, an outfit for purifying water, small compass, a 'dirty' silk handkershief (actually a map of France). Personal armament consisted of a revolver stuck down one boot, and a Commando knife down the other. Under our battle-dress we often had a civilian zipper jacket with a beret tucked away inside – though this was highly unofficial! We also had modified brass buttons on our trousers which could be used as makeshift compasses. Over all this lot one strapped on one's parachute/dinghy pack and then – somehow – clambered into the Hurricane's cockpit. I've heard that armoured knights of medieval times were hoisted on to their mounts by a sort of crane – I feel we could have usefully used something similar!

9. By Day, by Night

The year 1941 had seen Fighter Command made well aware of its inadequate overall strength for contemporary policies and responsibilities, and had brought a sobering crop of casualties in men and machines disproportionate to any achievements. The insistence by the Air Staff and sections of the War Cabinet that Sholto Douglas maintained what was clearly an unprofitable form of daylight offensive was, nevertheless, dictated by circumstances. Bomber Command had yet to be armed with sufficient squadrons of the new, four-engined, truly heavy, deep penetration aircraft it had long been promised to pursue any realistic strategic air bombing offensive. Until these became available the existing force could only continue using its obsolescent Wellingtons, Hampdens and Blenheims to fray the edges of Germany's vast industrial resources; accumulating an appallingly high cost in valuable air crew lives and causing relatively light damage to the Nazi war machine. At sea the struggle for the supremely vital ocean lanes of replenishment and reinforcement was reaching a critical peak, as the Allied navies and RAF's Coastal Command attempted to ward off an increasing stranglehold on Britain's lifelines across the oceans by Germany's underwater wolves – the U-boats. Added to such deep commitments was the need felt by the British government to assist the latest, unlikely ally to the war against Nazidom, Russia. Vast effort and resources were beginning to be diverted to assist the USSR's desperate defences against Germany's invasion; involving the divergence of labour and material which might well have bolstered the existing British Services' equipment and strength.

Such a variegation in priorities left the Air Staff with little alternative but to continue the only effective form of aerial offensive within its capability, irrespective of actual efficacy. Such a decision was at least partially justified. The daylight offensive sweeps gave plentiful opportunity for maintaining a fine operational razor-edge among the crews – a necessary moral advantage in war. Freshly-trained pilots emerging from the mushrooming training establishment could be inculcated gradually to the fighting scene, gaining vital experience in the most favourable circumstances. Tactics could be tried and tested, readjusted, practised, with invaluable lessons gained in methods and modes of the planning, leading and execution of massed fighter operations generally. All these facets, and many other more minor aspects of the fighter war, were necessarily adjuncts to the main operations, fitted in when and where it was possible, and principally very much of an *ad hoc* nature.

If the year's accumulated experience had created any shades of complacency in higher Service circles by early 1942, however, these were rudely shattered in mid-February. Three of Germany's principal ocean raiders, *Prinz Eugen*, *Scharnhorst* and *Gneisenau*, a constant Damocles' sword hanging over Allied naval and mercantile shipping since the outbreak of war, had been harboured in Brest since March 1941. Their presence on the Atlantic seaboard was a constant anxiety to the Admiralty which, necessarily, was forced to chain a proportion of its meagre western fleet to the role of watchdog, should any or all of the surface raiders ever move out of harbour and attempt to scour the Atlantic of Allied shipping. Though temporary moves of anchorage were made during mid-1941, the three ships eventually remained at Brest: a 'grey eminence' which cast a grave threat over Allied troop convoys intended to reinforce the North African campaign, and mercantile convoys generally. RAF Bomber Command kept a close reconnaissance watch on Brest throughout the subsequent nine months, and launched a series of bombing sorties against the raiders, though with virtually no outstanding success. At Allied headquarters in London a contingency plan to prevent the three vessels from reaching German waters was formulated as early as April 1941; a plan which relied mainly upon air operations due to the many contemporary commitments already undertaken by the Home Fleet. The air aspect of 'Fuller' – the code name for the overall executive plan – involved Coastal, Bomber and Fighter Commands, acting in concert once the operation was ordered into being. Fighter Command's succinct role was in support of all other air operations required, directed from 11 Group headquarters, with an additional watch-and-ward role of 'Jim Crow' patrols of two hours' daylight reconnaissance sorties between Ostend and Fecamp by single or pairs of fighters. Operation 'Fuller' was heavily in favour of the view that should the enemy ships attempt to return to Germany via the English Channel – a 360-mile-journey from Brest to the Dover Straits alone – this would be undertaken with a timing schedule which would allow the ships to pass Dover in darkness.

Meanwhile the German leader, Hitler, had become personally convinced that the Allies intended to invade Norway – based apparently on the various Commando incursions along the Norwegian coastline earlier in the year – and in December 1941 ordered the preparation of necessary plans to have all three capital ships moved from Brest to reinforce the other German naval forces in northern Norway. Despite intensive dismay at such a move expressed by the German admirals, active planning for such a break-out commenced on 12 January 1942 in a cloak of the highest secrecy, with a wide quota of ancillary deception and other cover plans. Extensive aerial cover was included in the operational directive – some 250 day and 30 night fighters, apart from bombers from *Fliegerkorps* IX tasked with attacking any British naval ships attempting to deny passage in the Channel area – and the fighter 'umbrella' was under the control of Adolf Galland's headquarters at Le Touquet. Every other possible contingency – mine-sweeping the route, torpedo flotillas for countering naval opposition, meteorological reports from U-boats, counter-intelligence bluffs *et al* – received meticulous attention. The date for the eventual move was then set at 1930 hours on the evening of February 11th, which starting time – if all proceed to plan – would bring the ships through the Dover Straits at approximately 1130 hours on the morning of the 12th – in *daylight*.

The subsequent fiasco of unco-ordinated efforts and individual heroism by the various RAF elements involved has been detailed in a host of post-1945 accounts, and has no place here. Fighter Command's participation was large. Twenty-one Spitfire squadrons from 11 Group, aided by three more from 10 Group and six more squadrons from 12 Group, were at varying times committed to the attack on the German trio of ships and their massive sea and air escorts. Of the total of 398 RAF fighters involved, 17 failed to return. Neither the fighter pilots nor any other British forces involved achieved their main purpose; the three German raiders reached port on February 13th unscathed, except for damage caused to the *Scharnhorst* by a sea mine. En route the German naval force had lost merely one E-boat, while Galland's air arm had lost eleven men and 17 aircraft; a minute price to pay for such an audacious and highly successful tactical operation. The subsequent official inquiry into the British failure to prevent this 'Channel dash' resulted in the Bucknill Report, which virtually whitewashed the incredibly unco-ordinated efforts by all forces involved, though laid heavy emphasis upon the outstanding courage and determination shown by all individual elements concerned. The ineffectiveness of the RAF fighters was due to several factors, not least the lack of harmonious liaison between 11 Group headquarters – commanded by Trafford Leigh-Mallory – and Coastal Command, the Royal Navy and other participants. This resulted in many of the pilots hastily despatched at minimum notice to the Channel being totally unaware of what they were to find there, or its significance. As Galland was to record later, 'The pilots of the RAF fought bravely, tenaciously and untiringly, but had been sent into action with insufficient planning, without a clear concept of the attack, without a centre of gravity and without systematic tactics.'[1]

The most poignant illustration of Fighter Command's total unpreparedness for the Channel operations was the case of the five fighter squadrons promised as cover escort for a daylight torpedo attack on the German ships by six Fairey Swordfish of 825 Squadron, Fleet Air Arm, commanded by Lt-Commander Eugene Esmonde, DSO. Based temporarily at Manston for Operation 'Fuller', the half-strength 825 Squadron was originally intended to undertake an attack under the cover of darkness – as assumed by the executors of the original 'Fuller' plan – and therefore required no fighter escort. Once it was realised that the ships were openly sailing through the Dover Straits in daylight, the need for a strong fighter protection for the antiquated Swordfish biplanes was crucial, if their crews were to have even the slightest hope of surviving. Of the five Spitfire squadrons from the Biggin Hill and Kenley Wings detailed to fly close escort to the eventual Swordfish sortie, only ten aircraft from 72 Squadron rendezvoused with Esmonde on time; the remainder were too late. Minutes later Esmonde and his faithful crews were shot into the sea as they attempted to penetrate the veritable wall of gun shell-fire and Luftwaffe fighters – only five crew members were retrieved. Esmonde's subsequent award of a posthumous

[1] *The First & the Last*; Methuen, 1955.

Victoria Cross not only acknowledged his personal unswerving devotion to duty, but also reflected the degree of utter determination displayed by all air crews flung hastily into the fury of the Channel battle. The tragic loss of Esmonde and the bulk of his Swordfish crews also epitomised the *ad hoc* nature of the British reaction, and – especially – the unnecessary sacrifices caused by ill-co-ordinated liaison between the various higher authorities in the RAF and Admiralty.

If the wide public (and Service) consternation and no little indignation over the outcome of the 'Channel Dash' operations imposed an undignified and critical air upon the opening weeks of 1942, Fighter Command's commander Sholto Douglas had many other, deeper problems to solve. The night defences continued to improve in efficiency and 'ironmongery', if rather slowly due to a continuing struggle to find a truly workable airborne radar interception system; the relatively minor night bombing operations undertaken by the Luftwaffe during the first four months of the year permitting concentration upon improvements in techniques and training. Then, on April 23rd, some 40 German bombers – Junkers 88s and Dornier 217s from KGs 2, 100 and 106 – launched the first of a series of pure terror bombing raids upon British cathedral cities; the so-termed 'Baedeker Raids' which continued until late October 1942. This renewal of night bombing brought the whole gamut of Britain's night defences into operation again, with a particularly heavy commitment for the night fighter squadrons. These still flew a variety of aircraft types, but were in the main equipped with Beaufighters with A.I. sets. However, on 13 December 1941, a new unit, 157 Squadron, was formed at Debden, to be equipped with de Havilland Mosquito night fighters and commanded by Wing Commander Gordon Slade. By the end of March 1942, the unit was based at Castle Camps and had 14 Mosquito Mk IIs on charge, each fitted with A.I. Mk V radar sets. On April 6th a second unit, 151 Squadron, a Defiant unit, received the first of 16 Mosquitos to be delivered by the end of that month. And it was to 151 Squadron that the distinction of the first Mosquito night 'victory' came when, on May 29th, Flight Lieutenant Pennington, in Mosquito DD628, damaged a twin-engined German bomber over the North Sea. The following night Squadron Leader Ashfield of 157 Squadron, in W4099, shot down a Dornier 217E-4 south of Dover.

The ubiquitous Mosquito – it was eventually to undertake virtually every possible role for a fast, twin-engined aircraft – was a classic design

120

from the outset. Of all-wood construction, it carried a two-man crew and – in the fighter variants – a nose armament of four .303-inch calibre Browning machine guns to supplement a belly battery of four 20mm cannons. With a maximum speed in excess of 360 mph, high ceiling, extended range endurance, and delightful handling and manoeuvring characteristics, the 'Mossie' came to be regarded by all its crews as a superb fighting vehicle, and postings to 'Mossie' squadrons were a much-sought 'bonus'. Apart from its obvious potential as a war weapon, the Mosquito gave its crews supreme confidence – a 'one-ness' twixt men and machine which is usually only found in the very best designs of aircraft. Bolstering that aura of confidence was the rugged nature of the 'Mossie'; despite its wooden construction, it could and did absorb terrifying punishment on occasion and still delivered its crew safely back to base. By the close of 1942 nine squadrons had been formed or re-equipped with Mosquito fighters.

The extended range, endurance and versatility of the Mosquito boded well for future night operations, not only in defence of the United Kingdom but also in the offensive intruder role. The existing Beaufighter units, though performing well and achieving satisfactory results against the Luftwaffe's night marauders, were limited to a degree when undertaking any form of offensive across France or the Low Countries. A rugged, pugnacious fighter, the mighty Beau needed strong handling to exploit its main virtues in combat. The Mosquito, equally tough, brought a delicacy of control which made it admirably suitable for deck-level intrusion, and possessed a turn of speed which enabled its crews to evade flak or fighter opposition if so desired. The first Mosquito intruder sortie was undertaken by Squadron Leader 'Sammy' Hoare, DFC, and his navigator, Pilot Officer Cornes of 23 Squadron in Mosquito DD670 in the early hours of 6 July 1942. Hoare patrolled the Caen area but found no targets. On the following night, however, again in DD670, he stalked a Dornier 217 east of Chartres and with three brief bursts of cannon-fire sent it down in flames at Montdidier. Just two nights later another 23 Squadron pilot in the same Mosquito shadowed a Dornier as it circuited its airfield, then shot it down. Continuing his patrol to Evreux he next tagged on to a Heinkel 111 preparing to land and shot this into the ground. For intruder operations Mosquitos were fitted with long-range fuel tanks, increasing normal endurance by one and a half hours, and producing an operational radius of approximately 600 miles. Although radar equipment

121

was not fitted, the intruder Mosquito crews were always in radio contact with base.

The fighter offensive by day continued during the aftermath of the disastrous 'Channel Dash' operations in the same pattern as before, but now Sholto Douglas was shouldered with a fresh responsibility for his command. The Allied authorities had decided to attempt a large-scale 'invasion' of German-occupied France in August 1942; a one-day 'raid' to test enemy reaction, and in effect a small-scale 'exercise' in planning and execution of a combined Services' rehearsal for an eventual 'spring across the Channel' – the invasion proper of Europe. As in the case of Hitler's 1940 Operation 'Sea-Lion' – the projected invasion of Britain – complete air superiority over the beach-head was an essential pre-requisite. Given generous time in which to plan his air 'umbrella', Douglas immediately clamoured for more aircraft and crews to supplement his existing squadrons. No. 11 Group would, necessarily, become the controlling authority for the tactical handling of all air operations in the project, and Leigh-Mallory, the Group commander, was substantially reinforced to bring his fighter strength up to more than 600 aircraft – a total of 56 squadrons of Spitfires, Hurricanes, Whirlwinds and other types. In support were four squadrons of Mustang fighter-recce aircraft for direct Army co-operation duties, plus five squadrons of Bostons and Blenheim IVs from 2 Group for ancillary duties. Further direct assistance was to be given by heavy bombers from RAF Bomber Command and the American Eighth Air Force which would attack Luftwaffe bases in the hinterland of the 'invasion' area. The objective selected for attack was Dieppe, and the date, 19 August 1942.

Minute by minute control of the air cover was anticipated by fitting out a landing vessel with a fighter direction team, equipped with ample radio apparatus, while 11 Group's SASO (Senior Air Staff Officer), Group Captain Harry Broadhurst, chose to pilot a lone Spitfire high above the battle area to keep an experienced eye on the panoramic air situation and advise Group HQ directly on any necessary changes in the original planning. Though highly conscious of the priority of protection of the actual invading forces on the surface, Fighter Command also anticipated the operation as a golden opportunity to draw up massive Luftwaffe opposition in circumstances dictated by the RAF – a veritable concentration in a single day of the underlying purpose of its drawn-out 'Circus' operations over the past year or more. At dawn on

August 19th the invasion fleet sailed for Dieppe, preceded by waves of Bostons laying smoke screens, bomber 'heavies' carpeting rear echelon Luftwaffe airfields, and low-flying Blenheims, Typhoons and Hurricanes attempting to blast the German coastal defences into rubble. In the next few hours the air effort became divided roughly into two main facets. Below 2,000 feet and mainly at zero altitude, Hurricane fighter-bombers kept up a series of head-on assaults against any German installations or transport found. High above the beach-head a gradually expanding maelstrom of combat ensued as the Luftwaffe's fighters and, later, bombers attempted to pierce the strong Spitfire cover; each side being continually reinforced as fuel tanks and ammunition boxes ran empty by fresh squadrons arriving on a planned schedule.

The experiences of the low cover 'Hurribombers' against point-blank, fierce German defences are possibly encapsulated by the personal account of Flight Sergeant (then) J. W. Brooks of 174 Squadron. Based at Manston normally, 174 was moved to Ford aerodrome on August 14th, though none of the pilots had any clue as to the reasons for this 'temporary detachment'. On the evening of August 18th they were carefully briefed about their part in the coming operation – code-named 'Jubilee' – as part of the air cover. The squadron was to be in the very first wave, before daybreak, and the main target was to be a battery of heavy naval guns on high ground at the rear of Dieppe covering the beach area. Each Hurricane was to carry a 500lb HE bomb under each wing – twice the normal weight in use at that period. Next morning, long before sun-up, Brooks led a section of three other Hurricanes in the full squadron battle order, and arrived over Dieppe less than an hour after take-off, and before the Allied landing craft had reached the French shoreline. Diving in line astern from 1500 feet, Brooks's section blasted their way through a hail of 40mm and other light flak shells, jinking urgently to avoid trees and other hazards, and plastering their target with the bombs. Strafing some German troop transport on the way out to the Channel, he returned to Ford, where it was found that three of 174's men were missing, including the Free French squadron commander. All Hurricanes had sustained bullet and flak damage, but such was quickly patched over, the fuel tanks were refilled, and guns re-armed, ready for the next sortie.

Sometime after lunch we were briefed to go out again. This time our target was a concentration of tanks and guns which were apparently moving in from north of Dieppe. We were also informed that our troops were now pulling out and we were supposed to cover them as best we could. Flight Lieutenant MacConnell (acting CO now) was to lead our eight serviceable Hurricanes. A different sight now met my eyes when we arrived over Dieppe. At 1500 feet I had a panoramic view in the brilliant sunshine. There was an extraordinary amount of rubbish floating around in the water, quite some way off shore. There were bright yellow dinghies which stood out against a surface of oil and sundry junk. There was a dogfight going on overhead and we all kept our eyes peeled for an attack. It was our job to avoid any conflict as this meant we would have to get rid of our two bombs and hence our mission would be wasted. We went in two lines abreast as pre-arranged and I could see the targets right ahead. They were slinging everything at us, or so it appeared. In the daytime it was difficult to see the amount of flak being fired at you, so if you were sensible you kept jinking about, not flying straight and level for one moment, and getting down as low as possible. I saw one of our Hurricanes get hit and catch fire. He dived straight at a bunch of armoured vehicles and blew up. I think this was 'Doofy' du Fretay, a Free Frenchman who loathed Germans. Then another friend, an Australian named Flight Sergeant Watson, blew up. I think one of his bombs got hit as he went in.

I flew straight at some transport and troops with my guns going and skipped my bombs at them. I passed over the top at a couple of feet and brought back with me a souvenir – the whip aerial of a German tank, wedged in my radiator. I wasn't sorry to get out of that lot and, together with Murray Thomas, joined up with MacConnell and we then went on a strafing run up to the coast. We formed up to go home – there were now just five of us – at about 200 feet, when I saw to my horror a big formation of Messerschmitt 109s and Focke Wulf 190s flying parallel to the coast. They passed directly over the top of us at no more than some 200 feet. It was possible to make out individual markings, and one I noticed had a big black oil streak underneath. I held my breath, as I'm sure the others did, since we had used most of our ammunition in ground attacks. Besides this we would have been slaughtered being outclassed, outnumbered and short of fuel. I watched them disappear into the smoke and confusion to the north. It was nice to see the English coast again and even nicer to get down in one piece, because I was sure I'd been hit somewhere vital. In fact all I had was a lot more holes in 'G' and she was still flyable. We had been on the ground only a short time when a Ju88, or a Dornier, came over Ford at very low altitude and dropped a stick of bombs across the grass, ducking in and out of some low cloud which was coming in from the sea. He was a very brave man.

Around tea-time we were stood down as the operation was considered over as far as we were concerned. We had begun the operation with (I think) seventeen pilots, and we now had eight left and some very patched Hurricanes. Next day we flew back to Manston.

Far above the savage land fighting the sky became a constant, shifting battle of fighters in hundreds, ranging in altitudes from zero to nearly 25,000 feet and sprawling across a cubic box of sunlit air stretching for up to fifteen miles in every direction from the beaches. The Luftwaffe reacted swiftly to the first indications of the cross-Channel invasion, throwing several *geschwadern* of Messerschmitt Bf 109s and Focke Wulf 190s into the fray. Each was engaged and prevented from reaching the Canadian troops and outlying Commandos on the beach zone. As the morning wore on reinforcements for each air force arrived in increasing numbers, going straight into battle as Dieppe came under their wings. The first few hours saw this aerial struggle become a straight fighter-v-fighter clash as several hundred single-seaters fought hard to break the purpose of their opponents. The air became a crazy composition of darting aircraft, twisting, diving climbing in the contortions of mortal combat; all against a background of falling wreckage, burning aircraft plunging to earth, white blossoming parachutes fluttering a delicate path through the tumbling chaos. Casualties on both sides mounted grimly, with the Luftwaffe gaining more than it was losing, yet still thwarted from reaching the invasion fleet. By mid-morning German bombers were hurled into the mêlée, but these fared no better. Fighter Command's tight umbrella remained intact, and by 1400 hours, as the battered survivors of the ground forces completed their planned withdrawal, the RAF's fighter pilots had flown nearly two and a half thousand individual sorties in total.

At dusk the various squadron Intelligence officers totted up the statistics of that one day's marathon fighting. The RAF had lost 106 aircraft, but claimed totals of 91 German aircraft destroyed, apart from nearly 200 more probably shot down or severely damaged. It was perhaps as well for their morale that the true German casualties' figures – 48 destroyed and 24 damaged – remained unknown until well after the war.

In attempting to tackle well-alerted, hugely strong and determined defences, the 'invasion' below them had been an overt disaster. Yet from the ashes were garnered invaluable lessons for the air commanders. Foremost was the unequivocal fact that the air umbrella had achieved its primary purpose; forbidding the Luftwaffe working space in the area above the battle zone, in which it might otherwise have caused devastating casualties among the ground and sea forces. Every attempt by the German fighters and bombers to reach the Dieppe beaches had been nullified or frustrated by the unending stream of Spitfires, resulting in hitherto unexperienced multi-fighter combat clashes which bore a resemblance to the desperate hours over Kent in the high summer of 1940. The whole Fighter Command organisation, its methods of control, on-going intelligence of the shifting patterns of combat, the meticulous timing of reinforcement for depleted squadrons – all augured well for any future large-scale invasion projects to be hurled against Hitler's vaunted *Festung Europa*. Tried and tested in the boiling crucible of bloody combat, the fighter control system *in toto* had distinguished itself, albeit at a heavy cost in men and machines.

One disturbing lesson to emerge from the operation was the clear superiority of the Focke Wulf 190 fighter over anything the RAF then flew on front-line operations. The Spitfire IX – the 'answer' to the Fw 190 – could barely hold its own against Kurt Tank's sleek design, especially when this was in the hands of any veteran German pilot. Though generally regarded by its pilots as the best Mark of Spitfire for aerial combat from 1941 onwards, the Mk IX was intended for medium to high altitude fighting, at which level it was undoubtedly a match for the contemporary Messerschmitt Bf 109s and the Fw 190. At low altitude, however, the Focke Wulf 190 had a clear edge, and was the principal type used in a campaign of hit-and-run bombing raids undertaken by the Luftwaffe against south-east England targets, including London, from late October 1942. These 'sneak' raids by fast fighter-bombers commenced in strength on October 31st, when a total of 90 Focke Wulf 190s, from JG2, JG26 and ZG2, raided Canterbury. Though 63 RAF fighters were sent to intercept, all but three of the Germans returned to base. On 20 January 1943, when 28 Fw 190s made a daring daylight attack on London, faulty reporting in the RAF defence organisation allowed all 28 to reach their target and bomb, but as the Germans turned for home nine were shot down by the defenders.

Although such 'nuisance' raids were sporadic, due mainly to the weather conditions, they caused civilian casualties, and the need for a fast low-altitude version of the Spitfire was realised with the introduction of the Mk XII, a Griffon-engined variant which first entered first-line service with 41 Squadron in January 1943. Another design capable of catching and destroying the Fw 190 was the Hawker Typhoon, stable-mate of the immortal Hurricane. Intended as a day interceptor originally, the Typhoon – 'Tiffie' – first entered RAF operational use with 56 Squadron in late 1941, but quickly exhibited disastrous failings in a prolonged saga of engine failures, shearing tails and a host of minor faults. This seven-ton 'monster', with its novel Sabre engine, proved a fairly awesome experience at first acquaintance to pilots used to the well-mannered, sensitive Spitfire or Hurricane; while its disappointing performance at high altitude negated the original intended role for the brute. In its favour were the four-20mm cannon battery housed in its thick wings, and the astonishing turn of speed when operated at low or deck level. The latter characteristics provided an ideal counter to the 'nuisance' sneak-raiding Fw 190. Nevertheless, the extended tale of woe created by the many early difficulties of Typhoon operations almost led to its withdrawal, and but for the stubborn championing of the design by (then) Squadron Leader Roland Beamont, DFC, of 609 Squadron the 'Tiffie' might never have continued in service. As one of the men involved in the early trials and testing of the Typhoon, 'Bea' Beamont was convinced of a great future for this heavy, fast and well-armed fighter. With 609 Squadron, based at Manston, he proceeded to prove his point in late 1942 by undertaking a series of both day and night low-level offensive strikes across occupied France. These 'Rhubarbs' were additional to the unit's 'routine' task of standing patrols over south-east England, during the course of which 609's pilots destroyed 14 Fw 190s in four months. Beamont's faith in the Typhoon was to be amply justified, and by mid-1943 eighteen squadrons had been re-equipped with Typhoons. In the final year of the European conflict, particularly, rocket and bomb-armed Typhoons were the spearhead of the Allied armies' advance from the Normandy beaches to Berlin, blasting a clearway forward for the infantry.

As the winter of 1942–3 extended the hours of darkness the Luftwaffe re-opened its night bombing assault on Britain. By early 1943, however, the British night defences had grown both in quantity and efficiency. Twelve squadrons were flying Beaufighters, some equipped with the latest A.I. Mk VIII 'centimetric' radar sets, alongside six operational units of radar-equipped Mosquitos, with four more in the process of receiving de Havilland's 'wooden wonders'. Between them these squadrons held more than 400 aircraft. In France and the Low Countries the Luftwaffe's bombing arm had recently been reinforced, with a total of some 120 Dorniers and Junkers 88s in KG2 and KG6 alone. These aircraft were the very latest, improved variants of each design, and opened their New Year's campaign by mounting 118 sorties against London on the night of January 17th. In co-operation with the recently installed radar-guided searchlights around the city, RAF night fighters accounted for five of the raiders, while a sixth was destroyed shortly after initial take-off by a marauding intruder. Interspersed with hit-and-run raiding by Focke Wulf 190 fighter-bombers, *Luftflotte* 3 continued its spasmodic attacks against principal cities in England for the next few months. The ever-increasing opposition they found waiting for them claimed a rising toll of casualties; KG2 alone lost 26 crews in the month of March alone. One slightly desperate innovation in the bombing programme came on the night of April 16th, when 28 Fw 190s, carrying bombs, attempted to raid London. With virtually no interference from the defences, three Fw 190s landed in error at West Malling, a fourth crashed, and two more failed to return to base; nearly a quarter of the force was lost.

The vulnerability of the Fw 190 became increasingly evident when tackled by Mosquito night fighters; on the night of May 16th/17th, No. 85 Squadron based at West Malling accounted for no less than five Fw 190s from a raiding force of 17 fighter-bombers, all from 1/SKG 10. Such was the improved efficiency of the night fighters that few of the bombing formations despatched against England during the first six months of 1943 escaped unscathed, and Luftwaffe casualties rose steadily. Although the Fw 190 raids petered out after June, the 'normal' night bombing assaults on British cities continued at irregular intervals throughout the summer months, albeit in relatively small numbers on any single foray. If such raids produced reasonably little damage – relative to the widespread destruction caused during the 1940–1 winter – the necessity for maintaining such an offensive by the Luftwaffe was a direct result of RAF Bomber Command's mounting aerial onslaught against German cities, which forced Göring to retaliate by Hitler's express orders. For the German bomber crews it was an unenviable task. The increased strength of the British air defences provided a formidable enough opposition to face on every sortie, while even in the area surrounding their base airfields the Luftwaffe crews were harassed nightly by the ever-present intruder Mosquitos. This constant menace meant that no German bomber was safe from sudden attack at any stage of a sortie, from take-off to eventual landing; a 'Damocles sword' suspended above them at any given moment of operations.

The introduction by the Germans of fresh aircraft designs, such as the twin-engined Messerschmitt 410 and Junkers 188, did little to

30 *The supremely aesthetic Spitfire, arguably the most beautiful warplane ever designed. This Spitfire Vb, R6923, was serving in 92 Squadron at the time of the photo, but had been one of the original cannon-armed Mk Ibs to serve during the Battle of Britain with 19 Squadron.*

31 *Hurricane pilots of 402 Squadron, RCAF, 'scrambling' at Digby, 1941. Note ground crew ever-ready to receive 'their' men, with parachute harnesses ready and trolley accumulators plugged in for fast start-up.*

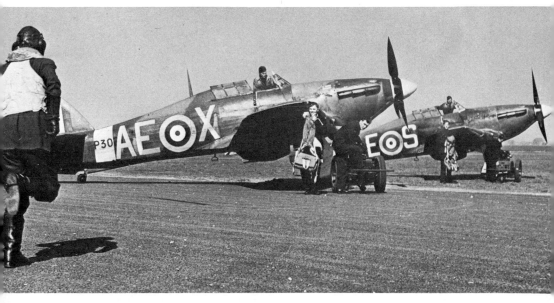

32 (Above) Hurricane IIb, BE417, AE-K at Warmwell in early 1942, being loaded with 250lb GP bombs. Note fabric patches doped over wing machine gun ports to prevent intrusion of dust etc.

33 (Top, right) The twin 20mm cannon wing installation of a Hurricane II, showing the Belt Feed Mechanisms (BFMs) and cannon shell belts.

34 (Right) The brutish Hawker Typhoon with its four 20mm cannon battery in the wings. The large nose 'scoop' intake was a hazard in the event of a pilot being forced to 'ditch' in the sea.

35 *(Left) Wing Leader: Alan Deere, DSO, DFC, a New Zealander who joined the RAF pre-1939, and fought through the Battle of Britain, before becoming a Wing Leader. Seated here in a Spitfire.*

36 *(Right) AVM T. Leigh-Mallory, controversial commander of 12 Group in 1940, who later became AOC-in-C, Fighter Command, and then commanded 2nd Tactical Air Force for the invasion of Europe in 1944.*

37 *(Below) Spitfire Mk XIIs of 41 Squadron, illustrating some of the 'stretching' modifications applied successively to the Spitfire throughout the war.*

38 *Through the camera. Messerschmitt Bf 109F about to 'die' at the hands of a Spitfire NCO pilot.*

39 *AM Sir Roderic Hill, commander of the ADGB 1943–4, and later AOC-in-C, Fighter Command until the end of the European war.*

40 *The Hawker Typhoon (rear) was supplemented by the sleeker Tempest by 1944. These two were from 486 Squadron.*

41 *Mosquito bite – the four 20mm cannons and four .303 machine guns of a DH Mosquito
'speak' . . .*

improve bombing results. However, a particular menace came from the Luftwaffe when it took a leaf out of Fighter Command's 'book' by introducing their own forms of intruder operations, whereby German fighters infiltrated the returning Bomber Command streams – a ploy making radar identification extremely difficult – and selected victims as these were about to land at base airfields. In August and September 1943, defending Mosquitos claimed 17 victims, among them 13 Me 410s or Fw 190s which had mingled with the heavy bombers seeking prey. The longer nights of October brought an increase in effort, when German night raiders operated on 21 nights of the month, mainly against London. Of these formations, 17 German aircraft were shot down by the Mosquito crews. Such steady losses did not deter Hitler, whose obsession with retaliatory bombing of Britain now reached a point where, on December 7th, he issued a directive to Göring for a heavy reprisal bombing phase – 'a massive blow' – against London. The new assault – code-named 'Steinbock' ('Ibex') – was to be undertaken with the first operational use of the four-engined Heinkel 177, intermixed with the usual Dornier and Junkers 88 *geschwadern*; while it was originally intended to employ at least 500 bombers *in toto*, each carrying a 70 per cent incendiary/30 per cent high explosive bomb load. Preparations for this new bombing attack phase were quickly put in hand, and in the third week of January 1944 the various units earmarked for 'Steinbock' were moved to advanced landing grounds along the French and Baltic coasts. In the late afternoon of January 21st Luftwaffe crews were called to briefing and then told, for the first time, that their target was London that same night. Only hours later a total of 227 bombers were en route to their common objective.

10. Shield and Buckler

As the first waves of Operation 'Steinbock' approached the English coast, the night defences swung into action. The German crews used *Düppel* anti-radar foil – the equivalent of the RAF's 'Window' – but although this created a certain amount of confusion among the GCI receivers, it did not prevent a number of successful interceptions throughout the prolonged series of bombing assaults. Before dawn at least nine of the raiders had fallen to the guns of the Mosquito crews alone, one of these being a Heinkel 177 destroyed by Wing Commander H. K. Kemp and his navigator Flight Sergeant J. R. Maidment of 151 Squadron. Flying Mosquito HK193, Kemp shot the giant bomber, from 1/KG40, into the ground near Hindhead – the first He 177 brought down over Britain. The night's 'massive blow' cost the Luftwaffe 25 aircraft, seven of these due to anti-aircraft gun fire or other causes, and the remaining 18 to aircraft of Fighter Command. Such a loss – it did not include a further 18 aircraft which were lost or crashed for reasons unconnected with enemy action – was insupportable; while the damage caused by actual bombing was remarkably small. If only on a more limited scale the 'Baby Blitz', as this latest series of night bombing raids was dubbed, was to continue until May 1944. Those first five months of 1944 cost the British civilian population – mostly in the London area – 1556 killed and nearly 3000 seriously injured. Nevertheless, the Luftwaffe had lost more than 300 bombers in the same period, representing almost two-thirds of the original force assembled for 'Steinbock'. Clearly, attacks on Britain were too costly ever to be maintained on such a scale.

While the command's night fighter arm extended its efforts to deny Britain's night skies to the dwindling Luftwaffe bomber force, planning had already commenced for the long-awaited Allied return to European soil – the invasion of France and establishment of a 'Second Front'. The over-riding prerequisite for any such venture was air supremacy over the invasion beach-heads – as it had been for Göring's Luftwaffe in the summer of 1940. This inescapable condition for success was just as valid for the allies in 1944 as it had been for the Axis four years before. The cliché 'He who controls the air, controls' was equally applicable. Recognition of this basic tenet of modern warfare presented Fighter Command with a schizophrenic problem. Formed, shaped, tested and well-established for a primary role of defence of the United Kingdom, the Fighter Command overall organisation was firmly rooted in Britain. To expect that intricately woven network of shield and buckler suddenly to expand across the Channel and then drop deep into France was not only impractical, but would dilute the still-vital need for protection of the base from which all offensive action must originate. Quite patently there was a need to create virtually a fresh air force specifically for the invasion programme; an air force self-sustained and independently controlled for direct participation in the coming operations.

The composition of such a 'new' air formation was, perforce, accomplished in stages. Fighter Command had an intensive air offensive in being already, and this could not be abruptly disturbed. Therefore, at least until the projected date of any actual invasion launching , all reorganisation, control and continuing operations remained under the aegis of Fighter Command headquarters. The first stage commenced on 1 June 1943 when 2 Group, Bomber Command – the only remaining light-medium bomber force – was transferred to Fighter Command; while two weeks later the Army Co-operation Command was disbanded. The 'move' of 2 Group coincided with the start of widespread, intensive offensive operations by Fighter Command's day squadrons in a series of systematic attacks on transportation – particularly rail communication – in France and the Low Countries. The Bostons, Venturas and Mitchells of the Group flew medium altitude bombing attacks, heavily escorted by Spitfires, while bomb-carrying and – recently introduced – rocket-firing Hurricanes and Typhoons carried out deck-level strafes of enemy communication systems. On 13 November 1943, with the appointment of Air Chief Marshal Sir Trafford Leigh-Mallory as its first supremo, the Allied Expeditionary Air Force (AEAF) came into being. This new air force comprised three main components. One, already in being, was the American 9th Air

131

Force, while the others – officially 'formed' two days later – were Second Tactical Air Force (2nd TAF), and the Air Defence of Great Britain (ADGB).

The Second TAF, commanded by Air Marshal Sir Arthur Coningham, robbed the former Fighter Command of 32 fighter squadrons, apart from various units from the old Army Co-Op Command; leaving the revived ADGB with merely ten day and eleven night fighter squadrons, though until any actual move to Europe ADGB could call on the employment of twelve other fighter squadrons for operations. Thus, on 15 November 1943, RAF Fighter Command *per se* ceased to exist, being replaced in prime function and purpose by the ADGB. To command the new UK air defence force came the former 12 Group commander, Air Marshal Roderic Hill. A former World War One fighter pilot, Roderic Hill was the antithesis of his predecessor, Leigh-Mallory. Highly sensitive, with a fine scientific brain combined with an artistic soul, Hill inherited no sinecure. Responsible for the whole aerial defence of Britain, he was additionally shouldered with the vital security of the unprecedented mass of Allied might then being assembled for the 'Overlord' operations – the eventual invasion of Europe. And for these twin tasks he was left with only a third of Fighter Command's former strength. His personal position as AOC-in-C, ADGB, placed Hill in a delicate position vis-à-vis Leigh-Mallory, commander of the AEAF. Both had their headquarters at Bentley Priory until June 1944, and as head of the AEAF, Leigh-Mallory was, to all intents and purposes, Hill's immediate superior, commanding both home defence and the tactical air force being prepared for 'Overlord'. Fortunately, Hill was left a fairly free hand in running his command, and Leigh-Mallory – almost wholly absorbed in working up the AEAF, and the many complicated pre-planning relationships vital to an inter-Service, inter-Allied force of such magnitude – gave Hill his consent to deal directly with the Air Ministry when expediency demanded such a by-passing of 'normal channels'. That 'permission' was to be a vital factor in Hill's subsequent handling of the ADGB's greatest challenge only months later.

Operation 'Overlord' commenced just before midnight of 5 June 1944, when advance paratroops left England to occupy certain tactical positions, and dawn on June 6th revealed the massive naval armada of landing craft bearing the initial troop waves across the Channel to their designated Normandy beach-heads. Above this apparently unending tide of invaders the AEAF provided a wide umbrella of protection, anticipating sudden and strong reaction from the Luftwaffe – which in the event did not materialise that day. Within days of the initial scramble ashore a Canadian fighter Wing had become based in France, and was soon reinforced by other tactical air units. Thus the AEAF began its gradual move onto the Continent, where it was to remain until eventual victory in Europe was achieved in May 1945. This transference of 2nd TAF to France immediately relieved Roderic Hill of his 'extraneous' duties in maintaining the offensive cutting edge of AEAF's fighter units up until D-Day (June 6th), but his prime task – defence of Britain – was sharply brought into focus only seven days later. In the early hours of June 13th a Royal Observer Corps post reported a 'flying object' crossing the North Downs 'making a noise like a Model T Ford going up a hill', and at 0418 hours this 'object' dived into the ground near Gravesend and exploded. Three similar 'objects' crashed and exploded at, respectively, Sevenoaks, Bethnal Green and in Sussex. The age of 'robot' warfare had arrived over England.

The 'flying objects' were, in fact, Fieseler 103 flying bombs – titled *Vergeltungswaffe 1* (V1), or 'Revenge Weapon No. 1' – comprised of a 2,000lb high explosive container with simple 'plank' wings, driven by a crude 600lb thrust pulse-jet engine. Capable of a cruising speed between 300 and 420 mph, the V1s were ground-launched initially, though a relatively small number were later to be air-launched from Heinkel 111 bombers, specially modified, from III/KG3 based in Holland. These first four V1s to reach England were from a small salvo of ten bombs launched – the other six crashed shortly after take-off – instead of an originally envisaged hail of 500 flying bombs to open the V1 'revenge' attack that day. British defence chiefs had long anticipated such an assault. Evidence from underground intelligence in Europe, photo-reconnaissance and a dozen other sources had gradually revealed that Hitler had instigated some form of 'new weapon' for attacking England; only the specific nature of such a weapon had eluded identification until the last few weeks prior to June 13th. Allied suspicions about the weapon had been focused for many months on the apparent factories and sites associated with it, and a prolonged bombing campaign against such objectives had been carried out by both RAF Bomber Command and the USAAF. A contingency plan for defences against this fresh threat had been drawn up, under the code-name 'Diver', and passed to Roderic Hill to instigate. Broadly, the

'Diver' plan was a combination of anti-aircraft guns and fighters, working in conjunction, with Hill's fighters committed to standing patrols along specified lanes whenever any assault was suspected as about to commence.

The paltry initial 'wave' of V1s on June 13th caused no immediate reaction from Hill's defences, and when there was no follow-up within the next 48 hours, Hill reserved the full use of the 'Diver' resources temporarily. Then, on June 15th, at about 10 pm, a total of 55 flying bomb sites commenced launching a steady salvo of V1s, aimed mainly at London, and within the next 24 hours sent a rain of 244 off their ramps. Of these only 144 reached the English coast and then lost 33 to the defences. Hill immediately brought the full resources of the *Diver* plan into play, and quickly expanded the strength of his forces in balloons, anti-aircraft guns and fighters. Of the latter he already possessed a few squadrons equipped with the latest Mk XIV Spitfire and the stable-mate successor to the Typhoon, the aesthetically-pleasing Hawker Tempest, each of which was fast enough to catch a V1 at low altitude and destroy it. To these he added a Wing of Mustang III fighters, 'borrowed' from Arthur Coningham's 2nd TAF. By mid-July he could muster 13 squadrons of single-engine fighters and nine Mosquito units to counter the robot bombs. This first month of operations, up to July 15th, saw the Germans launch 4361 of the tiny cruciform 'aircraft', of which roughly 3000 actually crossed the English coastal zones. The defences destroyed 1241 of the latter, 924 of these being accounted for by ADGB fighters.

Though the V1 was in theory a perfect target for either anti-aircraft gun or fighter, being forced to fly an unwavering course at reasonably low altitude, it presented peculiar problems for the defenders. Its sheer speed – badly under-rated in the original 'Diver' contingency planning – at very low heights baffled the anti-aircraft gunners generally. For the pursuing fighter it presented a very small target, with its wing-span of 17 feet 6 inches and a length of only 26 feet. To close to pointblank range before opening fire invited near-disaster too; the V1's 1870lb of Trialen high explosive could shatter anything within the same patch of sky if detonated by cannon-fire. After several pilots had been killed by exploding V1s, tactics were modified from the normal dive and close approach before firing, to a fast dive to overtake the target and then allow the V1 to pass ahead, when full deflection shooting was employed. One novel 'tactic' used by many pilots was to formate closely with the lethal robot bomb, then topple it from its course by literally tipping it sideways with the fighter's own wingtip; a method requiring iron-steady nerves and immaculate flying. A few pilots even flew deliberately head-on at the flying bombs, then banked sharply to create a slipstream turbulence ahead of the target and thus divert it from its implacable flight-path. Whichever method was used, each entailed a high risk factor to the pursuing fighter. An example of the extreme hazards involved is the record of one Tempest unit, 486 Squadron, RNZAF. Though many of this unit's pilots achieved double-figure victory tallies of V1s, three pilots were killed, 10 seriously injured, and 17 Tempests were destroyed or damaged beyond repair; usually resulting from the flames and/or wreckage from the flying bomb as it blew up.

The main offensive by the V1s – dubbed 'Doodlebugs', 'Buzz-bombs' or 'Jitterbugs' by the general public – continued apace until early September 1944, before a brief breathing space was 'granted' to the ADGB defences. By September 5th, a total of some 9000 flying bombs had been initially launched, of which just over a third had been destroyed en route by British arms. The increasingly successful countermeasures by ADGB resulted not only from experience hard-gained on actual 'Diver' operations – these being code-named 'Cross-bow' by the RAF – but largely as the result of a courageous decision by Roderic Hill. Until mid-July the defence system of combining anti-aircraft guns and balloon barrages with the pure fighter role had relied upon a mixture of all elements within the same main defence areas. The result had been that a number of fighters had been fired at by defence guns while intent on pursuit of any V1. Additionally, the radar reporting screens became cluttered with 'friendly' aircraft thereby obscuring many of the flying bombs as these came into view. Though holding a fairly free hand in the disposition of his defence resources, Hill had tended to act first and then inform his superiors at Air Ministry afterwards; a form of decision-taking tolerated in view of the emergency. From his first-hand experience, for Hill flew many personal sorties on 'Crossbow' patrols in order to see for himself the actual problems facing his pilots, he realised that this compression of a mixed defence organisation into a defined area had serious operating problems – as he later described it, 'a very fast game played on a very small ground'. Mutual interference between each arm of the defence set-up was perhaps inevitable, with no single factor gaining any great advantage from the overall situation. On July 13th, on being approached by General Pile, head of the anti-aircraft guns, and other senior staff officers, Hill accepted their views that a complete redistribution of areas of responsibility for fighters vis-à-vis guns was vital. Accordingly, on his own authority, he ordered the bulk of the guns to be moved to the coastal areas, facing out to sea, where their radar could be unimpeded and the gunners could have an unfettered field of fire. The fighters were, henceforth, to operate solely 'behind' the guns, thereby relieving them of any anxiety about being shot at by their own guns.

When, later, Hill informed the Air Staff of this bold decision – a move involving massive effort in minimal time by all concerned – the Air Ministry made their disapproval plain, but in the face of a *fait accompli*, and the critical circumstances, did not force Hill to reverse his orders. It was, however, made crystal clear to Hill that his entire future was in the balance, dependent wholly on the eventual outcome of the new disposi-tions of ADGB. Fortunately for Britain, and no less Roderic Hill, the Whitehall fears were not justified. Within weeks of the new disposition Pile's gun crews were recording increasingly high success, while the fighter pilots were able to operate with ample elbow room, unaffected by any need to restrict their tactics to slot in with gun zones. The fresh areas of responsibility were occupied quickly and from July 16th until September 5th the gun crews destroyed 1198 V1s, while fighters claimed a further 847. Then, in September–October, Allied troops on the Continent began to over-run many of the German-occupied areas which housed V1 launching sites, and the menace died down temporar-ily as these were hastily withdrawn to more safe areas of operation.

One significant addition to the ADGB's armoury arrived on the operational scene late in the 'Crossbow' battle, but managed to make its mark during the closing stages. This was the Gloster Meteor – the first Allied operational jet-engined fighter. No. 616 Squadron, based at Culmhead, was selected as the RAF's first jet unit, receiving its first example, EE219, on July 12th. Two weeks later 616 moved to Manston with a Flight of seven Meteors – the squadron was then mainly equipped with Spitfires – and on July 27th Flying Officer McKenzie, a Canadian, took off on the first-ever Meteor operational patrol. A succession of cannon-jams prevented the jet pilots from attaining any victories until August 4th, but on that date Flying Officer 'Dixie' Dean, in Meteor EE216, caught up with a V1, fired his cannons which promptly jammed, then coolly formated on the flying bomb and tipped it off-course with his wing-tip, sending it down to explode harmlessly in some woods four miles south of Tonbridge. Only minutes later, another 616 pilot, Flying Officer J. K. Roger, destroyed a V1 with two crisp two-second bursts of 20mm cannon shells. The RAF's jet-age had opened in the turmoil of combat over the green fields of Kent. By early September the jet fighters of 616 Squadron had claimed 13 flying bombs destroyed. Typical of the man, Roderic Hill found time to visit 616 at Manston and made a brief local flight in the new fighter to 'see for myself' – a trait which had already endeared him to his men throughout his command. In the event only one other fighter squadron, 504, received Meteors before the end of the war, and this unit became 'operational' too late to undertake wartime sorties.

The capture of the initial band of V1 launching sites in the Pas de Calais area led the Air Ministry and the British government to assume – indeed publicly state – that the flying bomb need engender 'no further fear of danger' due to the over-running of these bases. The statement was rashly premature, and within the following seven months more than 2000 bombs were aimed at London from fresh bases in Holland, with a small proportion being air-launched from the wings of Heinkel 111s of KG53. In this new phase of 'Crossbow' the interception of the air-borne V1s proved to be an awkward problem. The Heinkels flew low over the sea in their approach, nullifying radar detection to a great extent, then climbed briefly to launch their 'babies' in the requisite conditions before diving fast again for home. Intruder Mosquitos were often despatched to intercept the returning Heinkels with modest success, but the V1 continued to present problems by being launched mainly at night. Interception of such a small, fleeting target in the black of night was far more difficult than by day, requiring experience and a degree of good fortune. Nevertheless, certain pilots acquired the 'knack', among them Squadron Leader Joseph Berry, DFC of 3 Squadron, who ran up a final tally of more than 60 flying bombs destroyed. The gun defences achieved a high-scoring peak of success, and during this whole phase, from 16 September to 14 January 1945, claimed 331 victims. In the same period fighters downed 71 bombs and 16 Heinkel carrier-aircraft – all by night. The overall success of ADGB can be measured against the simple fact that only one in twenty V1s initially launched, by whichever method, actually reached a London target.

Apart from a final flurry in March 1945, the V1 menace was defeated soundly; the result of splendid co-operation between the anti-aircraft guns of General Pile and Roderic Hill's pilots in the main. During the whole V1 campaign, from 12 June 1944 until 29 March 1945, anti-aircraft gunners had claimed 1878, while fighters destroyed 1846. A further 231 were brought down by the floating balloon barrage 'apron' – a familiar 'ceiling' to Londoners during those months. In view of these officially confirmed figures, it seems curious that the Prime Minister, Winston Churchill, should then send a memorandum to the Secretary of State for Air in March 1945, in which he made the petulant comment, 'You have no grounds to claim that the Royal Air Force frustrated the attack by the "V" weapons. The RAF took their part, but in my opinion their efforts rank definitely below that of the anti-aircraft artillery, and still farther below the achievements of the Army in cleaning out all the establishments in the Pas de Calais, which so soon would have opened a new devastating attack upon us in spite of all the Air Force could do.'[1]

In the midst of the V1 assaults Roderic Hill had an even more potentially dangerous threat with which to contend. Allied intelligence had for some considerable time been patiently fitting together fragments of evidence of the existence of an even bigger robot weapon, the A4 rocket-bomb. On 2 September 1944 the Director of Intelligence (Research) had somewhat confidently reported that any threat from such a rocket 'would disappear when the area in Northern France and Belgium 200 miles from London was "neutralised" by the proximity of our land forces and the operations of our Tactical Air Forces.' Only four days later his view was reinforced by the Vice-Chiefs of Staff who opined that rocket attacks on London need no longer be expected. At Bentley Priory, Hill had necessarily studied such intelligence on the subject as he was provided, knowing full well that the ADGB would be regarded as the primary defence organisation to meet any such attack on Britain. Hill's own Intelligence staff promptly pointed out the flaws in the reasoning behind the Vice-Chiefs of Staff's broad statement, indicating that the latest information suggested strongly that long-range rockets could easily be launched from bases in western Holland. Their view was dramatically confirmed at 6.40 pm on September 8th when the first A4 rocket fell at Chiswick, followed within ten days by 26 more in various sections of London.

The A4 rocket was a 12.7 tons intercontinental missile, measuring 46

---

[1] *Triumph & Tragedy*, vol 6 of the Churchill Memoirs.

feet in length with a body diameter of five feet five inches. Its warhead carried 1650lb of high explosive. With a maximum velocity of 3600 mph, and capable of rising to a height of at least 50 miles in any planned war trajectory, the A4 would arrive on a target vertically at a speed calculated to be more than 2000 mph. In short, it was impossible to 'intercept' with any existing aircraft, and virtually immune to any known form of anti-aircraft gun then in existence. The only solution to prevention of A4 launchings was to eliminate its bases. This Hill proposed to Bomber Command and the Air Staff, and in the interim inaugurated a series of fighter reconnaissance and fighter-bomber attacks on suspected A4 sites on the Continent. A marked reluctance on the part of either Bomber Command or the Air Staff to divert any major portion of the contemporary bomber offensive against Germany resulted in little real effort being expended to implement Hill's requests in that context; while his continuing fighter offensive against the sites caused little significant relaxation in the mounting rocket attacks on England.

From the unheralded arrival of the first A4 – it was more usually referred to as the 'V2' – on 8 September 1944, until the ultimate launching of such a missile against England on 27 March 1945, a total of 1403 were actually aimed at British objectives, of which 1115 found a mark on British soil. Half of these plunged into the London Civil Defence Region, with the remainder scattering widely around the Home Counties and East Anglia. They killed 2754 civilians and seriously wounded a further 6523; slightly more than a third of civilian casualties caused by the more primitive V1 flying bombs. Unseen, unheard until the devastating explosion which announced their arrival, the A4s constituted the final desperate move of Hitler against Britain. Though Hill's fighter squadrons were powerless to intercept these harbingers of man's space age, they continued to harass the suspected launching sites and storage depots assumed to be supplying the massive robots. Then, by late March 1945, the Allied advance through France and the Low Countries over-ran all tenable firing sites and the menace from the stratosphere disappeared. By April 1945 the Allied Service chiefs ordered the cessation of all countermeasures against rocket or flying bomb attacks.

With the Allies firmly consolidated on the continent and driving eastwards towards the Reich by October 1944, the need for the temporary RAF reorganisation for D-Day was nullified. Coningham's 2nd

TAF, continually reinforced, could cope adequately with the needs of the armies in France; while in Britain the petering Luftwaffe bomber offensive required no extra effort from the triumphant night defences. Only the robot bomb attacks were now significant, and even these – at least, the V1 – were containable. Accordingly, with effect from 15 October 1944, the label of Air Defence of Great Britain was replaced by RAF Fighter Command for a second time, with Roderic Hill continuing as AOC-in-C of Britain's home-based fighter defences. The spasmodic conventional-aircraft attacks by the Luftwaffe against Britain ceased with two slightly desperate operations in March 1945. On March 4th, in the pre-dawn hours, more than a hundred German long-range night fighters infiltrated the 500-strong RAF bomber streams returning from night attacks on Ladbergen and Kamen. In Norfolk, Suffolk, Lincolnshire and east Yorkshire a total of 27 bomber airfields were strafed and harassed by these Luftwaffe intruders, who claimed 22 bombers shot into the ground and at least eight more seriously damaged. In balance just six intruders were brought down by the defences. Just two weeks later, on March 17th, the German intruders tried again, when 18 Junkers 88s left Holland and roamed above the east counties of England seeking prey. Their journey was 'unnecessary'; there were no heavy bomber operations by the RAF that night, and the Junkers' sole victim was an innocent aircraft undergoing night-flying practice training. It was the Luftwaffe's ultimate appearance over the United Kingdom – the death throes of a once proud force. On 8 May 1945 Europe rejoiced – it was 'VE Day' ('Victory in Europe') – and the war against Nazi Germany had come to its close; the struggle was over.

The cessation of war operations in Europe brought with it a momentary halt to the Fighter Command defensive system's *raison d'être*. No potential aerial threat to the sanctity of the United Kingdom was foreseeable in the immediate future; relief that the years of tension had ended brought with it a slow relaxation. Soon many of the hastily devised appendages to Dowding's original foundation structure were in the process of being disbanded or removed. Roderic Hill, having so successfully accomplished the myriad difficult tasks imposed upon his brief tenure of office in command, was quickly moved to the 'Whitehall Paper Factory', despite his expressed desire to complete a normal period of duty in Fighter Command as its AOC-in-C. With effect from 14 May 1945 Hill became Air Member for Training at the Air Ministry, where his uncommon expertise and above-the-ruck intelligence could now be devoted to the many problems of re-establishing the foundations for a peace-time air Service. His task at Bentley Priory was taken over by Air Marshal Sir James Robb, a 1914–18 fighter pilot of distinction with extensive experience in the field of air operations, and a practising pilot who had only recently been Commandant of the Central Flying School. Then, on 15 August 1945, came the announcement that all remaining hostilities in the Far East theatre against Japan had been concluded. The world was – at least for a moment – at peace.

Once the first fervour of celebrations had subsided it was possible to assess objectively the achievements (or otherwise) of Fighter Command to date. The years 1936–41 had seen it as a pure metropolitan aerial defence organisation for the protection of Britain and its coastal waters and approaches. Under Hugh Dowding's resolute and unwavering direction it had fulfilled its role, and during the supreme acid testing of 1940 had defended triumphantly. Above the green meadows and uplands of England the fighter pilots had salvaged a bright hope for eventual victory while defending their birthright of freedom from the oppressive cruelties of a Nazi dictatorship. In doing so they had fought a battle unique in the centuries-old saga of human warfare by meeting and defeating a strong, determined enemy in the skies alone. If the balance between defeat and ultimate victory during those fateful summer days had been razor-thin on occasion, this could hardly be wondered. Mustered in the sleepy days of a complacent peace, Fighter Command had been armed slowly – even reluctantly initially – and not always wisely, yet any 'fault' in the adolescent stages of its growth could not be laid at the feet of its pilots or its austere leader. Totally uncompromising in the pursuit of what he saw as his clear duty and responsibility, Hugh Dowding at least accomplished his prime aims, despite circumstances and a lack of support from the number of his civil and Service 'superiors' which might easily have daunted a lesser spirit. In doing so he and his valiant 'chicks' (as he termed his Battle of Britain crews) firmly secured Great Britain as the base for the subsequent offensive operations undertaken by all Allied Services which ultimately sounded the death-knell of Hitler's vainglorious fantasy of a 'Thousand Years Reich'. Had Dowding and his men failed, then the past 40 years might have been recorded now as the blackest era ever in the history of the human race.

In 1941 and 1942, under fresh guidance at the helm, the fighter arm recuperated, re-armed its muscles and teeth, then inexorably expanded, blossoming into a hydra-headed instrument of offensive power on an ever-increasing scale. The actual process of switching from a purely defensive role to an offensive spearhead was slow, a protracted transition complicated by a continuing vital need to guard the skies of Britain from both day and night assaults; while the divergent forms of offensive operations undertaken from 1941 necessitated entirely fresh tactical thinking and practice with the newer fighter designs entering service at squadron level. Experience in the new modes of aerial fighting was gained at no small cost in lives and machines, and the period 1941–2 became a time of part-frustration for the eager fighter pilots. There was seldom a lack of combat action available, yet end results too often appeared to be of little consequence. Casualties were high in relation to positive achievements, many of the former being men who had survived the savage clashes of 1940 only to be lost in relatively 'minor' sorties during the early months of the 'new' offensive operations across the Channel. The loss of such experienced veterans was doubly tragic, creating gaps in the field leadership which were difficult to fill at first. Epitomising Trenchard's confidence in the quality of 'his' airmen when he had often said that no matter what the situation, 'A man will emerge', new fighting leaders soon emerged in the squadrons, and the high standards were maintained.

Whatever the view of such daylight offensive sorties by individual pilots, these at least provided a continuous opportunity to increase and sharpen the experience of all pilots and thereby maintain the fighting 'edge' of the Command. A secondary consideration in maintaining pressure upon the now depleted Luftwaffe fighter force based in France was as an indirect aid to Russia. By compelling Göring to retain a certain minimum of defending fighter *geschwadern* along the 'western front' of Germany to combat the ceaseless day and nights forays by the Allied air Services, the RAF was effectively preventing such units being used to strengthen Hitler's offensive in the east. Even more important, from the Allied viewpoint, was the necessity for achieving aerial superiority in the west, in order that the projected strategic bombing offensive by the RAF and USAAF could be pursued from 1942. As Adolf Galland has stated succinctly: 'An air force is, according to its intrinsic laws, by nature an offensive weapon. Air supremacy is, of course, essential for this. If this has been lost, then the fighter force has to be strengthened first of all, because only the fighter force can achieve this essential supremacy so that the bomber, and with it the entire air force, can go over to the offensive once more.'[1] Galland was describing the contemporary situation within the Luftwaffe in mid-1942, deploring the lack of emphasis then on a strong Luftwaffe fighter defence force for the German homeland against the increasingly heavy bombing offensive then ensuing, but his statement applied equally to all contemporary air forces.

The introduction of the Spitfire IX and Hawker Typhoon in 1942 gave added fillip to the RAF's daylight operations, while the advent of the wooden de Havilland Mosquito fighter-bomber extended the long arm of that offensive by night, as 'Mossie' crews ranged at will across Europe, patiently stalking Luftwaffe bombers to their base airfields before destroying them, and creating havoc with German crews' morale by this ever-present nemesis. Aided by the very latest radar 'black boxes' the Mosquito crews became the bane of the Luftwaffe's bomber arm, and also provided a protecting presence increasingly for the nightly RAF bomber streams in German skies as aggressive shields against the German homeland's night fighters. The combination of these factors, plus the 'bonus' of the start of true operations by the first units of the American Eighth Air Force, were the real beginning of Fighter Command's genuine supremacy over western Europe; a superiority in the air which it was never to lose in the remaining years of the conflict, and an achievement which ensured ultimate victory. This supremacy was reinforced and confirmed throughout 1943 and early 1944, and was manifest during the opening stages of the Allied invasion of Normandy from 6 June 1944. Though 'split' into two formations as the 2nd Tactical Air Force and the ADGB by that date, the RAF fighter arm could by then boast more than a hundred firstline fighter squadrons, roughly 60 per cent of these being under Leigh-Mallory's aegis in 2nd TAF, and the remainder UK-based under Roderic Hill's direction for the continued defence and security of the United Kingdom itself. As the first landing craft of the Allied invasion fleet beached in Normandy that day, the sky above them was devoid of German aircraft; testimony to the pinnacle of air supremacy achieved by Fighter Command.

[1] *The First & the Last*; Methuen, 1955.

Effectively, the prime task of Fighter Command – defence – reached its peak in the closing months of 1944. Having gained a great measure of mastery over the V1 flying bombs – neither it nor any other form of defensive system could obviate the larger V2 missile threat – the Command virtually 'sat out' the final weeks of war, like some crouched tiger chained to its lair in the UK, but constantly on the *qui vive* to counter each dying gasp or tremor of the near-defunct Luftwaffe. Its 'back-up' organisation had by then reached its own peak of efficiency, with an all-embracing network of control, radar eyes and reporting procedures which could ensure immediate notification of any would-be invader in British skies, co-ordinated with the requisite means for despatching prompt interception and destruction of any such raider. The pathway to such a state of efficiency had been an uphill struggle of trial, error, and dogged perseverance, but that it had been achieved was in itself a mark of the spirit of dedication which had long been associ-ated with the men and women of Fighter Command and its ancillary formations.

As Europe resounded to the clamour of victory bells in May 1945, Fighter Command could look back on nine years of unremitting labour and sacrifice; years in which Churchill's dramatic phrase 'Blood, sweat and tears' had never been more aptly epitomised. The cost in human terms of that effort had been grievous. In the years 1939–45 alone, 3690 air crew members had been killed, while 1215 had been seriously wounded or crippled for life, and a further 601 had suffered imprison-ment in enemy hands. The tally of more than 5000 'victories' over enemy aircraft could never compensate for the toll of such tragic proportions in a single generation of such splendid youth. Among the ranks of the fighter pilots and crews had been an incredibly blended conglomeration of races, nationalities, creeds and colours. In common was their youth, and an eager enthusiasm for each task allotted, what-ever the circumstances. Individuals had occasionally attracted a modi-cum of fleeting international fame and publicity for their prowess, and some entered the annals of aviation legend as outstanding leaders and supreme examples of the fighter traditions of the RAF. Yet the vast bulk of the men who so willingly filled the cockpits of the Hurricanes, Spitfires, Beaufighters, Mosquitos, Typhoons and Tempests attracted no such public acclaim, and it was this 'silent majority' who truly gained the victory, and to whom must be offered the accolade.

Most were ex-civilians in a temporary uniform, with no small percentage comprising boys fresh from a school desk, and their light-hearted regard for the more obscure idiosyncrasies and esoteric rules of dress and conduct ingrained in the regular-serving RAF members too often bred a false image of irresponsible adolescence in the layman's mind. Nothing could be further from the truth. If such 'irresponsibility' was apparently manifested by the crumpled edge to a Service peaked cap, or a top tunic button carelessly undone to denote their calling, these were by symbols of a fierce pride and jealous regard inherent in any tight-knit fighting community. Such 'adolescents' fought an uncompromising life and death struggle for supremacy over a common foe virtually day or night, voluntarily laying unfulfilled lives on a borderline of possible sacrifice in order to help preserve an ideal. With the distinct possibility of death in some of its more horrifying forms accompanying them on every sortie, who would deny them a desire to fill the off-duty hours with gaiety and a disregard for the more tedious conventions created by their 'elders and betters'. Nearly thirty years before, in the 'War-to-end-wars' of 1914–18, the American fighter 'ace' Raoul Lufbery had said, 'There won't be any after-the-war for a fighter pilot', and the underlying fatalism of Lufbery's words reflected the outlook of many of this latest generation of fighter pilots.

The official historian's description of the Battle of Britain 'Few' as, 'In the main gloriously extrovert, they drank cheerfully of life with few questions as to the quality of the beverage; and if death struck the cup from their hands long before the dregs were reached, there were worse ends than one which was sudden, swift, and encountered in the service of what they held dear',[1] could have been applied equally to a majority of fighter pilots throughout the war. Yet for those many who 'failed to return', the words of John Milton were even more appropriate:

Nothing is here for tears, nothing to wail
Nothing but well and fair,
And what may quiet us in a death so noble . . .
Thither shall all the valiant youth resort,
And from his memory inflame their breasts,
To matchless valour and adventures high.'

[1] *Royal Air Force 1939–45* by D. Richards; HMSO 1953.

11. From the Cockpit

The saga of Fighter Command's achievements during the years 1936–45 is, inevitably, predominantly an account of tactics, strategy and aircraft, set against a backcloth of military and naval conflict and the more abstract 'scenery' of the larger political and Service necessities of each succeeding year of the period. At least, this is the general tenor of the bulk of literature published in the past forty years. Statistics and compounded hindsight may well be the stuff of archival records, but what of the men who flew and fought? The age-old Service cliché, 'Old men make wars – young men fight them', has never been better exemplified than by the overwhelmingly youthful men whose fighting was from the bucket seat of an aeroplane cockpit. Barely mature – so many did not live to even attain the legal mark of 'majority' – the fighter pilots fought a war of unique character in the history of human conflict. Encased in a machine capable of speeds beyond any previous experience, in a third-dimensional element into which man had first ventured a mere four decades before and still hardly comprehended, the fighter pilot's war was unlike that of any other fighting man. Like all wartime air crews, his existence was one of vast contrasts in physical and emotional reactions, usually pressed into mere minutes or even seconds.

In combat he sought and fought a human enemy whom he seldom saw. His target was a machine, not a human being, and pilots (of all nations) seldom gave prior thought to the pilot or crew within that machine. Indeed, many fighter pilots experienced shock when any enemy pilot was actually seen, and realisation that he was attempting to kill a fellow human penetrated his normally objective approach to combat. This 'detachment' from the physical act of deliberately taking a life was a common phenomenon experienced by many pilots even in

146

the days of highly individual combat during 1914–18. The legendary German fighter leader Oswald Boelcke had summarised his feelings, and those of his fellow fighters on such matters in a letter he wrote to his parents on 17 September 1916: '. . . we do not number the victims who have fallen, but the machines we have brought down. That you can see from the fact that it only counts as one victory when two inmates are killed, but that it still remains a "number" when both the inmates escape unhurt. We have nothing against the individual; we only fight to prevent him flying against us. So when we have eliminated an enemy force, we are pleased and book it as one up to us.'[1] Boelcke's impersonal attitude towards an enemy opponent was reflected by Gordon Taylor, a Sopwith Pup pilot with 66 Squadron in April 1917, who has recorded, 'We felt no real hate against the Hun. He hardly existed as a human individual. He was simply "the Hun", the opponent, the impersonal enemy. For myself – and I believe I was typical – I was not incapable of killing Huns, but I was certainly incapable of hating them. I hunted as a job, and for the thrill of the chase. Hate had no part in it.'[2]

With rare exceptions, this 'impersonal' view of German opponents was felt by a majority of RAF fighter pilots during 1939–45, despite the insistent propaganda engendered by Allied authorities and media, and the jingoistic fervour of armchair hawks and 'warriors' in non-combatant occupations. Whereas the foot-slogging infantryman was faced with direct encounters with a visible, human adversary attempting to kill him with cold steel or bullet, the fighter pilot fought a machine first and the man inside second; though he was highly conscious of the human brain against which he was pitted in such a life and death combat. Eminent psychologists emphasise that man is a hunter by nature and a killer by instinct, with the latter trait deeply buried (or at least firmly controlled) by all but a relative few, unleashed only in the direst situation or circumstance. In times of war, however, each man in uniform was expected – at least in theory – to be ready and capable of killing a fellow human to order, to summon an instinctive ability which most men privately found repugnant to their normal nature. While the professional Serviceman could rationalise such a paradox, having voluntarily donned his country's uniform and sworn on oath of allegiance to fight and, if necessary, kill, the bulk of fighter pilots in the RAF

[1] *Knight of Germany* by J. Werner; John Hamilton, 1933.
[2] *Sopwith Scout 7309* by Sir Gordon Taylor; Cassell, 1968.

during 1939–45 were 'non-professionals' without any such 'salve' to their innermost feelings on the subject. For these men their 'duty' was less clearly rational, though all were unpressed volunteers with little doubt as to their ultimate purpose and employment in the war.

Whatever private inner conflicts of conscience may have been experienced by individuals, these were rarely in evidence in the day-to-day actions and conversations of the fighter pilots. The introspective thoughts of men like the late Richard Hillary, author of *The Last Enemy*, were untypical of the vast majority; most men forced themselves to overcome instinctive finer feelings in their approach to their 'job' where it involved killing or destroying, and seldom pondered too deeply upon the moral 'rights' and 'wrongs' of their task. Life expectancy was too short for many, and off-duty periods were for relaxation of the body and mind, not deep philosophical or religious scruples. In any case, once committed to combat every ounce of mental and physical effort was needed in the quicksilver tournaments of the upper air; events occurred at a speed which baffled logical thought or reasoned argument. As one anonymous source expressed it, 'War is a conflict which does not determine who is right – but who is left.'

The view of warfare through an aeroplane's windscreen and gun-sight expressed by fighter pilots over the past sixty-five years is remarkably similar, irrespective of the period or type of combat experienced. Accounts have been recorded in private diaries, log books, and published literature illustrating the personal reactions of individual pilots to the widely varying circumstances in which each fought. Such accounts give the only real 'picture' of a fighter pilot's war; only those who have 'strapped on a kite' and engaged in mortal combat four and five miles above the green earth are truly qualified to present their story for posterity. The following personal stories are a minute selection of such first-hand impressions, each exemplifying a particular phase of World War Two, or facet of aerial fighting. None lay claim to being great literature – indeed, remarkably few pilots throughout the past 70 years have ever accomplished the talent for interpreting their most inner feelings and experience of combat flying into truly classic expression. Yet all are entirely authentic records of first-hand reactions to their roles – scraps of history in themselves. In deference to a long tradition in the RAF of self-denial and a preferred anonymity, each pilot is un-named.

Apart from several isolated combats during the first six months of the war, the first real fighting by the men of Fighter Command came with the evacuation of the British and Allied Expeditionary Force from Dunkirk in May 1940. The following was told by a Squadron Leader, awarded a DSO later:

We got a 'Stand By' early in the morning of the first day of the Dunkirk evacuation, and at 9 am we got our orders. There were 12 of us and, climbing to 20,000 feet, we headed across the North Sea. We kept well together and, of course, kept a radio silence. We knew every inch of the coastline to which we were heading, but even without that knowledge there was no mistaking Dunkirk. Only a few minutes after leaving Britain and at our height we could see the pillars of smoke rising from the burning town and the villages all the way up from Calais.

At 4,000 feet we were beetling along still looking for trouble when I saw a Hun formation of about 60 machines – 20 bombers and 40 fighters – at about 15,000 feet, and cursed the height we had lost. The fighters, all Messerschmitts, heeled over and came streaming down at us and the next second we were in the thick of it. That attack developed, like most dog-fights, into individual scraps. It was at about 10,000 feet that I found myself on the tail of my first Hun, a Messerschmitt 110. Most of my instruments had gone crazy in the course of the violent manoeuvring. I remember particularly that my gyro was spinning wildly and the artificial horizon had vanished somewhere into the interior of the instrument panel, calmly turning up its bottom and showing me the maker's stamp and the words 'Air Ministry Mark something-or-other'.

Down went the Messerschmitt again with me close on his tail. With the built-up speed of my dive my controls were freezing solid and I was fighting the stick hard to bring the Hun into the centre of my sights. Once there you can hold them for ever. I thumbed the trigger button just once, twice. I smelt cordite fumes blowing back from my Brownings as the 1200 squirts per minute went into him. I saw the little spurts of flame as the tracers struck. For a fraction of a second I saw the back outline of the pilot's head half-slewed round to see what was after him, before, presumably, he ceased to know.

I looked around for the rest but they were gone. My own scrap had brought me about 50 miles inland, so I turned and headed back, noticing with a shock that my petrol reserve was only just enough to get home provided I ran into no more trouble. Out over the North Sea and on my way back to our station I clicked on the radio and called up the pilots of my squadron one by one: 'How are you? Did you get any?' The first one came back jubilantly – he'd got one. Then the rest – two didn't answer . . .

Next day I saw some Junkers guarded by Messerschmitts bombing a torpedo boat and some small rescue craft packed with troops far below. Chancing the anti-aircraft fire from the torpedo boat, we plunged in. The

Huns never saw us coming. We all got one in that first dive. Stick back and screaming up again, we re-formed and then down once more. This time the Huns scattered. I got on to one Messerschmitt who was scramming for home and got a squirt in. There was a burst of smoke from his engine as he went down. I followed, then let him have it in full.

On the way back the first (pilot) to answer my radio call said he had got four! Then he suddenly said, 'Oh hell! my engine's packed up.' Then – 'I'm on fire'. There was silence for a second or two and he said, 'Yippee! There's a destroyer downstairs. I'm baling out'. A second later I heard him mutter, 'But how?' . . .

By August 1940 the Battle of Britain was reaching its peak of ferocity in the daylight fighting. A Flight Lieutenant in a Hurricane squadron recorded his first parachute escape:

We were flying east when three enemy aircraft were spotted west in the clouds overhead. I told our leader that I would climb with my Flight above the clouds and investigate. As I did this twelve Messerschmitt 109s emerged from the clouds. Still climbing, I made for the sun, turned, and gave the order to break and attack. Eighteen aircraft chased round and round, in and out of cloud, and I chose my first opponent. He seemed to be dreaming and I quickly got on his tail and gave him a short burst and damaged him. I flew in closer and gave him a second dose. It was enough. He dived, out of control, and I followed him down to 6000 feet. There I circled and watched him dive vertically into the sea. Only a tell-tale patch of oil marked where he had disappeared.

I opened the hood for a breath of fresh air and looked about the sky. There was no sign of either the enemy or my own Flight. I was alone, so I climbed back into cloud which was thin and misty. Three Messerschmitts, flying in line astern, crossed in front of me – so close that I could see the black crosses on their wings and fuselages. I opened fire on number three in the formation . . . and had the pleasure of seeing my bullets hit him. Pieces of his wings flew off. Black smoke came from just behind his cockpit. He dived and I fired one more burst directly from astern. We were doing a phenomenal speed – then my ammunition gave out – just as the other two Messerschmitts attacked me. I twisted and turned but they were too accurate. I could hear the deafening thud of their bullets. Pieces of my aircraft seemed to be flying off in all directions; my engine was damaged and I could not climb back into cloud where I might have shaken them off. Then came a cold stinging pain in my left foot. One of the Jerry bullets had found its mark. I was about to dive to the sea and make my escape low down, when the control column became useless in my hand. I knew the time had come for me to depart.

Everything after this was perfectly calm. I was at about 10,000 feet but some miles out to sea. I lifted my seat, undid my straps and opened the hood. The wind became my ally. A 'hand' – actually the slipstream catching under my helmet – seemed to lift me out of the cockpit. It was a pleasant sensation. I was in mid-air – floating down so peacefully – in the cool breeze. I had to remind myself to pull my ripcord and open my parachute. When the first jerk came I swung like a pendulum, but I soon settled down and was able to enjoy a full view of the world below . . . the beach some miles away, with soldiers, and the long lines of villas in a coastal town. There was no sensation of speed. As I floated down one of the Messerschmitts appeared. The pilot circled round me . . . would he shoot? . . . he didn't . . . he opened his hood, waved to me, then dived towards the sea and made off towards France. . . . the journey ended in a cucumber frame after I had pushed myself free of a house with my foot.

The awesome bomber armadas sent to Britain by Göring, usually with their attendant swarms of protecting Messerschmitt fighters, presented the RAF fighter pilots with unprecedented targets to tackle. Equally they presented an acid test in courage and determination. Deliberately to plunge into enemy odds of anything up to 100:1 was the action of either a fool or an exceptionally brave man – and Fighter Command had very few fools. One such encounter is described by an ex-Sergeant pilot of a Hurricane squadron:

When I first saw the 'bandits' reported by our controller, I really couldn't believe my eyes. There seemed no end to the procession – row upon row of ugly-snouted bombers stretching half-way to France, or so it seemed. I looked higher for their escorts – then caught a sun glint from a cockpit canopy and placed them; a large gaggle of tiny black aircraft wheeling up-sun. We'd already been told to forget the fighters and concentrate on the bombers, but, I remember thinking at that moment, where the hell do six Hurricanes start on this bunch? The leader's voice came over my earphones, calm as ever, and in that snooty accent of his he said, 'We'll take these johnnies from head-on. Line up behind me. Here we go, chaps' – and in we went in single file in the old practised manoeuvre.

I was the last in the line and watched each of the others ahead of me open up in turn on his selected Hun, his wing guns streaming cordite plumes and empty cartridge cases back towards me – we were pretty close in behind each other on the run-in. Then Harry in front of me lifted a wing and disappeared from my windscreen and I had my first clear view of the Germans. There seemed to be hundreds of them, in every direction – an exaggeration as I realised once I got back to base and thought about it more calmly – and I hiccupped with sheer fright! No time for thinking, selecting a target or any such nonsense; I just pressed the firing button and 'stirred' my control column like a pudding stick, thereby spraying bullets in every direction. I probably said a prayer too, though I'm not a religious man . . . Seconds later I was still flying straight through the Heinkels and Dorniers, some of which were missing my Hurricane by only inches, before I recovered from my fright and had the sense to dive clear. I presume the bombers' gunners had fired at me though I wasn't conscious of any firing except my own.

Once I reached a patch of clear air, I looked upwards, hoping to find my pals, but the sky seemed full of Germans only; not a Hurricane in sight. I took a very deep breath, pulled back the stick, and climbed fast. One black-looking Heinkel in full silhouette against the bright upper sky seemed to rush down at me. As it filled the gunsight I opened fire, and saw my De Wilde splash along the wings into the fuselage belly. I flashed past him, between his wing and tail unit and kept on going as fast as possible. Levelling out at about 21,000 feet, I twisted my neck in all directions – where were those fighters? At that moment there was a deafening crash in my ears and my instrument panel seemed to explode in front of me – I'd been caught napping by a German behind me. I ducked my head, then pulled the Hurricane sideways and down – fast. Whoever that Hun was, he didn't bother following – at least, I never saw him. At about 5,000 feet I pulled the nose up carefully – I had no idea whether he'd done any other damage to the aircraft – and decided I'd had enough for one sortie, so got lower and searched for familiar countryside to guide me home.

One nineteen-year-old Pilot Officer in a Spitfire squadron had his introduction to combat on August 15th, one of the fiercest day's fighting of the Battle:

I joined the squadron only two days before my first fight. The squadron commander, a weary-looking man with very pale blue eyes which seemed to look right through you, told me I'd be in B Flight, and when I reported to my new Flight commander, he said he'd keep me off ops for the next day if he could! I'd rather expected a week or so's grace to settle in – they'd assured me at the OTU that a new pilot never flew 'in anger' until he had proved himself able to fly decently. I had just fifteen hours in Spitfires in my log book! Obviously, I was going to be thrown in at the deep end. . . .

As it happened I didn't fly operations next day and spent the time trying to get as much gen on the Spitfire cockpit, guns, sights etc as possible from the B Flight ground crews – none of the pilots seemed to have either time or interest for the new 'sprog'; though they were extremely polite when spoken to. On the third morning the Flight commander cornered me early and told me which Spitfire was mine, whom I was to follow, and what the squadron call-sign was for R/T chatter. His only other advice was, 'Keep twisting your neck and eyes. These bastards come at you from everywhere'. About half an hour after lunch the squadron was brought to Readiness, and I strapped myself into 'my' Spitfire, all fingers and thumbs in my nervous excitement – a fact noticed by the gnarled Corporal fitter who quietly smoothed everything out, then with a reassuring grin, patted my shoulder like some naughty child before he jumped down from the wing. (Bless him, that pat on the shoulder was very much needed by a very frightened young pilot. . . .)

Watching my Flight commander like a hawk, I saw his gloved hand suddenly shoot up and twirl a finger – start-up signal – and punched my engine starter. Minutes later we were rumbling across the field, then full bore and off. Once up, we fell into loose formation and began climbing hard. Once we reached 20,000 feet, we levelled out and tightened up the formation. I was tucked in on the right of my leader, with a hefty Yorkshire lad just to my right – a nice 'protected' feeling which helped my morale. There was a long layer of woolly cloud high above us, and my imagination envisaged hordes of evil-grinning Germans peeking down at me (not us – ME), licking their lips at such a gift horse! The R/T crackled, and the leader's voice came through saying, '50-plus bandits at angels 15, due south, two miles. Yellow Section stay on top. The rest follow me'. Then his Spitfire's nose dipped and down we went in a shallow dive, with myself anxiously attempting to keep station with the leader. I switched on my sight, moved the safety cover off my gun button, and searched ahead for the Germans.

The German formation came into view almost immediately, about thirty or so Heinkels and Dorniers, with twenty or more Messerschmitt 109s weaving around above and behind them. I was fascinated – these were real Germans in real bombers! Things then happened so fast I hadn't time to concentrate on anything but flying. The 'boss' didn't bother with any fancy tactics but simply steepened his dive, yelled 'Tallyho! Pick your own targets', then opened up at a leading Heinkel. A fat Heinkel swam into my sights and I automatically fired, seeing my tracers slide into its perspex nose compartment and ricochet off the port engine cowling; then I was rushing over it and on to a second further back which started to bank away. My fire splashed along its rear fuselage but I doubt if they did any harm. Seconds later I was in empty air – things had happened so fast for me. I threw the Spit into a turn, hoping to come back onto the rear of the bombers but when I straightened out they'd gone. Instead I found the other Spits in a fight with a gaggle of 109s, twisting and turning all over the sky. Even as I watched one 109 seemed to split at the seams and fell apart, with dozens of burning pieces showering down like a giant firework on Guy Fawkes Night. I had no idea what I was supposed to do, tactically, so I plunged in bald-headed, trying to line up on one 109 with a green engine cowling. Before I could even press the

153

button, another Spitfire cut right across me and hammered him, and the pair fell away from me still fighting. I looked around frantically – upwards, sideways and over my shoulder – and got the fright of my life on seeing two 109s right behind me with obvious evil intentions on my tailplane. I rolled to the right and let the Spitfire drop, pulled the stick back into my stomach, and quickly shot upwards again to get as high as possible. As I climbed two Hurricanes shot down past me with a string of 109s chasing them – one second they were there and the next they'd vanished into the party way below. Again I looked around for a target. There were none at my height. I looked down – the sky was clear. Highly relieved (if the truth be known), I went home.

As the day battle petered out in November 1940, the Luftwaffe's night blitz increased. Fighter Command's piecemeal night fighter defences relied heavily upon location of a bomber by the searchlights initially, after which, with a large slice of luck, the lone night fighter pilot could – perhaps – close with and engage the raider. Few aircraft carried radar sets, and even these had a myriad of problems with recalcitrant equipment and the sheer lack of experience in using the 'black boxes' effectively. One of the individual Hurricane pilots who attempted to intercept a raid on Norwich epitomises the frustration and patience of all night fighters at that period:

The take-off into an utterly black night sky never ceased to terrify me. Once airborne and climbing I was always OK, but that initial run along the airfield and lift into the air was never a pleasant process. On this occasion I'd been sent off to free-lance over the Norwich area. The sky that night was really dark – I could not even see my wing-tips – and only the occasional searchlight beam or bursting flak from our guns below gave any visual relief from the darkness all round me. Trusting almost wholly to my instruments I managed to reach Norwich, then started looking for bombers. My only real guide was the searchlights' constant sweeping around the sky. After about an hour I was getting decidedly browned off with seeing nothing and was thinking of packing the whole thing in, when up ahead of me, just east of the city, I saw three searchlight beams suddenly converge into a cone, all concentrated in one apex. They had finally found a German and were hanging on to him like grim death. I put the Hurricane into top gear and flew a bee-line towards the bright cone of lights.

My luck held up until I came into fairly long firing range of the Jerry – it was a Heinkel 111 – then the lights lost him; either that or the Jerry pilot had finally outfoxed them with some quick move. Cursing, I fired my guns anyway on the off-chance of a strike on him, or even to tickle one of his gunners into replying, which would, of course, betrayed his location to me. However, that crew must have been experienced because nothing happened. I then decided to fly out to sea; perhaps I could spot him against the water below rather than black land. I flew in roughly the direction I thought he might take if he was on his return journey. After about ten minutes creeping around I caught a tiny flicker of light slightly higher and to my right. Turning towards this I piled on extra boost and caught up with it – exhaust flames and small sparking from two engines! Creeping up underneath the, as yet, unidentified aircraft, I found I was holding my breath as if he'd hear me coming! Finally I was just astern and below the aircraft, and I studied its outline as best I could. It had a fish-like snout and Spitfire-like rounded wings – a Heinkel. Satisfied, I lined up behind and below him, closed to roughly 200 yards, then fired all eight guns at a spot just ahead of his nose while lifting the nose of my Hurricane slightly. The idea was to rake him stem to stern and thus let him run right through my fire. He duly obliged and I saw a line of red sparks flash off him as he ran the gauntlet.

My burst must have woken the pilot, because seconds later he whipped sideways – and vanished. For the ensuing 15 minutes I searched in every direction but with no result. He'd got away. My morale sank and, utterly depressed, I set course for base. On arrival over the field I found no landing lights to guide me down – I was told later that 'there was a raid on', hence the black-out – and therefore, because of my fuel state, I was forced to land virtually blind – an unnerving experience which did nothing for my nervous system.

The years 1941–3 were mainly the era of the daylight fighter offensive sweep across France and the Low Countries. Each individual sortie was, in effect, a 'personal' invasion of enemy territory, with all the attendant hazards of such a perilous venture. This offensive can be split into two main forms; the high-level massed 'Circus'-type operations, and the deck-level strafing sorties designed to disrupt communications and to generally create confusion. The latter role was a particularly exhilarating, if distinctly dangerous form of flying for a fighter pilot. Normally forbidden to indulge in low flying back in Britain, he could 'let his hair down' with a vengeance over German-occupied lands. A Spitfire pilot, already awarded a DFC for his part in the Battle of Britain, was one of the early low-level raiders to penetrate enemy-occupied France in the beginning of 1941:

The dawn that morning was one of those really beautiful spring dawns which make you feel grateful for being alive; clear blue sky, no clouds, and a warm sun promising a perfect day's weather. The dew was still thick on the grass at our dispersal when we arrived to go to work. The target was a German MT (Mechanical Transport) park reported some 20 miles into France, not all that far from Abbeville's horde of yellow-nosed Messerschmitts, so we weren't looking on this sortie as a soft touch by any means. Six Spitfires, led by myself, were to go direct to the vehicle park and clobber it as best we could; then back home fast using the remaining ammo on any targets of opportunity en route. I'd been briefed by the squadron 'Spy' (Intelligence Officer) about a couple of fairly vicious flak posts near the beachline at our point of entry to France, and duly passed this gen on to my chaps.

In terms of operations it was a straightforward sortie – straight in and straight out; a joyride before breakfast. I led them out and we took off altogether in one Vic, thus saving time on formating in the air. We kept very low on the run to the coast, then dropped to near sea-level for the Channel crossing; no point letting Jerry know we were coming if we could avoid it. My plan was to cross the French coastline on the deck, then climb quickly to 2,000 feet to line up on the objective, and finally to attack in a shallow dive from that height and get in close to the target. The sea in the Channel was almost pond-smooth, making height judgement difficult at that hour of the morning, and I've never been very happy with flying over water anyway. However, we got across without any snags and the French beaches soon appeared under our noses and we roared inland. Luckily for us the flak gun teams must still have been asleep because we got no reception from them.

Once across the beaches I flipped my wings to signal for the climb – I'd ordered complete R/T silence up to the attack time – and we rose to roughly 2,000 feet. Almost dead ahead was the vehicle park, a cluster of wood huts and large barn-type buildings – presumably an old French farm being used for MT maintenance now. I then broke radio silence to give the order 'Form up', and we formed into two sections of three Spitfires in line-abreast, then said, 'In we go!' My own target was a line of lorries conveniently in parade dressing, end-on to me, while my numbers two and three on either wing took the buildings each side of the centre courtyard. At about 800 yards I commenced firing and saw my bullets run in a line along the parked lorries, with the day tracers bouncing off at all angles. About halfway along the line I must have hit a petrol tank because there was an almighty whoof of flames and smoke which almost engulfed me seconds later as I flew through it. I kept my firing button depressed until the smoke cleared and ran out the other side, banking sharply to port and slightly climbing. On looking back I was just in time to see the second wave of Spits begin their run-in. The centre man, a recently-arrived Flying Officer from Canada, must have misjudged his height because he went straight into the side of a large barn and exploded, scattering flaming wreckage all over the park. His port wing man was pushed sideways by the blast but seemed OK as he flattened out and flew towards me; while the starboard Spit emerged from the chaos in one piece and turned in my direction too.

By now I was halfway round the target and decided to have one more run. Telling the other four to form up and circle, I turned back into the target. By now there were Jerries scampering about all over the place, and as I lined up my sight on a big gantry type of apparatus, a machine gun on the roof of one square building opened up at me. It was too late to change direction to deal with him, so I hunched down in my seat and went in, my guns opening up as the gantry thing filled my windscreen. Something bright red flashed across my vision – presumably tracer from that gun – and I felt rather than heard a rattling sound outside the cockpit, like pebbles on a tin roof. My ammo splashed all over the gantry, and then I was clear. Once beyond the target in open country, I looked for my section, spotted them circling at about 1,000 feet north, and climbed to join them. Once up front I said 'Let's go home' and led them down to deck level for the return trip.

The loss of the Canadian didn't particularly bother me personally – I'd hardly had time to get to know him – but I was bloody angry at losing one of my Section in such a stupid way. We hedge-hopped all the way to the coast; I felt sure the Jerries had 'phoned Abbeville or some other Luftwaffe field, and I had no wish to be bounced by Messerschmitts when my fuel and ammunition were so low. It was no time to go making noises like a hero; I just wanted to get back in one piece. At the coast those pre-briefed flak posts were waiting for us, but by keeping below the tree-tops we ran through fast and I vented my feelings by firing two short squirts at one lone gunner actually on the beach who was trying to hit me. He 'disappeared' in a flurry of sand and shingle as my ammo ripped across his position; then we were out over the Channel.

When I'd tucked my Spitfire into our dispersal, I walked round the kite looking for damage, remembering that noise I'd heard over the target. Just above the port wing root was a neat collection of small bullet holes, and when my rigger lined up the entry and exit holes of these with a length of twine, he showed my how lucky I'd been. The burst must have passed through the cockpit inches from my ankles. After de-briefing by 'Spy', I sent my batman to gather the lost Canuck's personal gear to take to the Stores Officer for disposal. He told me later that the Canadian had hardly unpacked his suitcase.

By July 1944 the V1 'Doodlebug' – flying bomb – assault on Britain was getting into its stride by day and by night. The Air Defence of Great Britain (ADGB) made every effort to thwart these 'malignant robots' from reaching a civilian target, and night fighters were despatched on 'watching' patrols along the French coast in the hope of catching the bombs before they reached England. In that same month one member of a Mosquito two-man crew engaged in anti-V1 sorties was a Lieutenant (A), RNVR, loaned to the RAF for such duties:

From 7,000 feet up the French coast shone clearly below us in the light of the full moon. Our patrol line took us south from Cap Gris Nez to Saint Valery and then back again at 6,000 feet. We did the northward trip at a different height so as to lessen the chance of collision with one of our fellow-patrollers on the opposite course. We had to stooge up and down just off the French coastline and wait for the flaring white light that meant another load of death was on its way to London. In mid-Channel, we knew, were other night fighters on the same job as ourselves; while others, we suspected, were actually inside France, also on the job.

Sandy, my pilot, didn't go much on this business. Nor did I. We had been taken off intruding to help in this anti-V1 campaign, in which the tactics were as follows. On sighting the V1 the pilot placed his aircraft above the line of flight, as near as he could judge, and switched on his navigation lights to warn other aircraft that he was in the chase. Thus positioned the pilot would wait until the V1 passed in front of and below him. Then he opened the throttles and put the nose of the Mosquito down, using the extra speed gained in the dive to hold the small target in range long enough to shoot it down. My job, as observer, was to read out the ranges to Sandy as they appeared on the radar screen. Some form of range-taking was necessary since, by night, the exhaust flame of the buzz-bomb looked just as near at widely different ranges.

I was watching a rather spectacular raid which Bomber Command was putting on just inside the coastline when, looking back, I saw a light. 'That looks like one, Sandy!' I said, 'Just down to port'. Sandy turned slightly to port to look more closely. 'I think you're right', he said and swung the Mosquito out from the shore a little. We turned starboard again and had another look back for it. Then happened what we had seen many times. Before anyone could get on its tail the V1 toppled over and the light went out in the waters of the Channel. We turned northwards and prepared to make our way back to Gris Nez. But that dud was the herald of many live ones. Soon they were crossing the coast at several points, and the sky seemed full of the red, green and white navigation lights on the pursuing fighters.

We spotted another that looked within our range. Out we charged again, throttles well open. When we judged that we were on the line of flight and over our target, we looked for it. It was not below us on my side and Sandy couldn't see it on his, and we wondered if it had gone into the 'drink'. I craned my head backwards and saw it still coming along. We waited for it to overtake us, but it came no closer. 'Must be one of the slower ones', said Sandy. For doodle-bugs came in two main speed categories. One lot, the more numerous, tore through the sky at about 400 mph; the others, either through defect or intentionally, reached only about 250 mph. We turned back, throttling down, and keeping the target carefully in sight. Sandy eased the Mosquito in behind it and down to its level, some 2,000 feet above the sea. The ranges came down and down on my radar set. I read them out, 1,000 feet . . . 900 . . . 800 . . . 700 . . . 600 . . . and as I said '600' I looked up from my set, knowing that Sandy would fire at that range. He aimed at the flaring light right in front of us. As the aircraft shook to the thump of the cannons I saw the little flickering white lights from around the flying bomb's jet, which told of strikes on our target. Then a great shower of red sparks mingled with the white glow of the jet.

Sandy pulled out, and we waited for the V1 to fall into the sea, its fuel tank, as we thought, holed by our cannon shells. But nothing happened, so we went in again. Once more the flicker of the strikes, again the red shower from the exhaust light. Again Sandy pulled the Mosquito aside; too many of our squadron's aircraft had come back to base battered and torn by the terrific blast of a buzz-bomb's explosion at close range. Others had never come back but had perished from unknown causes. Altogether, the squadron had lost more aircraft and crews on this type of operation than in the similar period on the apparently more dangerous job of night intruding. So Sandy turned aside once more. Again, nothing happened and again we went in, this time to closer range, 400 feet.

Sandy put his sights on the target, pressed the firing button and we saw the strikes. Then, suddenly, the V1 seemed to stand still in mid-air, so violently did it slow down. We passed it close on our starboard side, my side of the Mosquito, as Sandy and I sat side by side in the nose of the aircraft. For one ghastly moment we were dead-level with it. There, almost at our wing-tip, was the buzz-bomb, and I could see every detail of it as clear as day, for it was glowing a fiery red. I thought, 'It's going to explode right in my face!' With a gulp I found my voice. 'Hard port, Sandy!' I yelled, 'Turn hard port!' He did so and as I looked back I saw our hard-hit target topple over in a stall and plunge into the Channel.

When the war ended, most fighter pilots greeted the peace with a natural relief; they had come through, they had survived – it was enough for the moment. A few indulged themselves by having one last fling in a favourite aircraft; a personal 'farewell' to the machine in which they had gone to war and which had succoured them and brought them home safely again and again. In the unnatural silence and solitude of a peaceful sky, such men tenderly put the aircraft through every manoeuvre, gracefully exploiting the freedom of an upper air devoid of adversaries, and paying their individual tribute to a superbly concocted machine which had always seemed to have a near-human life of its own. As they left the cockpit for the very last time, the pilots may have been forgiven for a pang of regret. None knew better than they the horrors of war, yet few could honestly swear that they would miss what had been the most exciting years of their lives. The esoteric tight-knit comradeship of a fighting squadron had been unique. Some fellow pilots had been bonded in a friendship deeper than any blood relationship. Now it was over – the last links had been severed.

42 *Night crews of 29 Squadron's Mosquitos at Hunsdon in September 1944.*

43 *Squadron Leader Joseph Berry, DFC, who claimed 61 robot V1 flying bombs in 1944. He was killed by flak on 2 October 1944 when commanding 501 Squadron, AAF in north-west Europe.*

44 *The result of point-blank range fire. Mosquito of 85 Squadron, piloted by E. R. Hedgecoe, after getting too close to his Junkers 188 night victim on 24/25 March 1944.*

45 *J. E. Johnson, DSO, DFC, whose ultimate tally of 38 victories made him the top-scoring RAF fighter pilot in the European operational zone. Seen here in France in 1944.*

46 *Gloster Meteor EE528, piloted by a member of the RAF High Speed Flight in 1946; one of three Meteor F4s used for training in the successful attempt on the World Speed Record.*

47 *Standard Meteor F4s of 66 Squadron being re-armed with their 20mm cannons at Duxford 1949.*

48 *De Havilland Venom NF2s of 23 Squadron, with their unit badge on the nose and colour bars on the tail booms.*

49 *North American Sabre jet fighters carrying the shark-teeth markings of 112 Squadron (based then in Germany); one of the 'interim' designs purchased by the RAF to replace Meteors and Vampires, pending introduction of the Hunter.*

50 *Gloster Javelin FAW7s of 23 Squadron, fitted with DH 'Firestreak' missiles.*

51 *Wingless wonder. A Bristol Bloodhound ground-to-air defence missile. In background is its launcher control.*

52 *Hawker Hunter F6s in tight echelon, and fitted with long-range 'slipper' fuel tanks under wings.*

53 *The magnificent English Electric Lightning interceptor, seen here in the markings of 74 'Tiger' Squadron – first unit to be equipped with the type.*

54 *'Feeding time' – an HP Victor 1 Tanker being 'milked' by a pair of Lightnings.*

55 *A formation which exemplifies Fighter Command's principal fighters for the years 1939–68. From left: Hurricane, Spitfire, Meteor, Hunter and Lightning.*

12. Phoenix Rising

As the widespread celebrations of the 'peace' erupted in every Allied country in the world, and victory parades and fly-pasts marked the official cessation of armed hostilities, the first war-weary men and women doffed their familiar uniforms and quietly began their return to 'Civvy Street'; either to pick up the traces of a long-interrupted career and family life, or to face the uncertain prospect of a new mode of living – according to respective individual experience or age. With an efficiency greatly in contrast to the near-chaotic arrangements for demobilisation in 1918–19, the Services' release programme for war-enlisted personnel swung smoothly into gear even before the advent of peace. For many ex-fighter pilots this was a moment of anti-climax and indecision. The keyed-up tensions of months or even years of existence in a front-line squadron had ceased too abruptly for many to grasp immediately the aftermath; a void which was difficult to readjust to on a mental plane. Once most had accepted the bald fact that their 'services were no longer required', a number toyed with the thought of making flying their permanent career, either in the RAF or in civilian air lines. They were, in a majority of cases, to be swiftly disillusioned. The RAF had yet to sanctify any form of peacetime establishment or general policy of future recruitment, and in any case had a rich embarrassment of trained, experienced air crews readily to hand from which to select any future 'recruits'. Civil air lines, logically, gave priority to ex-bomber or to ex-transport or ex-Coastal Command crews: men with long practice in handling multi-engined aircraft *et al*. Ex-fighter pilots found – relatively – few openings for a flying career outside the RAF because their experience had no comfortable parallel in any civil occupation in aviation.

The coming of peace also heralded a completely new era for Fighter

161

Command and, indeed, the world aviation scene. While the sky continued to reverberate with the roar and whistle of piston-engined aircraft, an entirely new note had already penetrated the familiar aerial cacophony – the high-pitched whine of the jet propulsion engine. Pioneered and initiated operationally by Germany, the jet-powered aeroplane was almost simultaneously developed by Britain, Italy and America, and was on the verge of sweeping aside some forty years of dependence on propellers. Such a revolutionary change could not come about overnight however. Too little was known as yet about the many problems inherent in such a design concept which appeared to offer unlimited speeds and unprecedented performance range. In most countries which had already experimented with jet aircraft, conventionally-engined machines had already nudged the unknown; experiencing the thresholds of ultra-high speed with their associated effects of compressibility and shock waves on the borders of the so-termed 'sound barrier' – that calculable rate of speed at which sound travels through air at any given altitude.

Within Fighter Command the Gloster Meteor had already reached squadron level, albeit in small numbers, and had a modicum of operational experience. In its F.3 version the 'Meat-Box' formed the equipment of the first post-war jet fighter Wing at Bentwaters, comprised of Nos. 56, 74 and 245 Squadrons, and soon after equipped a second jet Wing at Boxted, with Nos. 222, 234 and 263 Squadrons. Fitted with uprated Derwent 5 engines, the Meteor F.4 variant was selected as equipment for the reconstituted RAF High Speed Flight in late 1945 for an attempt on the existing world's air-speed record. On 7 November 1945, flying Meteor EE454, Group Captain H. J. Wilson, DFC, established a new record speed of 606 mph over Herne Bay, Kent; and a year later, on 7 September 1946, Wilson raised this figure to 616 mph, flying another F.4, EE549. Within the following three years standard versions of the F.3 and/or F.4 equipped a total of 26 squadrons in the RAF and Auxiliary Air Force. In its production version for the RAF the Meteor carried a nose armament of four 20mm Hispano cannons, and later was part-modified for the carriage of under-wing rockets of wartime vintage; an outdated package of weaponry inconsistent with the potential performance of the aircraft design.

Although too late to see operational service during the European war, a second successful jet design to enter RAF service shortly after was the de Havilland Vampire, the first squadron to take delivery being

No. 247 in early 1946. By September of the same year, 247 was joined with Nos. 54 and 72 Squadrons to form the Command's first Vampire Wing, based at Odiham, Hampshire. In the event, Fighter Command equipped a total of 17 squadrons (including the Auxiliary units), while Vampires were also flown by a further 23 squadrons in the various overseas theatres and commands then existing. Of remarkably compact design, the Vampire also packed a four-20mm cannons' punch, and quickly proved itself delightful to handle for any pure aerobatic flying; a trait exploited by the pilots of 54 Squadron during the next four years when they were among the pioneers of jet formation aerobatic displays for the public displays that were beginning to come back into fashion in the late 1940s. In July 1948 six of the squadron's Vampires made aviation history by becoming the first RAF jets to cross the Atlantic, led by Squadron Leader R. W. Oxspring, DFC, and refuelling in stages at Iceland, Greenland and Labrador en route.

A third promising fighter which emerged too late for the war was the twin-engined (piston) de Havilland Hornet, a sleek all-wood construction design based closely on its stable-mate, the superb Mosquito. With a full war-load of four 20mm cannons in its belly, three-inch rocket projectiles and HE bombs under its slender wings, the Hornet was still fully aerobatic, and could achieve speeds well in excess of 400 mph; the fastest piston-engined fighter ever to see firstline operational service with the RAF. Despite its exceptional performance range, ease of maintenance, and all-round popularity with its crews, the Hornet saw only brief use within Fighter Command, being supplanted by Meteors by 1951, although the type soldiered on with highly active operational service in Malaya – 'Operation Firedog' – until 1955. Only four squadrons, Nos. 19, 41, 64 and 65, were Hornet-equipped in the UK.

The gradual transition from piston-engined fighters to an all-jet force was but one prime consideration facing Air Marshal Robb on becoming the latest AOC-in-C, Fighter Command. The atomic bomb now dominated the strategies of aerial warfare, and Robb perforce was responsible for preparing his command to meet a possible nuclear assault on the United Kingdom – a task which (theoretically) could only be viable if it could offer a guaranteed 100 per cent success rate of preventing any hostile aircraft carrying a nuclear device from penetrating within striking range of Britain's coastline. The age-old contention that 'the bomber will always get through' could no longer be tolerated – just a single nuclear-armed bomber could wreak more havoc than any multi-bomber stream had ever achieved in history. The need for the earliest possible warning of any such intending invader was obvious, but the Command's reporting and radar control organisation, excellent as it was for the type of potential hostile recognised in the late 1940s, would quickly become obsolete for the new jet-engined designs being developed by Russia. Re-equipment of existing squadrons with jet interceptors of vastly improved performance was paramount, in parallel with the required up-dating of the ground system. It was an awesome responsibility to bear, and no little effort would be needed by all aspects of the defences if these were to be ready for their latest role in the ever-diminishing time available.

With the new potential performance ranges offered by the jet engine, combined with the vital necessity for new concepts in fighters for the interceptor role, a new generation of RAF fighters was conceived, and the RAF looked forward optimistically to a future when, once more, it could truly be regarded as its homeland's premier defence force. Yet, in 1946, there had been little cause for such optimism. Demobilisation of its vast wartime strength in personnel and aircraft quickly reduced the RAF's fighter force to a mere 26 squadrons, of which three were transparently 'non-operational', and all suffered from true depletion in adequate manning and updated equipment. The realistic Robb, after assessing the initial peacetime strength of his new command in late 1945, duly reported to the Air Ministry that if Britain was attacked in the near future, Fighter Command would be unable to defend the country. Moreover, he added, it would need at least two years to rebuild, reorganise and restrengthen if it was to meet even the needs of the role required from it by 1945–6 standards. His report was never intended as a reproach, or as any form of 'bureaucrat-bashing'; it was an objectively-viewed statement of the facts, phrased to leave no doubt as to existing state and placed on record as a basis for serious consideration by the air hierarchy in order to have put in hand all necessary rectification of the situation.

The reaction from the Air Staff was to agree in broad principle to a complete re-thinking about the Command, its ground control system and early warning capability. Equally a programme of 'development research' was to be undertaken, to probe the new 'mystery' areas of high speed and high altitude operational flying. This foisting of two distinctly separate responsibilities upon his command led Robb, in 1946, to report to his Whitehall masters, 'It is estimated that during the period of research and experiment the effectiveness of the air defences provided over the active area will approximate to that achieved under the old system during the war.' It was a diplomatic yet succinct exposition of Robb's view of the weakness and obsolescence of his command's contemporary capability, apart from including an inferred protest at being shouldered with tasks which normally should have been undertaken by the RAF and other scientific establishments created for such experimentation and pure research. Nevertheless, the RAF High Speed Flight, under the aegis of Fighter Command, eagerly undertook successive experiments aimed at reaching speeds in the region of the elusive sound barrier. Its pilots, including Neville Duke, 'Bill' Waterton, and the commanding officer Group Captain E. M. Donaldson, utilised souped-up versions of the RAF's then standard jet fighter, the Meteor, for these trials, but soon realised that their aircraft were simply not capable of piercing the speed of sound 'barrier'. The existing jet engines certainly had sufficient reserve power, but the Meteor's (and Vampire's) airframe design was incapable of becoming supersonic without a distinct possibility of total disintegration; in layman's terms, they were 'the wrong shape'. The ramifications were obvious – no contemporary RAF frontline fighter was ever likely to operate at supersonic performance in the forms then existing. In view of known progress towards true transonic designs in aircraft under trial in both the Russian and American air services at that time, it was a disquieting thought.

Regrettably, this situation was highly exacerbated by a particularly obtuse decision by the recently-created Ministry of Supply which laid down that all research into supersonic flight would be undertaken by the use of small, radio-controlled vehicles launched from conventional airborne aircraft; *not* by pure aircraft designs. As Peter Wykeham expressed it: 'This was probably one of the worst decisions in the history of British aviation, costing the aircraft industry untold technical progress, and losing it in five years the hard-won lead it had gained in aerodynamic design.'[1] In the event the experimentation with unmanned devices proved both enormously wasteful and, more significantly, pointless. The after-effects of such an unnecessary diversion of effort (and costs) were to seriously delay proper concentration upon the design and introduction of true transonic fighters for Britain's defence arm.

[1] *Fighter Command*; Putnam, 1960.

If the British aviation industry was severely hampered by lack of official urging in the context of transonic exploration, it continued – albeit slowly, and by trial and error – to pursue privately its own experiments in the long-established tradition which had, in the past, given the RAF some of its most outstanding aircraft eventually. At de Havilland's, John Cunningham regained the International Altitude Record by taking a pressurised-cabin version of the Vampire to a height of 59,492 feet; while J. D. Derry, DFC, set up a new 100-km closed circuit course record of 605.23 mph in the swept-wing DH 108, and in the same design eventually achieved Mach 1 in 1948. Meantime, the company had developed the DH 112 Venom (originally designated Vampire FB8) to Specification F.15/49 as a successor to the Vampire in firstline squadrons – an interim-stage fighter-bomber to fill the gap between the already out-dated Meteor and Vampire and the latest generation of jet fighters taking shape on the industry's drawing boards which would much later emerge as the Hawker Hunter and Supermarine Swift. The first prototype Venom, VV612, made its first flight, at Hatfield, on 2 September 1949; and delivery to the RAF eventually commenced in April 1952. Another Air Ministry specification F.3/48 was responsible for the Hawker P.1067 design, from which was to come the magnificent Hunter fighter. Yet another future RAF fighter, the delta-wing Gloster Javelin, also had its origins in a 1948 specification, although it was to be February 1956 before this twin-jet engined two-seater – the first of its particular type in the world's air forces – actually began to equip an RAF squadron. Undoubtedly the distant future looked reasonably bright in terms of aircraft equipment for Fighter Command, but to James Robb, and his successor Air Marshal Sir William Elliott who took up the reins of command in November 1947, the contemporary scene was unpromising.

With little alternative readily available the command was forced to continue to rely on the Meteor and Vampire as its main jet force, while wartime designs, such as the Spitfire and ubiquitous Mosquito, continued to 'take up the slack' in overall strength. In the immediate post-bellum period such a situation was not as dangerous for Britain as may have been thought by the more fanatical fringe of aviation stalwarts. The likelihood of an aerial assault from any quarter was reasonably remote, and in any case any such attack would have been made by aircraft of virtually 1945 standards, with equal vintage weaponry. In consequence, in the Meteor and Vampire Fighter Command possessed excellent modern interceptors perfectly capable of fulfilling their designated role. Equally, although the back-up radar and other facets of the ground control had hardly progressed from its wartime efficiency levels, it remained – at least temporarily – adequate for its purpose.

If such a 'balance' in power produced any euphoria in governmental minds, this *status quo* was rudely shattered during the summer of 1949. Until that time both British and American scientific intelligence had assumed confidently that the state of British and American nuclear development would not be equalled, let alone overtaken, by Russia before 1952 at the earliest. Then, in 1949, clear evidence of a Russian nuclear device being exploded successfully necessitated a rapid re-assessment of the Anglo-American position in the nuclear arms race and armament generally. Combined with known Russian development in the jet bomber field, a strong potential threat to western security now existed. British reaction was swift, and the Air Ministry initiated virtual 'crash' specifications for a wide range of surface-to-air and air-to-air missiles, and air-to-ground radar or TV-guided bombs and devices. It also placed extra emphasis on the urgent need to speed up all existing development programmes in the transonic fighter field, and gave extra importance to the jet bomber production envisaged years earlier when the English Electric Canberra and – later – V-bombers' series were first mooted and tested in prototype.

The combination of a potentially hostile nation possessing both nuclear weaponry and a carrier jet bomber presented an entirely fresh dilemma for Fighter Command and its whole defence organisation. Patently the existing interception system of sub-sonic fighters and wartime-orientated reporting control *et al* was seriously obsolete. To permit even a single nuclear-armed raider to slip through the defences would invite disaster on a scale unprecedented in human history. The long and hard-won tradition and experience of Britain's aerial shield was, for all practical purposes, wiped clean from the slate; the command would need to start almost from scratch to rebuild and re-form to meet entirely fresh situations. It meant new ideas and concepts in aircraft designs and strategical thinking, unblinkered by all past practice. Sober consideration by British Service chiefs recognised that any real attack could not be mounted immediately; there was a 'breathing space' in which to prepare any countermeasures. Yet any such 'gap' was now disturbingly short, compared with the period of grace which the western powers had confidently expected to be available to them.

167

If the western powers' Service and civil hierarchy appeared to have been caught napping by Russia's speedy entry into the nuclear age – and there can be little argument that this was so – it did not mean that such a situation had not been at least considered and partly catered for in the Air Ministry's forward planning for the aerial defences of the United Kingdom. Production orders were able to be placed for the first Hawker Hunters in October 1950, and a month later for the Supermarine Swift. Within ten months both types had made their first testing flights. In November 1951 the first Gloster Javelin delta-wing all-weather fighter made its 'maiden' flight. Nevertheless, all three were still sub-sonic in performance. The crucial need for even these designs was underlined by a review of Fighter Command at UK bases in June 1950. Of the 33 squadrons, including the Auxiliary units, eleven were Meteor-equipped, and five flew Vampires. Of the remaining seventeen squadrons, no less than twelve were soldiering on with the final variants of the aged Spitfire; three relied on Mosquitos and the other pair had DH Hornets. In other words, more than half were operating piston-engined fighters, with ten-year-old weaponry. None were capable of piercing the Mach 1 speed barrier. Russia's 'jump' had achieved surprise in probably the most important criterion – time.

In the same month as the review mentioned, an event on the other side of the globe occurred which was to have even more impact on the RAF's outlook. On 25 June 1950 North Korean forces crossed the '38th Parallel' into South Korea and precipitated a long and bloody war which enmeshed most of the western (and eastern) powers. Sixteen nations pledged support for South Korea, including Britain, and all came under a unified USA command leadership from July 8th. Within six months the British government announced plans to expedite British rearmament, and called up its reservists, at the same time postponing demobilisation of many long-term regular Servicemen *pro tem*. Part of this programme was a ten-fold increase in the annual RAF intake of student pilots (from 300 to 3,000), with an additional plea for some 500 ex-navigators to volunteer for further service. The Royal Auxiliary Air Force was placed on three months' continuous training.

The main United Nations fighters to oppose the North Korean air service were the Gloster Meteor 8, in Australian squadrons, and the American F-86 Sabre jet. By the close of 1951 intensive combat experience had proved conclusively that neither design was any real match for the Russian MiG-15 jets employed by the 'North Koreans' (many of whom were Russian 'volunteers' wearing appropriate Korean uniform). Several experienced RAF fighter pilots were 'attached' to USAF squadrons to gain experience of a modern, all-jet mode of aerial combat, and were able to confirm the inferiority of Britain's Meteors for such fighting. The marginal difference in performance between the American Sabre and the Russian MiG-15 was compensated by the much superior experience and training of the American pilots; and by the close of the Korean agony years later, Sabre pilots could honestly claim some 16 MiG-15s shot down for every Sabre lost in combat. Nevertheless, the Sabre's weak point was its armament. It used wing batteries of six .50 machine guns – weapons which had armed the Thunderbolts and Mustangs of 1943–5. At combat closing speeds nudging Mach 1 level, such guns were effectively too slow in rate of fire to concentrate sufficient fire-weight on any target.

This question of updated weapons for modern jet fighters in the 1950s was particularly highlighted in the context of the RAF's first-line aircraft. At the end of the war in 1945, Fighter Command's aircraft were armed with .303-inch calibre machine guns and/or 20mm cannons; weapons conceived a decade or more previously, and concepts in fighter armament already considered obsolete in the German Luftwaffe in 1939. Bearing in mind the simple basic requirement of any fighter aircraft as a vehicle to convey appropriate armament from point A to point B and thereafter destroy a target – i.e., a flying gun platform – the whole field of airborne armament deserves studying in relation to any particular period of combat history. In the context of RAF Fighter Command, the lack of any progress in development of armament specifically for its front-line defensive aircraft can be judged by comparison with the armament used operationally by the Luftwaffe in precisely the same role in 1943–5. By 1944 Messerschmitt 262 twin-jet fighters defending Germany from the Allied bomber streams were armed with six 30mm MK 108 guns and 48 rockets; while it was intended within the year to uprate such offensive power by a replacement installation of a 50mm MK-214A gun. Other armament used operationally by the Me 262 during the closing month of the European war included a battery of 48 R.4/M missiles attached below the wings. The efficacy of this latter installation can be judged by an attack made by just six Me 262s on a box of B-17 Fortresses in early 1945, when 14 B-17s were destroyed for no German losses.

Even before 1939 German armament specialists had recognised the

169

basic precept that an airborne gun needed to satisfy criteria entirely different to those applied to guns for use in the army or navy. Britain's 'convenient' and continuing reliance on adapted infantry weapons for use in air combat had reduced the potential effectiveness of even her latest fighter designs before 1940. The operational introduction of the 20mm Hispano cannon in 1940 was timely, but in essence, a stop-gap born of necessity. Its continued use throughout the rest of the war, though justified in terms of readily-available production stocks and replacements etc., did nothing to progress British airborne armament parallel with the increasing performance ranges of succeeding fighter designs, and – from a purely technical viewpoint – was outdated when the first Meteor jets entered RAF squadron service in 1944. The same could be said of the lack of urgent progression in the design and ballistic qualities of the ammunition employed – something already studied and advanced greatly by the German ballistic experts during the war.

The continued use of the 20mm Hispano cannon as the standard armament for British fighters in the post-1945 era, especially in the command's first jet fighter, was stark evidence of the failure of British and Allied air technicians to reap the rich harvest of scientific data and 'ironmongery' which became available to them in the post-war Allied occupation of Germany. A wealth of ultra-modern armament, either in operational use and/or under advanced development was – in the main – overlooked, destroyed, or simply ignored. Some of the finest German scientists in this field of research were literally told that their long years of practical experience and knowledge were 'of little or no value' to the Allied authorities; thereby driving such men into the highly appreciative hands of Russian authorities who proceeded to exacerbate the situation by inaugurating a deliberate campaign of suppressing or actually destroying documents and hardware to prevent such vital material falling into Allied hands. Even items relative to German fighter armament transferred to Britain received scant attention in relation to its importance. The few more visionary British officials who realised the value of culling this wealth of scientific data, and therefore attempted to offer employment to the aircraft-gun designers who had worked for the Mauser and Rheinmetall-Borsig firms, were in the event over-ridden by 'higher authority'.

Though it was reprehensible in many ways, this general lack of interest in picking the brains of some of the most inventive and ingenious armament technicians then existing was simply an extension, and perhaps an inevitable product, of the traditional methods of approach by past British aeronautical manufacturers and designers to the creation of any operational aircraft for the RAF. Put at its simplest, aircraft were designed to meet certain performance criteria, and – all too often – armament was then 'stuck on' as almost an afterthought. It was a 'Christmas tree' mentality which was (and indeed still is to a much smaller degree) clearly evidenced by many of the RAF's frontline aircraft designs throughout its long history. Only after World War Two was serious consideration given to producing both aircraft and appropriate armament as a single entity – as a true weapons 'system'. It is perfectly true that there were examples of 'half-way', interim designs in which the design's intended armament was considered from the outset, yet in virtually every case the ultimate machine to emerge from the factory for issue to the RAF had been very considerably modified – in the weaponry context – from the original thoughts. And even then Service testing under combat conditions often forced re-thinking as theoretical 'advantages' quickly exhibited distinct disadvantages at the sharp end.

Even allowing for the time necessary to design and produce any new automatic weapon – usually estimated conservatively as anything from five to ten years – the failure of British officialdom to grasp the abundant material and data from German sources in 1945 was to add a totally unnecessary five or six years' delay to the progression of truly modern defence weapons for Fighter Command's task in the 1950s and 1960s. Compounding this picture of lethargy was the post-1945 adoption of the 30mm Aden gun as a successor to the obsolete 20mm Hispano for future RAF fighters. The original Aden automatic gun was copied from the Mauser 40mm (via a Chinese adaptation), and thus – like every other major air gun used by the RAF, with the exception of the Vickers 40mm 'S' cannon – of non-British origin. Though used in various forms by the Luftwaffe (i.e., guns of the same barrel calibre), the type had been considered inadequate by German armament experts as early as 1941. Yet Britain calmly intended to equip post-war designed jet fighters with such a weapon for use in the prime defence role of the late 1950s. Admittedly, it was originally adopted simply as an interim between the wartime reliance on conventional cannons and the envisaged future airborne missiles, but its use in fighters only entering service in the mid-1950s illustrated the tardiness of Britain's entry into the missile era of the fighter arm of the RAF.

171

Life on the fighter squadrons in Britain in the first decade of peace gradually returned to a semblance of its 'golden era' in the 1930s, when the RAF had been described in cynical quarters as the 'finest flying club in the world'. The drab camouflage markings of the wartime period were gradually replaced by a return to the 'silver' paintwork of pre-1938 days on fighter aircraft, the first such scheme being promulgated in early 1946, which stated that all fighter aircraft were to be in either natural metal or glossy aluminium finish. Two years later official approval was given for the colourful heraldry of individual squadron markings to be applied to aircraft in modified form; usually the squadron badge on the nose section. Night fighters of this period continued to employ a form of camouflage in grey and green overall. The actual change from wartime drabs to peacetime 'silver' was a gradual process during the first three years, but by 1950 most day fighters were resplendent in silver finish, with extensions of bright colour markings along the flanks (or noses) of the airframe. Another pre-war custom to be revived slowly was the fashion for squadrons to form an aerobatics formation or even Flight internally; an 'art form' of flying with a long RAF tradition which has continued to this day in ever-increasing precision, skill and pure showmanship of a superb standard. Pilots, too, began to revive – perhaps, 'continue' would be a more appropriate description – the old custom of adorning their flying overalls with full-size cloth and wire unit badges. All these manifestations were an indication of the individual and corporate pride in being identified with a specific unit and, especially, with any fighter squadron.

Of the men themselves, there continued to be far more civilian volunteers for pilot training in the RAF than there were establishments to fill. Within the ranks of the RAF, too, were many hundreds of young airmen, particularly ex-Halton apprentice 'regulars', who had volunteered for air crew duties as early as 1944–5 and who had yet to be remustered to air crew u/t (under training). Thousands of young men – a majority too young to have seen wartime service – eagerly applied to enlist in the RAF for flying duties, thus permitting the much-reduced post-bellum RAF to be highly selective in its recruitment for the foreseeable future. Of the more senior pilots already on the squadrons, most posts from Flight Lieutenant to Wing Commander were filled by ex-operational men from the war; both regulars and those who had elected to extend their 'duration (of the war) only' engagements to a permanent career. Many were well beribboned with gallantry and campaign medals, though almost all had 'dropped' one or even two ranks from their acting status of 1945. Such veterans provided a continuation 'spine' of hard experience and intimate knowledge of the operation of fighter aircraft, and incidentally served as inspiration and example for the freshly-joined, peacetime-trained youngsters steadily filling the squadrons.

If actual pay and short-term promotion prospects were not of the most encouraging during this build-up period, there was a host of compensations 'in kind' for the newly-graduated fighter pilot; not least the simple fact that he was now a *fighter* pilot; inheritor of a tradition established by many of the now legendary names of military aviation history. Inevitably perhaps, the immediate post-war RAF inherited too the pre-war, and wartime, policy of mixing commissioned and non-commissioned pilots on any squadron. On obtaining his 'wings' brevet, a new pilot was then automatically promoted either to Sergeant or Pilot Officer, according to the view taken of his purely non-flying qualities of character, background and education. It was a policy of curiously mixed origins; ostensibly on a foundation of selection of future 'leaders' and eventual very senior staff officers, but undeniably a continuing manifestation of the peculiar 'class' distinctions which are inherent in the British character. Leaving aside the incurable matter of 'class' prejudices, the justification of deciding a pilot's future potential for higher responsibilities of command was, to say the least, questionable in relation to the criteria applied by contemporary 'selection' and 'commissioning' boards of interviewers. For merely one example, one Sergeant pilot during 1940 later became Chief of the Air Staff. . . .

In most matters relating to actual flying and operations, rank played little part on the fighter squadrons, and all members of a particular unit regarded themselves as of equal status in this context. Nevertheless, the segregation of pilots off-duty into their respective ranks and therefore RAF standing was not entirely conducive to the integration of effort and mutual co-operation in the prime role which marked the very best squadrons. It needed only one class- or rank-conscious junior officer, or even Flight commander, to disrupt the otherwise smooth operational efforts of any individual unit. In general, though, such situations were thankfully few and easily remedied by any squadron commander who kept a close eye on the internal running of his unit. Diplomacy was at a premium in such matters, particularly in view of the conscious higher policy of returning the peacetime RAF to the more discipline-conscious

173

standards of the pre-1939 Service. The situation began to be rational-ised by the mid-1950s when, in Germany initially, all fighter pilots were in future to be only commissioned officers, and existing NCO fighter pilots were shunted into other flying duties – often prosaic duties such as 'driving' the normal Station Flight transport aircraft on most RAF stations in the UK. The pros and cons of such a general decision created a fair amount of criticism and dissatisfaction among the younger SNCO pilots, but – objectively speaking – at least provided a basis for future harmony and policy in regard to the manning of RAF fighter squadrons.

13. Beyond Sound

The first real step towards an all-jet Fighter Command came with the introduction of the Hawker Hunter in July 1954, when No. 43 'Fighting Cocks' Squadron at Leuchars received their latest equipment. Along with Nos. 54 and 222 Squadrons, the 'Cocks' were issued initially with Hunter F.1 versions, but quickly discovered that above certain altitudes pilots could not use the four-gun (Aden 30mm) pack as firing caused engine surge. The F.2 version, with an Armstrong Siddeley Sapphire engine in place of the F.1's Rolls-Royce Avon, did not suffer such a drawback, and entered RAF service with 257 and 263 Squadrons at Wattisham at the close of 1954. The Hunter design thereafter was progressively modified and improved; the most-built variant being the F.6 which first saw squadron service in 1956, and within two years equipped every RAF day fighter unit in Europe. With a maximum speed of 715 mph at sea-level (or Mach .95), a climb to 45,000 feet in just over seven minutes, and range (with drop tanks) of over 1800 miles, the F.6 was an admirable interceptor for its time. Its 4×30mm Aden guns armament could be supplemented by 2,000lb of bombs on wing carriers, or several alternative war loads on pylons *et al*. In all, 14 UK-based squadrons came to use the F.6 Hunter, and all pilots were unanimous in their praise for the design's liquid manoeuvrability and pleasant controls. These handling characteristics were exemplified when a formation aerobatics team from 111 Squadron, nicknamed the 'Black Arrows', made their first public performance in April 1957. In less than two years the sleek black Hunters of 'Treble-One' Squadron had become, without question, the finest aerobatics team in the world, reaching a peak of perfection with a 22-aircraft loop in immaculate formation at the 1958 Farnborough Air Show. Three years later the 'Arrows' were superseded as Fighter Command's representative

175

aerobatics team by the royal-blue Hunters of 92 Squadron, the 'Blue Diamonds', who worthily upheld the standards pioneered by 'Treble-One'.

Nearly two years after the Hunter's operational debut, 46 Squadron, based at Odiham, began receiving its first delta-wing fighters, the Gloster Javelin 'all-weather' interceptors. The performance of the Javelin, which was incidentally the first delta-wing fighter for the RAF, was inferior to the Hunter, but its twin jet engines and two-man crew, apart from the ample space for installation of multi-radar 'boxes' and other equipment, made it highly suitable for night interception defence units. Its appellation 'all-weather' was perhaps a misnomer, implying an aircraft which could defy anything the mighty elements cared to manifest; shortly after its introduction to squadron service a scheduled fly-past over London was cancelled with an Air Ministry 'spokesman's' ironic explanation, 'Due to weather conditions . . .' The initial Mk 1 Javelins issued to the RAF were generally considered by many pilots to have been the best version Javelin to see squadron use. It was undoubtedly a 'pilot's aeroplane', with all vital equipment and controls close to hand, easy to operate, and simple to check. From a 'cold start' the Javelin could be airborne ('wheels-up') from a tele-briefed 'Scramble' order in less than two minutes, and its ceiling of 45,000 feet was reached quicker than in subsequent Marks. The cockpit was well designed, comfortable, although actual cockpit lighting was considered 'archaic' by most contemporary standards. Its handling qualities were thought to be excellent, though at speeds exceeding Mach 0.91 the elevators became virtually inoperative, and the aircraft could be '. . . a bit of a beast' at very low or very high altitude. Its greatest fault, from a pilot's viewpoint, was its poor stall recovery characteristics. Normal stall recovery was almost impossible in a Javelin Mk 1, which quickly deterred most pilots from operating the design to its operational limits.

In February 1954, only weeks before the first Hawker Hunters joined 43 Squadron, another swept-wing jet fighter, the Supermarine Swift, began to equip 56 Squadron. Produced as a 'safeguard' design should the Hunter prove a disappointment, the Swift in fact was a somewhat dismal failure in its intended role of day interceptor. The Swift's performance was so severely limited, and its handling qualities so poor for operational employment, that despite prodigious labour, modifications, and trials, subsequent Swift variants could not produce the characteristics vital for a firstline defender, and the type was eventually used, in Germany only, as a 'fighter-reconnaissance' machine. The Swift's only real claim to fame was when a Mk 4 prototype, WK198 piloted by Lt-Commander Mike Lithgow, set a new world air speed record of 737.7 mph on 25 September 1953, and subsequently broke several other associated records. In Service use the Swift was under-armed – usually only two 30mm Aden guns and supplemental rockets or bombs – which, combined with the design's undesirable longitudinal control characteristics and no little engine deficiencies, condemned the type for Fighter Command's needs.

If the Hunter was the only real advance in updated equipment to reach the command's operational squadrons by the end of the first decade of 'peace', this was no fault of Britain's aviation industry. Due to the disastrous decisions taken by 'higher authorities' immediately after the war, to pursue research into transonic flight by means of unmanned or robot vehicles rather than manned aircraft, the industry had been forced to shelve or even cancel several distinctly promising aircraft designs – not least of these being the Miles M.52 supersonic research aircraft in 1946. Only in the early 1950s was the industry really able to pick up the traces again and surge ahead with true transonic research. In this interim period the RAF generally, and Fighter Command in particular, was left with no alternative but to improvise with 'stretched' and 'improved' versions of such jet aircraft as had already entered service i.e., the Meteor, Vampire and English Electric Canberra. Each design, excellent in its contemporary climate of operational needs, was to produce long lines of new variants for virtually every possible RAF role in both Bomber and Fighter Commands for many years. Even by 1948 the folly of the 'unmanned vehicle' research programme was realised by the Ministry of Supply, and talks were held with the leading British aeronautical industrialists with a view to inaugurating supersonic aircraft research as quickly as possible.

Of the several new aircraft design projects then undertaken, the most significant – from Fighter Command's point of view – was that of the English Electric Company, where, under the direction of its designer W. E. W. Petter, the company in effect 'leap-frogged' the more normal stage of producing first a research aircraft and then a Service fighter design. Instead Petter's team produced a supersonic fighter designated the P.1, and used this concept to meet the Air Ministry's 1949 Specification (F.23/49) for a supersonic day fighter/interceptor. It was a bold step into the future by any conventional standards, and was to

177

produce the English Electric Lightning fighter – acknowledged on its eventual appearance as the finest fighter in the world. In effect the company had undertaken the design and production of a transonic aircraft, capable of full operational Service use, in one scratch-to-squadron stage; the outcome was a superb fighter by any possible criteria. The first prototype P.1, WG760, made its initial test flight from Boscombe Down on 4 August 1954 in the highly capable hands of Wing Commander Roland Beamont, and reached a speed of Mach 0.85. Only a week later the same P.1 achieved a speed in excess of Mach 1 – the speed of sound – in level flight; the first aircraft in Britain to fly supersonically in such circumstances.

Within four years of Beamont's initial flights, the first Lightning (as the design was now named) production Mk 1 was flying; and in July 1960 No. 74 'Tiger' Squadron, based at Coltishall, Norfolk, began to receive the first examples of this magnificent new fighter. By then the Lightning's original design chief, Petter, had left the English Electric Company to join the Folland Company; and from 1950 the Lightning design team had been headed by F. W. Page. The Lightning was received with loud acclaim by its Service pilots; here at last was an interceptor with both the 'urge' and the 'punch' to tackle anything a potential aggressor cared to send against them. Handling was excellent – a 'pilot's aeroplane' – and day-to-day flying, servicing and general turn-round maintenance presented no insurmountable problems for air or ground crews, even on such an unconventional, heavy 'brute'. The considerable advance exemplified by the Lightning – the Mk 1a was rated at a maximum speed of Mach 2.3 (1500 mph) at 36,000 feet, and had a Service ceiling of more than 60,000 feet – could be illustrated in contemporary terms by the simple fact that the design was capable of twice the performance of the Hawker Hunter. Its greatest significance to Fighter Command, however, was that the Lightning had been produced from the outset as an integrated weapons system, not simply a fast gun-platform or carrier. In other words, its airframe, engines, armament, radar fire-control and auto-controls were wholly co-ordinated in a single overall concept. As such the Lightning was the first RAF single-pilot fighter ever in such a guise. The built-in radar fire-control and locked-in navigational and 'homing' equipment were such that, when using air-to-air missiles, a Lightning pilot was not necessarily in visual contact with his target when he fired.

The introduction of the Lightning – the RAF's first 'jump' across the elusive sound 'barrier' into a transonic, nuclear-shaded era of aerial defence – was timely for the immediate and near-future security of the United Kingdom. That it actually entered service was virtually a close decision, for in April 1957 the then Minister of Defence, Duncan Sandys, presented to Parliament a Defence White Paper which seriously compromised the RAF's future in several vital aspects. The two main ploys of this ill-advised statement for future defence policies which affected the RAF were the intention substantially to run down overall RAF strength in aircraft and replace these with a form of nuclear deterrent i.e., a V-bomber 'quick reaction' force capable of delivering atomic bombs; and a bland statement that 'fighter aircraft will in due course be replaced by a ground-to-air guided missile system'. This latter intention clearly indicated a run-down in manned aircraft – and hence a need for trained pilots – within Fighter Command. Indeed, the only major role for such a future command was envisaged as merely defenders of the V-bomber base airfields – chained watchdogs in a purely defensive role. Added to the government decision, announced in the same year, that National Service would end after 1960, the effect of the Sandys' paper on RAF morale – and civilian recruiting for the Service – was depressing. Recognised now as possibly the most mistaken policy statement in the history of UK defence, the Sandys Paper cast a deep shadow over a number of aeronautical projects in being which were on the brink of fruition, leading to cancellations of such future RAF weapons as the superb TSR2 low-level strike aircraft and the Blue Streak stand-off bomb. Not for the first time by a long chalk, the RAF was to be expected to carry heavy and far-ranging responsibilities with a vastly reduced means of fulfilling such responsibilities.

If the immediate effect of this statement was to give every RAF fighter pilot serious doubts about his future career prospects, it must be pointed out that the Air Ministry had rather different ideas about the future use of certain missiles. In July 1958 the first Bristol-Ferranti Bloodhound ground-to-air defence missiles entered service at RAF North Coates, but the Air Staff's clear intention was for these to be used in conjunction with manned fighter defences, not as replacements for piloted aircraft. In similar vein, the introduction later of THOR intermediate range ballistic missiles (IRBMs) to Bomber Command were supplemental to the various Victor, Valiant and Vulcan V-bombers in more conventionally-equipped squadrons. It might have been

179

considered a minor psychological error for such collections of 'wingless wonders' to be officially labelled as Squadrons, but tact in the abstracts of hangar-floor-level RAF matters had never been recognised by the men at the sharp end as any particularly obvious characteristic of Whitehall hierarchy.

The general reaction in non-RAF circles to the Sandys' Defence Paper was vociferous, noisy and, occasionally, fiery; particularly on the question of the apparent determination by the existing government to run down all manned aircraft. In 1958, partly in view of this widespread criticism, but partly to appease some of Britain's more outspoken NATO partners, the Minister of Supply affirmed a production order for the English Electric P.1b – forerunner of the superb Lightning – and the Chief of the Air Staff, Sir Dermot Boyle, convened a meeting of industrial, professional and Service heads to outline and explain the RAF's future commitments and how these were to be met. Among his main points was the clear intention of the RAF to continue to need and use manned aircraft 'for as far into the future as can be foreseen', alongside flexibly graduated deterrents such as the guided missile and nuclear bomb. Boyle also stated that by the beginning of 1963, after the cessation of National Service, the aim was to recruit and maintain an all-regular RAF of 120,000 airmen, all ranks. This diplomatic rebuttal of the rumoured prospect of an 'unmanned', all-robot RAF was also strengthened in the autumn of 1959 when the Prime Minister, Harold Macmillan, addressed cadets and staff at the RAF's Cranwell College, and laid especial emphasis on the Service's continuing need for the human element.

Such reassurances notwithstanding, the damage to the morale and, particularly, air crew recruitment of the RAF could not be repaired immediately. The evidence for this necessitated yet further reassurance from the Secretary of State for Air, Julian Amery, in 1961 when he bluntly stated that the RAF was still not getting sufficient pilots and navigators to train, and commented that it was his belief that this was due to 'the widespread belief that there is no future in flying and that in a few years the Air Force will have nothing but ground-based missiles.' Encouragement for this view that the RAF would continue to require jet aircraft crews was the existing pilot training scheme. In August 1955 all-jet instruction had commenced at No. 2 Flying Training School (FTS) at Hullavington when the Jet Provost (replacement for the piston-engined Provost trainer) came into use regularly. The first pilot to benefit from the new syllabus went solo after just eight and a half hours' instruction in dual flying. Though later the RAF was to revert to *ab initio* instruction on piston-engined trainers before graduating to jet aircraft, it at least pointed the way forward. Further 'bait' to recruitment of air crew officers was the Short Service Commissions' scheme introduced in 1961. Hitherto, post-1945 commissions had entailed a minimum of 16 years service, or reaching age 38, whichever was later. The SSC scheme permitted an officer to 'retire' after eight years or twelve years, with respective gratuities of £1500 or £4000. Those opting to remain in service were guaranteed an engagement to age 38, with further opportunity to 'sign on' until age 55 if selected.

With the Hunter and Javelin already in service, and now the Lightning, the government was already looking to the future requirements for the RAF. In 1961 an operational requirement for a vertical/short take off and landing (V/STOL) ground-attack design was referred to in Parliament; while development of the Hawker P.1127 Kestrel had already been agreed. From the Kestrel was eventually to come the Hawker Siddeley Harrier: the first VTOL operational fighter to enter regular squadron service in any air force in the world. Such official preparations boded reasonably well for a future RAF to rely as ever on manned aircraft, and helped assuage the gloom and false philosophies of the Sandys Paper. Nevertheless, wide-ranging changes in overall strategy and organisation were about to affect Fighter Command. In December 1960 the Minister of Defence announced a fresh aspect of UK air defence policy for the immediate future. Henceforth the United Kingdom was to be but one of four NATO air defence regions, and thus RAF Fighter Command was to operate under the aegis of the Supreme Allied Command Europe (SACEUR), based then in Paris. Accordingly, the AOC-in-C, Fighter Command, Sir Hector McGregor, assumed an additional title of Commander UK Air Defence Region with effect from 1 May 1962.

The interdependence of Britain upon NATO's early warning defence organisation had been evident since 1954, and the command was well practised in co-operation with Britain's NATO allies' air services; but the concept of direct control from 'outside' the command and country raised serious doubts in a large number of minds. It smacked too heavily of the situation which had faced Hugh Dowding in early 1940, when near-hysterical demands for Fighter Command strength to be severely diluted merely to boost French inadequacies had hovered on the brink of stripping Britain of its only sure aerial shield. Objective assessment of the relative situation pertaining in the early 1960s, however, brought the hard realisation that Britain's future security in any nuclear-headed conflict could never be guaranteed by withholding the RAF in isolation. Only as a completely integrated partner and segment of an overall NATO alliance and organisation could Britain have any chance of being defended from a nuclear holocaust in the event of war. This theme of integration of the armed services was exemplified in Britain on 1 April 1964, on which date a unified Ministry of Defence, with overall authority vested in a single Secretary of State for Defence, merged the previously separate Army, Navy and RAF ministries. Henceforward the Air Council became the Air Force Board, while the Secretary of State for Air became re-titled Minister of Defence for the RAF.

Thus, Fighter Command, and indeed the RAF generally, entered the 1960s with the same basic responsibilities and roles in relation to its mother country as in years past. Nevertheless, the command was no longer simply an esoteric national safeguard in isolation. Henceforth, increasingly so, it was to be one segment of an integrated western European shield against any form of aggression or threat to international peace. For the moment it at least retained its individual title as a distinct formation within the RAF's structure, but its days as a succinct community, virtually self-controlled, were numbered as the western allies adapted their strategy to meet the needs of a twentieth century nuclear-power-muscled struggle for superior status – and the hovering abstract nightmare of a possible nuclear holocaust. Essentially, the roles of Fighter Command's pilots were of watch and ward in the aerial approaches to the United Kingdom, and a smaller but no less important forward reconnaissance capability, though the latter task was mainly allotted to the squadrons in France and western Germany. The constant, round-the-clock vigilance necessary to protect Britain from aerial invasion was linked with a radar network whose tentacles and ultra-sensitive antennae stretched to limits undreamed of in the anxious months of 1940; an intricate 'spider's web' which would shimmer in warning vibration at the slightest touch, and thereby alert pilots and crews seated and strapped into interceptors with engines idling for instant take-off and investigation.

In a sense Fighter Command had come full circle. Born as a purely defensive force for metropolitan protection, it had fulfilled that role superbly when Britain had been under mortal threat in 1940 and, later, in 1944. In the interim years it had also stretched its muscles and pursued a strike, offensive role in tactical and part-strategical support of the Allied intention to recapture a fettered Europe from the black clutch of Nazidom. For many years after the war the command had reverted to a mainly defensive role, but always retained a capability for 'leaning forward' in the offensive pattern. By the late 1950s, however, Britain's true strike power lay with the V-bomber force, poised constantly for any necessary nuclear 'retaliation', though ostensibly labelled as a 'deterrent'; part of the so-termed 'Trip-wire Strategy' then in vogue among western military chiefs. Under this mode of 'defence' Fighter Command became a kennelled watch-dog protection for the V-bomber bases, ensuring security of the bomber take-off platforms. Even to have attempted to provide a more traditional 'all-round' aerial interception defence was by then overtly impossible to guarantee – and to permit even a handful of nuclear bomb-armed invaders to slip through the curtain would be catastrophic in result. In December 1962, as a result of the Nassau Agreement, the nuclear deterrent responsibility was passed to the Royal Navy, and the RAF, though maintaining V-bomber power to add to the 'flexible weapons' policy of the western allies, turned more towards becoming a force of strategic mobility. The latter role was partly of necessity as former overseas bases were rapidly closed down, but proved to be a short-lived policy.

In 1968 the 'Trip-wire Strategy' – massive nuclear retaliation – was officially declared 'dead', and was replaced by a policy of 'flexible response'. This foresaw an initial phase in any future war of 'conventional' (i.e., non-nuclear) warfare, involving 'conventional' weaponry and machines. Whether such a policy resulted from 'adapting' strategic thinking to the stark facts of weaponry actually available is a moot point for debate. Certainly in 1968 – the fiftieth anniversary of the original formation of the Royal Air Force – British military air power was at its lowest quantitative level in 20 years; possessing an *overall* total of 2526 aircraft of *every* type – of which only 1902 were actually considered 'operational'. The majority of the latter, even then, were not first-line strike aircraft, capable of taking offensive action. This state of affairs was a direct result of governmental decisions in 1965, when virtually 'at a stroke' the incumbent politicians abruptly cancelled the development and future production plans for several new aircraft designs which the RAF was depending on for eventual re-equipment.

183

Far advanced strike designs, like the TSR2 and Hawker P.1154, were calmly assigned to oblivion on the grounds of 'economy'. It was the real start of an era of reduction and 'pruning' of the RAF which has continued even to the present day. In his book *The Royal Air Force. The Past 30 Years*,[1] ex-RAF author A. G. T. James commented on this governmental cut-back, 'in the economic climate of 1965, no British government regardless of complexion could have accepted the costs of equipping even one or two RAF squadrons with this magnificent aircraft' (referring to the TSR2 specifically); yet it is difficult to evaluate 'costs' when these are balanced against possible total destruction of Britain's industrial capacity, and indeed its whole future.

If the RAF was dismayed by the 'economic' cuts imposed in 1965, it was to suffer even worse shocks three years later when a further programme of budget reductions and sweeping cancellations of orders for promised replacement aircraft were introduced. These cuts included cancellation of orders for 50 American F-111 swept-wing strike fighters intended to fill the gap made by the earlier discarding of the TSR2. For Fighter Command this latest alarming political decision meant a further tightening of its belt. The command's ageing Javelins and Meteor NF fighters were obsolescent, while the magnificent Lightning, still being improved and modified, would obviously now have to continue in frontline service until at least the 1980s before any foreseeable replacement was likely to be available for squadron service. One 'stop-gap' design which was at least immediately available for use was the McDonnell Douglas Phantom, which had already been produced in two main variants for the RAF; the FG1 for air interception duties, and FGR2 for tactical reconnaissance. Indeed, the first Phantom, an FGR2, XT891, arrived at 228 OCU, Coningsby, on 23 August 1968, and within a year a total of 168 Phantoms had reached the UK for the RAF.

Before that first Phantom graced the skies of Lincolnshire, Fighter Command, as a separate formation, ceased to exist. Future planning for a re-structured Royal Air Force to meet the foreseeable commitments of the UK's aerial arm had begun some years earlier, culminating in a study undertaken by Air Vice-Marshal Denis Spotswood from 1963. His eventual recommendations included a merging of the RAF's existing four commands into just two – Strike Command and Air

[1] Published 1976 by Macdonald & Jane's.

Support Command. Consequently, on 30 April 1968, Bomber Command and Fighter Command were amalgamated to become the new Strike Command, with (by then) Air Chief Marshal Sir Denis Spotswood as the new command's first AOC-in-C. Within the new command structure, the former Fighter Command role was re-labelled as No. 11 (Fighter) Group – a worthy continuation of the old command's prime defence Group of nearly three decades before. Thus the unbreakable chain of tradition became linked to its latest inheritors; or in the classic phrasing of Sir Walter Raleigh in 1922: 'The Royal Air Force is strong in the kind of virtue that propagates itself and attains to a life beyond a life. The tradition is safe . . .'

Appendix 1

Air Officers Commanding-in-Chief, RAF Fighter Command
(Ranks, titles & decorations as at date of appointment)

AM Sir Hugh C. T. Dowding, KCB, CMG   14 July 1936
AM W. S. Douglas, CB, MC, DFC   25 November 1940
AM T. L. Leigh-Mallory, CB, DSO   28 November 1942
AM R. M. Hill, CB, MC, AFC   15 November 1943
       Fighter Command retitled Air Defence of Great Britain wef 15 November 1943;
       retitled Fighter Command again wef 15 October 1944.
AM Sir James M. Robb, KBE, CB, DSO, DFC, AFC   14 May 1945
AVM Sir William Elliott, KBE, CB, DFC   17 November 1947
AM Sir Basil E. Embry, KBE, CB, DSO, DFC, AFC   19 April 1949
AM Sir Dermot A. Boyle, KBE, CB, AFC   7 April 1953
AM H. L. Patch, CB, CBE   1 January 1956
AM Sir Thomas G. Pike, KCB, CBE, DFC   8 August 1956
AM H. D. McGregor, CB, CBE, DSO   30 July 1959
AM Sir Douglas G. Morris, KCB, CBE, DSO, DFC   8 May 1962
AM F. E. Rosier, CB, CBE, DSO   3 March 1966
       Fighter Command merged with Bomber Command to form Strike Command on 30
       April 1968.

Appendix 2

Fighter Command — Squadron Dispositions

(1) JULY 1936

Squadron	Aircraft	Station
1	Fury I	Tangmere
3	Bulldog	Kenley
17	Bulldog	Kenley
19	Gauntlet	Duxford
25	Fury I	Hawkinge
29	Demon	North Weald
32	Bulldog	Biggin Hill
43	Fury I	Tangmere
46	Gauntlet	Kenley
54	Bulldog	Hornchurch
56	Gauntlet	North Weald
65	Demon	Hornchurch
66	Gauntlet	Duxford
74	Gauntlet	Hornchurch
111	Gauntlet	Northolt
600 AAF	Demon	Hendon
601 AAF	Demon	Hendon
604 AAF	Demon	Hendon

(2) JULY 1938

Squadron	Aircraft	Station
1	Fury I & II	Tangmere
3	Hurricane	Kenley
17	Gauntlet II	Kenley
19	Gauntlet	Duxford
25	Fury II	Hawkinge
29	Demon	Debden/Martlesham
32	Gauntlet II	Biggin Hill
41	Fury II	Catterick

Squadron	Aircraft	Station
43	Fury I	Tangmere
46	Gauntlet II	Digby
54	Gladiator	Hornchurch
56	Gladiator	North Weald
64	Demon	Church Fenton
65	Gladiator	Hornchurch
66	Gauntlet II	Duxford
72	Gladiator	Church Fenton
73	Gladiator/Hurricane	Digby
74	Gauntlet II	Hornchurch
79	Gauntlet II	Biggin Hill
87	Gladiator/Hurricane	Debden
111	Hurricane	Northolt
151	Gauntlet	North Weald
213	Gauntlet	Wittering
600 AAF	Demon	Hendon
601 AAF	Demon	Hendon
604 AAF	Demon	Hendon
607 AAF	Demon	Usworth
608 AAF	Demon	Thornaby

(3) AUGUST 1939

Squadron	Aircraft	Station
1	Hurricane	Tangmere
3	Hurricane	Kenley
17	Hurricane	Kenley
19	Spitfire	Duxford
23	Blenheim IF	Wittering
25	Blenheim IF	Hawkinge
29	Blenheim IF	Debden
32	Hurricane	Biggin Hill
41	Spitfire	Catterick
43	Hurricane	Tangmere
46	Hurricane	Digby
54	Spitfire	Hornchurch
56	Hurricane	North Weald
65	Spitfire	Hornchurch
66	Spitfire	Duxford
72	Spitfire	Church Fenton
73	Hurricane	Digby
74	Spitfire	Hornchurch
79	Hurricane	Biggin Hill

Squadron	Aircraft	Station
85	Hurricane	Debden
87	Hurricane	Debden
111	Hurricane	Northolt
151	Hurricane	North Weald
213	Hurricane	Wittering
501 AAF	Hurricane	Filton
504 AAF	Hurricane	Hucknall
600 AAF	Blenheim IF	Kenley
601 AAF	Blenheim IF	Biggin Hill
602 AAF	Spitfire	Abbotsinch
603 AAF	Spitfire	Turnhouse
604 AAF	Blenheim IF	Hendon
605 AAF	Hurricane	Castle Bromwich
607 AAF	Gladiator	Usworth
609 AAF	Spitfire	Yeadon
610 AAF	Spitfire	Hooton Park
611 AAF	Spitfire	Speke
615 AAF	Gladiator	Kenley
616 AAF	Gauntlet	Doncaster

(4) 7 JULY 1940 (0900 hrs)
11 GROUP:

Squadron	Aircraft	Station
1	Hurricane	Northolt
25	Blenheim IF	Martlesham & North Weald (1 Flt each)
32	Hurricane	Biggin Hill
43	Hurricane	Tangmere
54	Spitfire	Rochford
56	Hurricane	North Weald
64	Spitfire	Kenley
65	Spitfire	Hornchurch
74	Spitfire	Hornchurch
79	Hurricane	Hawkinge
87*	Hurricane	Exeter
92*	Spitfire	Pembrey
111	Hurricane	Croydon
145	Hurricane	Tangmere
151	Hurricane	North Weald
213*	Hurricane	Exeter

*Transferred to 10 Group wef 18 July 1940.

Fighter Command

Squadron	Aircraft	Station
234*	Spitfire	St Eval
238*	Hurricane	Middle Wallop
257	Hurricane	Northolt
501 AAF*	Hurricane	Middle Wallop
600 AAF	Blenheim IF	Biggin Hill
601 AAF	Hurricane	Tangmere
609 AAF*	Spitfire	Warmwell
601 AAF	Spitfire	Biggin Hill
615 AAF	Hurricane	Kenley
FIU Flt	Blenheim IF	Tangmere

12 GROUP:

Squadron	Aircraft	Station
17	Hurricane	Debden
19	Spitfire	Duxford
23	Blenheim IF	Wittering
29	Blenheim IF	Digby
46	Hurricane	Digby
66	Spitfire	Coltishall
85	Hurricane	Debden & Martlesham (1 Flt each)
222	Spitfire	Kirton-in-Lindsey
229	Hurricane	Wittering
242	Hurricane	Coltishall
253	Hurricane	Kirton-in-Lindsey
264	Defiant	Duxford
266	Spitfire	Digby
611 AAF	Spitfire	Digby

13 GROUP:

Squadron	Aircraft	Station
3	Hurricane	Wick
41	Spitfire	Catterick
72	Spitfire	Acklington
141	Defiant	Turnhouse
152	Spitfire	Acklington
219	Blenheim IF	Catterick
245	Hurricane	Turnhouse
249	Hurricane	Church Fenton
504 AAF	Hurricane	Castletown
602 AAF	Spitfire	Drem
603 AAF	Spitfire	Dyce (A Flt) & Montrose (B Flt)
616 AAF	Spitfire	Leconfield

* Transferred to 10 Group wef 18 July 1940.

(5) 7 SEPTEMBER 1940 (0900 hrs)

10 GROUP:

Squadron	Aircraft	Station
56	Hurricane	Boscombe Down
87	Hurricane	Exeter & Bibury
92	Spitfire	Pembrey
152	Spitfire	Warmwell
213	Hurricane	Exeter
234	Spitfire	Middle Wallop
238	Hurricane	St Eval
247	Gladiator	Roborough (1 Flt only)
604 AAF	Blenheim IF	Middle Wallop
609 AAF	Spitfire	Middle Wallop

11 GROUP:

Squadron	Aircraft	Station
1 (RAF)	Hurricane	Heathrow
1 (RCAF)	Hurricane	Northolt
17	Hurricane	Debden
25	Blenheim IF	Martlesham
41	Spitfire	Rochford
43	Hurricane	Tangmere
46	Hurricane	Stapleford
66	Spitfire	Kenley
72	Spitfire	Croydon
111	Hurricane	Croydon
222	Spitfire	Hornchurch
249	Hurricane	North Weald
253	Hurricane	Kenley
257	Hurricane	Martlesham & North Weald (B Flt)
303 (Polish)	Hurricane	Northolt
501 AAF	Hurricane	Gravesend
504 AAF	Hurricane	Northolt
600 AAF	Blenheim IF	Hornchurch
601 AAF	Hurricane	Tangmere
602 AAF	Spitfire	Westhampnett
603 AAF	Spitfire	Hornchurch

12 GROUP:

Squadron	Aircraft	Station
19	Spitfire	Duxford
23	Blenheim IF	Wittering
29	Blenheim IF	Digby
64	Spitfire	Church Fenton & Ringway (B Flt)

191

Squadron	Aircraft	Station
74	Spitfire	Kirton-in-Lindsey
85	Hurricane	Church Fenton
151	Hurricane	Digby
229	Hurricane	Wittering & Bircham Newton (B Flt)
242	Hurricane	Coltishall
264	Defiant	Kirton-in-Lindsey
266	Spitfire	Coltishall & Wittering (A Flt)
302 (Polish)	Hurricane	Church Fenton
310 (Czech)	Hurricane	Duxford
611 AAF	Spitfire	Digby
616 AAF	Spitfire	Coltishall

13 GROUP:

Squadron	Aircraft	Station
3	Hurricane	Castletown
32	Hurricane	Acklington
54	Spitfire	Catterick
65	Spitfire	Turnhouse
141	Defiant	Turnhouse
145	Hurricane	Dyce (A Flt) & Montrose (B Flt)
219	Blenheim IF	Catterick
232	Hurricane	Sumburgh (1 Flt only)
605 AAF	Hurricane	Drem
607 AAF	Hurricane	Usworth
610 AAF	Sptifire	Acklington
615 AAF	Hurricane	Prestwick

(6) AIR DEFENCE OF GREAT BRITAIN (ADGB), 6 JUNE 1944

Squadron	Aircraft	Station
1	Spitfire	Predannack
25	Mosquito	Coltishall
33	Spitfire	Lympne
41	Spitfire	Bolt Head
64	Spitfire	Deanland
68	Beaufighter	Fairwood Common
74	Spitfire	Lympne
80	Spitfire	Detling
96	Mosquito	West Malling
118	Spitfire	Skeabrae & Sumburgh
125	Mosquito	Hurn
126	Spitfire	Culmhead
127	Spitfire	Lympne

Squadron	Aircraft	Station
130	Spitfire	Horne
131	Spitfire	Culmhead
137	Typhoon	Manston
151	Mosquito	Predannack
165	Spitfire	Predannack
219	Mosquito	Bradwell Bay
229	Spitfire	Detling
234	Spitfire	Deanland
263	Typhoon	Harrowbeer
274	Spitfire	Detling
303	Spitfire	Horne
307	Mosquito	Church Fenton
309	Hurricane	Peterhead
316	Mustang	Coltishall
345	Spitfire	Shoreham
350	Spitfire	Frieston
402	Spitfire	Horne
406	Beaufighter	Winkleigh
418	Mosquito	Holmesley South
456	Mosquito	Ford
501	Spitfire	Frieston
504	Spitfire	Castletown/Digby/Acklington det's
605	Mosquito	Manston
610	Spitfire	Harrowbeer
611	Spitfire	Deanland
616	Spitfire	Culmhead

(7) JUNE 1950

Squadron	Aircraft	Station
1	Meteor	Tangmere
19	Meteor	Church Fenton
23	Mosquito	Church Fenton
25	Mosquito	West Malling
29	Mosquito	West Malling
41	Hornet	Church Fenton
54	Vampire	Odiham
56	Meteor	Waterbeach
63	Meteor	Waterbeach
64	Hornet	Linton-on-Ouse
65	Hornet	Linton-on-Ouse
66	Meteor	Linton-on-Ouse
72	Vampire	North Weald

Squadron	Aircraft	Station
74	Meteor	Horsham St Faiths
92	Meteor	Linton-on-Ouse
141	Mosquito	Church Fenton
222	Meteor	Leuchars
245	Meteor	Horsham St Faiths
247	Vampire	Odiham
257	Meteor	Horsham St Faiths
263	Meteor	Horsham St Faiths
264	Mosquito	Acklington
501 AAF	Vampire	Filton
502 AAF	Spitfire	Aldergrove
504 AAF	Meteor	Wymeswold
600 AAF	Meteor	Biggin Hill
601 AAF	Vampire	North Weald
602 AAF	Spitfire	Abbotsinch
603 AAF	Spitfire	Turnhouse
604 AAF	Spitfire	North Weald
605 AAF	Vampire	Honiley
607 AAF	Spitfire	Ouston
608 AAF	Spitfire	Middleton St George
609 AAF	Spitfire	Yeadon
610 AAF	Spitfire	Hooton Park
611 AAF	Meteor	Hooton Park
612 AAF	Spitfire	Dyce
613 AAF	Spitfire	Ringway
614 AAF	Spitfire	Llandow
615 AAF	Spitfire	Biggin Hill
616 AAF	Meteor	Finningley

(8) JUNE 1960

Squadron	Aircraft	Station
19	Hunter	Leconfield
23	Javelin	Coltishall
25	Javelin	Waterbeach
29	Javelin	Leuchars
33	Javelin	Middleton St George
41	Javelin	Coltishall
43	Hunter	Leuchars
46	Javelin	Waterbeach
56	Hunter	Wattisham
64	Javelin	Duxford
65	Hunter	Duxford

Squadron	Aircraft	Station
66	Hunter	Acklington
72	Javelin	Leconfield
74	Lightning	Coltishall
85	Javelin	West Malling
92	Hunter	Middleton St George
111	Hunter	Wattisham
151	Javelin	Leuchars

Bibliography

Published books on the individual and more general facets of RAF fighter exploits abound in the aviation literature of the past 60-plus years. Even after reduction of this mountain of reading matter to within the strict parameters of the subject of RAF Fighter Command, the serious researcher is still left with a formidable list of titles. The following tabulation is therefore a personal selection of what I consider to be the more important books to be consulted in the context of this subject, and is by no means intended to appear as any comprehensive listing.

OFFICIALLY SPONSORED HISTORIES:
RAF Yearbook, 1938, L. Bridgman; Gale & Polden, 1939
Destiny can Wait, PAF Association; Heinemann, 1949
Royal Air Force 1939–45, 3 Vols, D. Richards & H. St G. Saunders; HMSO, 1953–4
RCAF Overseas, 3 Vols, RCAF; Oxford UP, 1944–5
New Zealanders with the RAF, 3 Vols, H. L. Thompson; 1959
Air War against Germany & Italy, 1939–45, J. Herington; 1954
Air power over Europe, 1944–5, J. Herington; 1954
The RAF in the World War, 4 Vols, N. Macmillan; Harrap, 1942–5
The Defence of the United Kingdom, B. Collier; HMSO, 1957

SQUADRON/UNIT HISTORIES:
Twice Vertical (1 Sqn), M. Shaw; Macdonald, 1971
43 Squadron, J. Beedle; Beaumont Aviation, 1966
Tiger Squadron (74 Sqn), J. I. T. Jones; W. H. Allen, 1954
I Fear No Man (74 Sqn), D. Tidy; Macdonald, 1972
242 Squadron History & Notes, A. E. M. Barton; Private publishing
Squadron 303, A. Fiedler; P. Davies, 1942
Defence until Dawn (488 NZ Sqn), L. Hunt; 1949
Treble-One (111 Sqn), R. P. D. Sands; Private pub., 1957
The Flying Sword (601 Sqn), T. Moulson; Macdonald, 1964

Glasgow's Fighter Squadron (602 Sqn), F. G. Nancarrow; Collins, 1942
603 Squadron. A. S. Kennedy; Private publishing
Under the White Rose (609 Sqn), F. Ziegler; Macdonald, 1971
Twenty-One Squadrons (AAF), L. Hunt; Garnstone Press, 1972
Squadrons of the RAF, A. V. Robertson; *FLIGHT*, 1938
Fighter Squadrons of the RAF, J. D. R. Rawlings; Macdonald, 1969

BIOGRAPHY & GENERAL:
Dowding & the Battle of Britain, R. C. Wright; Macdonald, 1969
Years of Command, S. Douglas; Collins, 1966
The Central Blue, J. Slessor; Cassell, 1956
Fighter Command, P. Wykeham, Putnam, 1960
To Know the Sky, P. Hill; Wm Kimber, 1962
Empire of the Air, Templewood; Collins, 1957
Fighter Aces of the RAF, E. R. C. Baker; Wm Kimber, 1962
Aces High, C. Williams & C. Shores; Spearman, 1966
New Zealanders in the Air War, A. Mitchell; Harrap, 1945
RAAF over Europe, F. Johnson; Eyre & Spottiswoode, 1946
Raiders Approach, H. T. Sutton; Gale & Polden, 1953
Combat Report, H. Bolitho; Batsford, 1943
Fighter Pilot, P. Richey; Batsford, 1942
Squadrons Up, N. Monks; Gollancz, 1940
AASF, C. Gardner; Hutchinson, 1940
Reach for the Sky, P. Brickhill; Collins, 1954
War Eagles, J. S. Childers; Heinemann, 1943
The Big Show, P. Clostermann; Chatto & Windus, 1952
Flames in the Sky, P. Clostermann; Chatto & Windus, 1953
Spitfire Pilot, D. M. Crook; Faber & Faber, 1942
Spitfire, B. J. Lane; J. Murray, 1942
Fly for your Life, L. Forrester; Muller, 1956
Arise to Conquer, I. R. Gleed; Gollancz, 1942
The Flying Sailor, A. Jubelin; Hurst & Blackett, 1953
Against the Sun, E. Lanchbery; Cassell, 1955
The Mouchotte Diaries, R. Mouchotte; Staples Press, 1956
The Way of a Pilot, B. Sutton; Macmillan, 1942
Biggin Hill, G. Wallace; Putnam, 1957
Scramble, J. R. D. Braham; Muller, 1961
Sailor Malan, O. Walker; Cassell, 1953
Nine Lives, A. C. Deere; Hodder & Stoughton, 1959
Wing Leader, J. E. Johnson; Chatto & Windus, 1956
One of the Few, J. A. Kent; Wm Kimber, 1971
Ginger Lacey – Fighter Pilot, R. T. Bickers; R. Hale, 1962
Where No Angels Dwell, S. Johnstone; Jarrolds, 1969

Shoulder the Sky, G. Thomas; A. Barker, 1959
Duel of Eagles, P. Townsend; Weidenfeld & Nicolson, 1970
Double Mission, N. L. R. Franks; Wm Kimber, 1976
Fighter Leader, N. L. R. Franks; Wm Kimber, 1978
Faces from the Fire, L. Mosley; Weidenfeld & Nicolson, 1962
The Guinea Pig Club, E. Bishop; Macmillan, 1963
Eagle Day, R. Collier; Hodder & Stoughton, 1966, reissued by Dent, 1980
Spitfire, B. Robertson; Harleyford, 1960
Night Fighter, C. Rawnsley & R. C. Wright; Collins, 1957
Cover of Darkness, R. Chisholm; Chatto & Windus, 1953
Night Flyer, L. Brandon; Wm Kimber, 1961
Night Intruder, J. Howard-Williams; David & Charles, 1976
Operation Sea-Lion, P. Fleming; Simon & Schuster, 1956
The Narrow Margin, D. Wood/D. Dempster; Arrow, 1969
Battle over Britain, F. Mason; McWhirter Twins, 1969
The Greatest Air Battle, N. L. R. Franks; Wm Kimber, 1979
The First and the Last, A. Galland; Methuen, 1955
The Luftwaffe War Diaries, C. Bekker; Macdonald, 1965
RAF, The Past 30 years, A. G. T. James; Macdonald & Jane's, 1976
The Hawker Hurricane, F. Mason; Macdonald, 1962
The Gloster Gladiator, F. Mason; Macdonald, 1964
The Gloster Meteor, E. Shacklady; Macdonald, 1962
Hurricane at War, C. Bowyer; Ian Allan, 1974
Mosquito at War, C. Bowyer; Ian Allan, 1973
Beaufighter at War, C. Bowyer; Ian Allan, 1976
Mustang at War, R. Freeman; Ian Allan, 1974
Typhoon & Tempest at War, R. Beamont/A. Reed; Ian Allan, 1974
Spitfire at War, A. W. Price; Ian Allan, 1974
Spitfire Special, T. Hooton; Ian Allan, 1972

Picture Credits

1 *Aeroplane*
2 Courtesy Dr D. I. L. Gleed
3 C. A. Sims
4 Ministry of Defence (Air)
5 Ministry of Defence (Air)
6 Sport & General Agency
7 Imperial War Museum
8 Hawker-Siddeley Aviation, Kingston
9 Vickers Aviation
10 Author's Collection
11 Imperial War Museum
12 Imperial War Museum
13 Author's Collection
14 Wing Commander F. Smith, DFC
15 Author's Collection
16 Author's Collection
17 Graphic Photo Union
18 Author's Collection
19 Crown copyright
20 Wing Commander G. McLannahan, DFC
21 P.N.A. Ltd
22 Author's Collection
23 J. B. Cynk
24 Public Archives of Canada
25 Public Archives of Canada
26 British Official
27 Associated Press
28 Imperial War Museum
29 British Official
30 Imperial War Museum
31 Fox Photos
32 P.N.A. Ltd
33 Author's Collection
34 Author's Collection
35 Author's Collection
36 Imperial War Museum
37 Imperial War Museum
38 Imperial War Museum
39 Author's Collection
40 Imperial War Museum
41 Author's Collection
42 Author's Collection
43 Director of Publicity, NZ
44 Imperial War Museum
45 Imperial War Museum
46 Gloster Aircraft Co
47 Ministry of Defence (Air)
48 Ministry of Defence (Air)
49 R. A. Brown
50 Ministry of Defence (Air)
51 Bristol-Siddeley
52 Ministry of Defence (Air)
53 Author's Collection
54 RAF
55 Ministry of Defence (Air)

Index

Index

Names

Amery, J. 180
Ashfield, G. *Sqn Ldr* 81, 120

Bader, D. R. S. *Sqn Ldr* 53, 68, 69, 70, 89, 92, 102
Baldwin, S. 14
Ball, A. *Capt* 21, 33
Bartley, A. C. *Flt Lt* 69
Beamish, F. V. *Gp Capt* 89
Beamont, R. P. *Wg Cdr* 49, 127, 178
Berry, J. *Sqn Ldr* 137
Birkenhead, Lord 15
Boelcke, O. *Haupt* 34, 147
Boyle, Sir D. *MRAF* 180
Braham, J. R. D. *Wg Cdr* 85
Broadhurst, H. *Gp Capt* 122
Brooke-Popham, Sir R. *ACM* 24
Brooks, J. W. *Flt Lt* 114, 123
Brothers, P. M. *Wg Cdr* 102

Camm, S. 25
Chamberlain, N. 28, 37, 39
Chisholm, R. A. *Wg Cdr* 85
Churchill, W. S. 16, 44, 45, 46, 47, 48, 49, 75, 113, 138, 144
Clisby, L. R. *Fg Off* 51
Coningham, Sir A. *AM* 132, 134, 139
Cooper-Slipper, M. *Fg Off* 71
Cornes *Plt Off* 121
Cornthwaite *Sgt* 19
Courtney, Sir C. *AVM* 30
Crowley-Milling, D. *Wg Cdr* 102
Cunningham, J. *Wg Cdr* 81, 83, 85, 100, 166

Dean *Fg Off* 136
Deere, A. C. *Wg Cdr* 74, 102
Derry, J. *Sqn Ldr* 166
Dick, N. R. D. *Plt Off* 113
Donaldson, E. M. *Gp Capt* 165
Dönitz, K. *Adm* 109

Douglas, S. *ACM* 48, 86, 87, 88, 93, 94, 107, 108, 109, 110, 113, 115, 120, 122
Doutrepont, G. *Plt Off* 69
Dowding, Hon D. H. *Plt Off* 41
Dowding, Sir H. C. T. *ACM* 17–19, 26–33, 35, 38–40, 42–9, 51, 53–6, 59–64, 66, 67, 73, 79, 80, 82, 86, 87, 88, 140, 141, 181
Du Fretay, M. H. *Plt Off* 124
Duke, N. F. *Wg Cdr* 165
Dundas, H. C. *Wg Cdr* 102

Ellington, Sir E. *ACM* 29
Elliott, Sir W. *ACM* 166
Esmonde, E. *Lt-Cdr* 119, 120

Farquhar, A. *Sqn Ldr* 41, 42
Fink, J. *Oberst* 70
Finucane, B. F. *Wg Cdr* 100, 102, 104

Galland, A. 60, 64, 71, 92, 118, 119, 142, 143
George, L. 14
Gibson, G. P. *Flt Lt* 85
Gleed, I. R. *Wg Cdr* 100
Göring, H. W. 54, 60, 64, 67, 73, 74, 86, 87, 94, 128, 131, 142, 151
Gray, C. F. *Wg Cdr* 74

Halahan, P. J. H. *Sqn Ldr* 51
Hankey, Sir M. 16
Hawker, L. G. *Maj* 34
Hill, Sir R. *ACM* 132–41, 143
Hillary, R. *Flt Lt* 148
Hitler, A. 16, 18, 31, 37, 54, 55, 73, 83, 84, 89, 102, 113, 118, 122, 126, 129, 133, 138, 141, 142
Hoare, Sir S. 14
Hoare, B. R. O'B. *Sqn Ldr* 121
Hülsemeyer, C. 79

James, A. G. T. 184
Jones, J. I. T. *Gp Capt* 103

Kain, E. J. *Fg Off* 43, 51, 99
Kemp, H. K. *Wg Cdr* 130

Kent, J. A. *Wg Cdr* 74, 75
Kingcome, B. F. *Wg Cdr* 74, 102
Kreipe, W. *Maj* 52

Lacey, J. H. *Flt Sgt* 72
Law, B. 14
Leigh-Mallory, T. *AM* 68, 86, 87, 119, 122, 131, 143
Lithgow, M. *Lt-Cdr* 177
Lock, E. S. *Flt Lt* 92, 100
Lufbery, R. *Maj* 145

McConnell, W. W. *Flt Lt* 124
McCudden, J. T. B. *Maj* 21, 33
McGregor, Sir H. *ACM* 181
McKenzie *Fg Off* 136
Macmillan, H. 180
Maidment, J. R. *Flt Sgt* 130
Malan, A. G. *Gp Capt* 34, 35, 52, 74, 77, 90, 97, 100, 102
Mannock, E. *Maj* 21, 33, 35
Milne, R. M. *Wg Cdr* 102
Mitchell, R. J. 25
Mottram, A. *Plt Off* 88
Mould, P. W. O. *Plt Off* 43, 99
Mungo-Park, J. C. *Sqn Ldr* 92

Neil, T. *Flt Lt* 100
Newall, Sir C. *MRAF* 30, 46, 48

Ortmans, V. *Fg Off* 92
Ostermann, H. 61
Oxspring, R. W. *Sqn Ldr* 163

Page, F. W. 178
Park, Sir K. *AVM* 27, 35, 51, 52, 56, 59, 64, 66, 67, 68, 69, 70, 71, 87
Pennington *Flt Lt* 120
Petter, W. E. W. 177, 178
Phillipson, J. *Sgt* 81
Pile, Sir F. *Gen* 136, 138
Pinkerton, G. *Flt Lt* 40
Pohle, H. *Haupt* 41
Proudman, G. V. *Fg Off* 42

Raleigh, Sir W. 185
Rankin, J. E. *Wg Cdr* 102
Rawnsley, J. *Flt Lt* 83, 85
Richthofen, M. von *Rittm* 33
Robb, Sir J. *ACM* 141, 163, 164, 165, 166
Roger, J. K. *Fg Off* 137
Romer, C. F. *Maj-Gen* 15
Ryder, N. *Flt Lt* 74

Salmond, Sir J. *MRAF* 15, 16
Sandys, D. 179, 180, 181
Sassoon, Sir P. 34
Sinclair, Sir A. 45

Slade, G. *Wg Cdr* 120
Sorley, R. *Sqn Ldr* 24
Spotswood, Sir D. *ACM* 184, 185
Stephenson, P. J. T. *Plt Off* 71
Stevens, R. P. *Sqn Ldr* 81, 84

Tank, K. 126
Taylor, Sir G. 147
Thomas, M. *Fg Off* 124
Trautloft, H. *Oberst* 71, 92
Trenchard, Sir H. *ACM* 14, 16, 22, 78, 105, 142
Tuck, R. R. S. *Wg Cdr* 53, 100

Vincent, S. *A Cdre* 71, 109
Voase-Jeff, R. *Flt Lt* 99
Voss, W. *Obltn* 33

Waterton, W. A. *Sqn Ldr* 165
Watson, C. B. *Flt Sgt* 124
Watson-Watt, R. 18, 19, 79, 80
Wavell, Earl 17
Wells, E. P. *Flt Lt* 74
Wilson, H. J. *Gp Capt* 162
Wright, A. *Plt Off* 88
Wykeham, Sir P. *AM* 87, 165

Places

Abbeville 88, 156, 157
Aston Down 103
Avebury 83

Barking Creek 40
Bawdsey Manor 19
Bedford 27
Bentley Priory 17, 19, 27, 35, 38, 39, 46, 47, 62, 86, 88, 132, 138, 141
Bentwaters 162
Berlin 54
Bethnal Green 133
Bethune 111, 113
Biggin Hill 68, 69, 71, 88, 119
Birmingham 81
Boulogne 68, 89
Boxted 162
Brest 117, 118
Brooklands 25, 68

Caen 121
Calais 68, 149
Canterbury 68, 69, 126
Cap Gris Nez 158
Castle Camps 120
Chartres 121
Chatham 39
Chelmsford 77
Chiswick 138

Coltishall   178
Coningsby   184
Cosford   105
Cotentin   59
Coventry   82
Cranwell   41, 46, 90, 98, 102, 105, 180
Croydon   39, 42
Culmhead   136

Debden   120
Dieppe   122, 123, 124, 125
Dover   52, 56, 68, 114, 118, 120
Drem   40, 41
Dungeness   68
Dunkirk   51, 52, 53, 55, 57, 58, 64, 65, 149
Durrington   83
Duxford   25, 68, 70, 71

Eastchurch   105
Eastleigh Airport   20, 25
Evreux   121

Farnborough   175
Fecamp   118
Firth of Forth   40, 41
Flowerdown   105
Ford   81, 123

Geneva   16
Gosnay   113
Gravelines   114
Gravesend   133
Guernica   37

Halton   98, 102, 105, 172
Hatfield   166
Hendon   20
Heston   103
Hindhead   130
Hornchurch   40, 53, 113
Hullavington   180

Ingrave   82

Kamen   140
Karinhall   54
Kenley   119

Ladbergen   140
Lammermuir   41
Le Touquet   88, 118
Leuchars   175
Lille Marque   49
Lille Vendeville   49
London   15, 26, 39, 54, 55, 60, 65, 67, 68, 69,
    70, 71, 82, 83, 117, 126, 128, 129, 130, 134,
    137, 139, 158, 176

Maidstone   68, 69
Manston   83, 119, 123, 124, 127, 137
Mersea Island   39
Middle Wallop   68
Montdidier   121
Munich   28, 29, 99

Northolt   25, 71
North Berwick   41
North Coates   179
North Weald   40
Norwich   154

Odiham   163, 176
Orby   83
Ostend   118

Paris   42, 48, 181
Pas de Calais   59, 89, 137, 138
Portland   72

Rochford   41, 77
Rye   68

St Abbs Head   42
St Athan   49
St Omar   113
St Valery   158
Sevenoaks   133
Sopley   83
Southampton   72
Southend   40, 41, 77
Stanmore   17, 27
Staplehurst   69
Stornoway   110

Tangmere   26, 81, 103
Thames Estuary   18, 39, 58
Tiree   110
Toul   43
Tunbridge Wells   82

Uxbridge   15

Vaenga   113
Valenciennes   50
Vassincourt   43
Versailles   16
Villacoublay   72

Waldringfield   83
Wattisham   175
West Malling   128
Willesborough   83
Winchester   17
Windsor   68
Wittering   103
Woolston   72
Woolwich   17